EARLY MEDIEVAL CHANTS FROM NONANTOLA

PART II

RECENT RESEARCHES IN THE MUSIC OF THE MIDDLE AGES AND EARLY RENAISSANCE

Charles M. Atkinson, general editor

A-R Editions, Inc., publishes seven series of musicological editions
that present music brought to light in the course of current research:

Recent Researches in the Music of the Middle Ages and Early Renaissance
Charles M. Atkinson, general editor

Recent Researches in the Music of the Renaissance
James Haar, general editor

Recent Researches in the Music of the Baroque Era
Christoph Wolff, general editor

Recent Researches in the Music of the Classical Era
Eugene K. Wolf, general editor

Recent Researches in the Music of the Nineteenth and Early Twentieth Centuries
Rufus Hallmark, general editor

Recent Researches in American Music
John M. Graziano, general editor

Recent Researches in the Oral Traditions of Music
Philip V. Bohlman, general editor

Each *Recent Researches* edition is devoted to works
by a single composer or to a single genre of composition.
The contents are chosen for their potential interest to scholars
and performers, then prepared for publication according to the
standards that govern the making of all reliable historical editions.

Subscribers to any of these series, as well as patrons of subscribing institutions,
are invited to apply for information about the "Copyright-Sharing Policy"
of A-R Editions, Inc., under which policy any part of an edition
may be reproduced free of charge for study or performance.

Address correspondence to

A-R EDITIONS, INC.
801 Deming Way
Madison, Wisconsin 53717

(608) 836-9000

RECENT RESEARCHES IN THE MUSIC OF THE MIDDLE AGES
AND EARLY RENAISSANCE • VOLUME 31

EARLY MEDIEVAL CHANTS FROM NONANTOLA

Part II
Proper Chants and Tropes

Edited by James Borders

A-R Editions, Inc.
Madison

EARLY MEDIEVAL CHANTS FROM NONANTOLA

Edited by
James Borders
and
Lance Brunner

*Recent Researches in the Music
of the Middle Ages and Early Renaissance*

Part I.   Ordinary Chants and Tropes
Volume 30

Part II. Proper Chants and Tropes
Volume 31

Part III. Processional Chants
Volume 32

Part IV. Sequences
Volume 33

© 1996 by A-R Editions, Inc.
All rights reserved
Printed in the United States of America

ISBN 0-89579-329-6
ISSN 0362-3572

∞ The paper used in this publication meets the minimum requirements of the American National Standard for Information Sciences—Permanence of Paper for Printed Library Materials, ANSI Z39.48-1984.

Contents

Preface	ix
Acknowledgments	ix
Abbreviations	x
Introduction to the Proper Tropes and Prosulae	xi
Proper Tropes	xi
Prosulae	xi
The Nonantolan Repertories of Proper Tropes and Prosulae and Their Transmission	xii
A Note on Performance Practice	xiii
Notes	xiii
Critical Apparatus	xiv
List of Manuscript Sigla	xiv
List of Works Cited	xv
Editorial Methods	xvi
Commentaries	xvii
Plates	lxxii

Proper Chants and Tropes

1. Introit: Ad te levavi; *Sanctissimus namque Gregorius*	1
2. Introit: Ad te levavi; *Almipotens verus Deus*	2
3. Introit: Ad te levavi; *Ecce iam Christus*	3
4. Introit: Dominus dixit; *Verbo altissimi patris*	4
5. Introit: Lux fulgebit; *Hora est iam nos*	5
6. Introit: Lux fulgebit; *Ecce iam venit hora*	6
7. Introit: Lux fulgebit; *Iam surgens aurora*	7
8. Introit: Puer natus est nobis; *Hodie salvator mundi per virginem*	7
9. Introit: Puer natus est nobis; *Hodie exultent iusti natus est*	9
10. Introit: Puer natus est nobis; *Hic enim est de quo prophetae*	10
11. Introit: Etenim sederunt principes; *Hodie inclitus martyr Stephanus*	11
12. Introit: Etenim sederunt principes; *Grandine lapidum*	12
13. Introit: Etenim sederunt principes; *Qui primus meruit*	12
14. Communion: Video caelos apertos; *Magnus et felix*	13
15. Introit: In medio ecclesiae; *Aeterno genitus genitore*	14
16. Introit: In medio ecclesiae; *Ille qui dixit*	15
17. Introit: In medio ecclesiae; *Amor angelorum et gaudium*	15
18. Introit: In medio ecclesiae; *Dilectus iste domini*	16
19. Offertory: Iustus ut palma; *Florebit iustus ut palma*	17
20. Introit: Ex ore infantium; *Hodie te domine suggentes*	18
21. Introit: Statuit ei dominus; *Venite populi ad conlaudandum*	18
22. Introit: Statuit ei dominus; *Hic est Silvester*	19
23. Offertory: Veritas mea; *Usque in saeculum saeculi*	20
24. Introit: Ecce advenit; *Hodie descendit Christus*	21
25. Introit: Ecce advenit; *Forma speciosissimus*	22
26. Introit: Ecce advenit; *Haec est praeclara dies*	22
27. Introit: Suscepimus; *Adest alma virgo*	23
28. Introit: Suscepimus; *Psallentes legimus*	24
29. Introit: Domine ne longe facias; *Ingresso Iesu*	25
30. Introit: Domine ne longe facias; *Suspensus ligno patri*	27

31.	Introit: Resurrexi; *Hora est surgite/Quem quaeritis*	28
32.	Introit: Resurrexi; *Christus de sepulchro resurrexit*	29
33.	Introit: Resurrexi; *Hodie resurrexit leo fortis*	30
34.	Offertory: Terra tremuit; *Ab increpatione et ira*	31
35.	Communion: Pascha nostrum; *Laus honor virtus*	32
36.	Introit: Gaudeamus; *Cuncti fideles Christi*	33
37a.	Introit: Gaudeamus . . . Senesii; *Sanguine sacrati Christi*	34
37b.	Introit: Gaudeamus . . . sanctorum omnium; *Sanguine sacrati Christi*	35
38.	Introit: Viri Galilaei; *Quem creditis super astra*	36
39.	Introit: Viri Galilaei; *Hodie redemptor mundi ascendit*	37
40.	Introit: Viri Galilaei; *Terrigenas summos affatur*	38
41.	Introit: Viri Galilaei; *Hodie rex gloriae Christus*	38
42.	Introit: Spiritus domini; *Hodie spiritus sanctus procedens*	39
43.	Introit: Spiritus domini; *Hodie spiritus sanctus processit*	40
44.	Introit: Spiritus domini; *Cum essent apostoli*	40
45.	Introit: De ventre matris meae; *Hodie exultent iusti . . . Iohannes*	41
46.	Introit: De ventre matris meae; *Deus pater clamat Iohannem*	43
47.	Introit: De ventre matris meae; *Audite insulae*	44
48.	Introit: Nunc scio vere; *Beatissimus Petrus catenis*	45
49.	Introit: Nunc scio vere; *Hodie sanctissimi patroni nostri Petri*	46
50.	Introit: Nunc scio vere; *Divina beatus Petrus*	46
51.	Introit: Os iusti; *A domino impletum*	47
52.	Introit: Os iusti; *In iubilo vocis*	48
53.	Introit: Confessio; *Hodie beatus Laurentius levita*	49
54.	Introit: Confessio; *Prunas extensa*	50
55.	Introit: Confessio; *Qui tibi dedit Laurenti*	51
56.	Introit: Gaudeamus . . . Mariae . . . assumptione; *Exaudi virgo virginum*	52
57.	Introit: Gaudeamus . . . Mariae . . . assumptione; *Ave beata Maria*	53
58.	Introit: Gaudeamus . . . Mariae . . . assumptione; *Nos sinus ecclesiae*	54
59.	Introit: Vultum tuum; *O quam clara nitet*	55
60.	Introit: Benedicite dominum; *Qui patris in caelo*	56
61.	Introit: Mihi autem nimis; *Nobile apostolici admirans*	56
62.	Introit: Mihi autem nimis; *Admirans vates proclamat*	57
63.	Introit: Mihi autem nimis; *Consortes tuorum effecti*	58
64.	Introit: Statuit ei dominus; *Divini fuerat*	58
65.	Introit: In omnem terram; *Festis nunc in apostolicis*	59
66.	Introit: In omnem terram; *Hodie beatissimus Andreas*	59
67.	Introit: Benedicta sit; *Splendor et imago patris*	60

Prosulae

1.	Gradual: Universi, ℣ Vias tuas domine; *Venturum te cuncti*	61
2.	Offertory: Ad te domine, ℣ 2 Respice in me; *Invocavite altissime*	61
3.	Offertory: Deus tu convertens, ℣ 2 Misericordia et veritas; *Possessor polorum Deus*	61
4.	Gradual: Qui sedes domine, ℣ 2 Qui regis Israel; *Qui sedes in alto throno*	62
5.	Offertory: Benedixisti domine, ℣ 2 Ostende nobis domine; *Misericors ac clemens*	62
6.	Offertory: Ave Maria, ℣ 1 Quomodo in me; *A supernis caelorum*	62
7.	Offertory: Deus enim fermavit, ℣ 2 Mirabilis in excelsis; *Dierum noctuque*	63
8.	Alleluia ℣ Dies sanctificatus; *Audi nos te deprecamur*	63
9.	Alleluia ℣ Dies sanctificatus; *Alme caeli rex immortalis*	63
10.	Offertory: Tui sunt caeli, ℣ 3 Tu humiliasti; *Proles virginis matris*	64

11. Tract: Commovisti, ℣ 2 Sana contritiones eius; *Sana Christe rex alme*	64
12. Tract: Qui confidunt, ℣ 2 Montes in circuitu eius; *Mons magnus est*	64
13. Tract: Deus Deus meus, ℣ 11 Libera me de ore; *Pater unigenitum tuum*	65
14. Alleluia ℣ Pascha nostrum; *Iam redeunt gaudia*	65
15. Alleluia ℣ Pascha nostrum; *Christe tu vita vera*	65
16. Offertory: Angelus domini; ℣ 2 Iesus stetit; *Christus intravit ianuis*	66
17. Alleluia ℣ Vos estis; *Rex Deus omnipotens*	66
18. Alleluia ℣ Vos estis; *Sicut tu Christe*	66
19. Alleluia ℣ Dum complerentur; *Erant omnes nostri linguis*	67
20. Alleluia ℣ Dum complerentur; *Pentecosten advenisse*	68
21. Alleluia ℣ Serve bone et fidelis; *Alme cuncti sator orbis*	68
22. Alleluia ℣ Serve bone et fidelis; *Serve et amice bone*	68
23. Alleluia ℣ Concussum est mare; *Ante Deum semper gloriae*	69
24. Alleluia ℣ Concussum est mare; *Concussum et percussum*	69
25. Alleluia ℣ Concussum est mare; *Angeli Michael et Gabriel*	69
26. Alleluia ℣ O quam pulchra est; *Psallat turba devota*	71
27. Alleluia ℣ Dilexit Andream; *In dulcedine amoris*	72
28. Alleluia ℣ Verba mea; *Alma domine noli claudere*	72
29. Alleluia ℣ Deus iudex iustus; *Arbiter singulorum facta*	73
30. Alleluia ℣ Ad te domine levavi; *Alma voce canamus*	73
31. Alleluia ℣ Eripe me; *Laudes debitas vocibus*	74
32. Alleluia ℣ Eripe me; *Et ab insurgentibus Deus*	74
33. Alleluia ℣ Eripe me; *Lingua cor simul clamitet*	74
34. Alleluia ℣ Benedictus es domine; *Semper sonet nostra lingua*	75
Index of First Lines of Proper Chants	77
Index of Chants by Feast Day	81

Preface

Early Medieval Chants from Nonantola contains all the tropes, prosulae, Ordinary chants, sequences, and processional chants found in three troper-prosers from the northern Italian monastery of San Silvestro di Nonantola: Bologna, Biblioteca Universitaria 2824; Rome, Biblioteca Casanatense 1741; and Rome, Biblioteca Nazionale Centrale 1343. These related manuscripts, which represent the lion's share of complete medieval music books with diastematic Nonantolan notation, were presumably copied in the abbey's scriptorium between the late eleventh and early twelfth centuries. Together they provide a sense of the expanded repertory of chant performed at this northern Italian monastery during the period.

The present work is divided in a way that loosely parallels the organization of the manuscript sources, which is: (1) Ordinary chants by category; (2) fraction antiphons; (3) Proper tropes, prosulae, antiphons *ante evangelium*, and sequences by feast; (4) processional antiphons, responds, hymns, and litanies by occasion. (Complete inventories of the three Nonantolan tropers are found in the general introduction.) The first part of this edition contains all the chants for the Ordinary of the Mass with associated tropes and prosulae. The second contains all tropes and prosulae for the Mass Proper with their associated chants. The third includes *confractoria*, antiphons *ante evangelium*, and processional chants. The fourth contains the forty-one sequences of the Nonantolan repertory, including the earliest readable versions of a number of Notker's compositions. Within each category the chants are arranged according to their use during the yearly liturgical cycle. The reader will note the similarity of this plan to the *Beneventanum Troporum Corpus*, edited by John Boe and Alejandro Planchart, Recent Researches in the Music of the Middle Ages and Early Renaissance, vols. 16–28 (Madison, 1989–).

The general introduction outlines the development of Nonantola's chant repertory and describes the three manuscript sources in detail; it concludes with complete inventories. Each volume contains introductions to the individual repertories along with commentaries on the chants with Latin texts and English translations. Summary lists of manuscript sigla for the sources cited in the edition are found before the commentaries, along with a bibliography of works cited and a discussion of editorial methods. Transcriptions of the texts and music comprise the bulk of each volume. Finally, an alphabetical index of the contents of the volume (individual trope verses or first lines of complete chants) is also included.

This edition is intended to meet the needs of a wide variety of users. Students of Romance philology and of medieval Latin may wish to consult manuscript spellings, which are generally retained. Significant text variants are also reported. Singers and conductors will find the translations supplied in the commentaries to be helpful. Musicologists and scholars of the liturgy can consult the readings and variants to compare them with other versions of the chants and tropes. It is also hoped that specialists will use the commentaries in the first and second volumes in their studies of chant transmission. Most important, the editors hope that these volumes will spark the interest of students, enabling them to study and perform the chants found in this edition.

Acknowledgments

At the outset I wish to express my sincere thanks to those people who contributed to my work on this edition. I owe the greatest debt of gratitude to my friend and fellow Chicagoan F. Joseph Smith, who with supreme patience (both with me and the Nonantolan scribes) vetted the Latin texts, corrected my translations, and offered much encouragement. I am also grateful to John Boe, who guided my early efforts by sharing with me the preface, editorial methods, and selected commentaries from the Kyrie volume of the *Beneventanum Troporum Corpus* prior to its publication. Lance Brunner and Alejandro Planchart encouraged me to undertake this project early in my career, and I remain grateful to them. Some enthusiastic graduate students at the University of Michigan, too numerous to name individually (but you know who you are!), helped me turn my transcriptions and comments into an edition in a memorable seminar some years ago. I also wish to thank Jonathan Besancon, who assisted with the collation of musical variants; David Vayo, who copied a great deal of the music with great accuracy; and Robyn Stilwell, who provided me with a clean text to submit to the publisher. Let me also express my gratitude to the editorial staff of A-R Editions, whose intelligence, editorial skill, and tenacity I have come to admire greatly. Last but certainly not least I thank my wife, Ann Marie Borders, for her patience and love.

James Borders

Abbreviations

AH *Analecta Hymnica Medii Aevi.* 55 vols. Edited by Clemens Blume, Guido Maria Dreves, and Henry Marriott Bannister. 1886–1922. Reprint. New York, 1961.

AMS *Antiphonale Missarum Sextuplex.* Edited by René-Jean Hesbert. Brussels, 1935.

BTC I *Beneventanum Troporum Corpus I. Tropes of the Proper of the Mass from Southern Italy, A.D. 1000–1250.* Edited by Alejandro Enrique Planchart. Recent Researches in the Music of the Middle Ages and Early Renaissance, vols. 16–18. Madison, 1994.

CAO *Corpus Antiphonalium Officii.* 6 vols. Edited by René-Jean Hesbert. Rerum ecclesiasticarum documenta, series maior, vols. 7–12. Rome, 1963–79.

CT *Corpus Troporum.* Stockholm, 1975–.

GR *Graduale sacrosanctae Romanae ecclesiae de tempore et de sanctis.* Tournai, 1945.

GT *Graduale triplex.* Solesmes, 1979.

JAMS *Journal of the American Musicological Society.*

MGG *Die Musik in Geschichte und Gegenwart.* 17 vols. Edited by Friedrich Blume. Kassel and Basel, 1949–78.

MQ *The Musical Quarterly.*

New Grove *The New Grove Dictionary of Music and Musicians.* 20 vols. Edited by Stanley Sadie. London, 1980.

OT *Offertoriale triplex cum versiculis.* Solesmes, 1985.

RdCG *Revue du chant grégorien.*

RISM Répertoire International des Sources Musicales.

Introduction to the Proper Tropes and Prosulae

Because numerous surveys of medieval chant address the origins and histories of Proper tropes and prosulae,[1] this introduction will focus on the contents of the three Nonantolan tropers and the issue of their transmission. However, before addressing the central question surrounding the development of late chant at Nonantola—namely, how did chants from so many geographical regions find their way to the abbey?—let us briefly examine the natures of these pieces.

Proper Tropes

Proper tropes are lines of text and music added to the Proper chants of the Mass, especially the Introit, Offertory, and Communion. With respect to their structure and relation to the items elaborated, there are two types: introductory and intercalated. Introductory tropes are comparatively long pieces performed, as the name would indicate, as preludes to standard items of the Proper. Examples of this type include no. 5, *Hora est iam nos*, which precedes the Introit for the second Mass on Christmas Day, *Lux fulgebit*; no. 14, *Magnus et felix*, which introduces the Communion for St. Stephen, *Video caelos apertos*; and no. 31, *Hora est surgite/Quem quaeritis*, preceding the Easter Sunday Introit, *Resurrexi*. In these and other introductory tropes, the singers—presumably a small group of soloists—invite the assembled monks to begin the Proper chant. Sometimes this was done by establishing a dramatic context for performance. The introductory trope *Magnus et felix*, for example, relates to the beginning of the Introit *Videos caelos apertos* as follows (in English translation): "He who endured the rain of stones sees Christ standing before him and says: 'I see the heavens opened . . .' "

Intercalated tropes, on the other hand, were combined with one another to form what are called trope complexes. These generally include a brief opening line of text and music plus as many as four additional ones sung between phrases of the standard chant. (Individual lines or elements are given in square brackets in this edition. As will be discussed below, different trope elements were connected with a given chant at different centers.) The texts of intercalated tropes generally relate closely to the chants they elaborate.[2] This is true not only musically—chant and tropes are in the same mode—but also with respect to the meaning of the texts. This connection is often achieved by the tropist updating the Old Testament text of the standard chant with an account of the New Testament events that the liturgy commemorates. Thus, for example, the tropes accompanying the Introit for the third Mass on Christmas Day (nos. 8–10) describe the Nativity, which was foretold in the standard Introit text drawn from the book of the prophet Isaiah.

Intercalated tropes are not typically rubricated in the Nonantolan tropers unless they are the first in a series of such items. Introductory tropes, on the other hand, are invariably preceded by identifying rubrics suggesting that they were performed first in a series of elaborations. Although this possibility cannot be confirmed since there is no surviving ordinal describing the performance of chant at Nonantola, it would follow that intercalated tropes were typically sung in connection with other tropes. For instance, the Introit trope complex *Christus de sepulchro resurrexit* (no. 32) was likely sung after the introductory trope *Hora est surgite/Quem quaeritis* (no. 31), which in turn was followed by the singing of the entire Introit and the appointed Psalm verse.[3] The combination of introductory trope plus one or two trope complexes, the standard chant and its repetition, Psalm verse, and lesser doxology would have greatly extended the performance of Introits on major feasts at Nonantola and other centers where troping was practiced. Considering that the Introit was merely the first in series of Proper and Ordinary chants, many of them troped, these Masses would have taken hours to complete.

Prosulae

Besides Proper tropes, prose texts (without new music) were added to certain of the lengthy melismas of Alleluias as well as Gradual, Tract, and Offertory verses. These pieces, which modern scholars call prosulae, following the terminology of some medieval sources, were not uncommon at Nonantola; this edition contains thirty-four. Prosulae were considered a genre distinct from tropes in the Middle Ages. Indeed, Nonantolan scribes generally identified them as *prosae*, not *tropi*. Hence in this volume they are numbered separately from Proper tropes.

The prosulae sung at Nonantola ranged in length from relatively short pieces of less than thirty syllables (e.g., nos. 8, 9, and 13) to elaborate works comprising two or three distinct sections (nos. 11, 26, and 28). This variation in scope, which at first glance would seem significant to the definition of the genre, must however be understood in relation to the different lengths of melismas to which the texts were underlaid. Simply stated, the longer the melisma, the longer the prosula. In addition to length, the melodic structure of certain melismas affected the text structure of some prosulae. This is most apparent in melismas with internal repeats or other parallelisms. For example, two identical leaps of a perfect fourth (d to g), which open successive phrases of a melisma in the second verse of the Tract *Qui confidunt,* probably led the author of *Mons magnus est* (no. 12) to create parallel text phrases: *Mons magnus est, mons terribilis est* ("The mountain is great, the mountain is awesome").

Some prosulae stand quite apart from the texts they elaborate in their subject matter. For example, no. 1, *Venturum te cuncti dixerunt* ("All the prophets have spoken of your coming"), does not relate closely to the Psalm text that encloses it: *Vias tuas domine/notas fac mihi* ("Your ways, O Lord, make known to me"). Perhaps for this reason different prosulae were combined with the same standard chants at different centers.[4] In other cases, however, the authors of prosulae artfully incorporated words of the standard Proper texts into their structures (e.g., no. 4, *Qui sedes in alto throno;* no. 11, *Sana Christe rex alme;* and no. 12, *Mons magnus est*).

The Nonantolan Repertories of Proper Tropes and Prosulae and Their Transmission

The three Nonantolan tropers together preserve Proper tropes and prosulae for forty-one occasions, including twenty-four feasts of the Temporale[5] and seventeen of the Sanctorale plus the Common of the B.V.M.[6] In all, there are a total of sixty-seven introductory tropes and trope complexes and thirty-four prosulae for the Proper of the Mass. (An index of individual trope verses and prosulae is found at the end of this volume; inventories of the tropers appear in the "General Introduction" to Part I.)

As with the Ordinary tropes, Rn 1343 and Rc 1741 preserve more Proper tropes than Bu 2824, though the latter manuscript yields three trope complexes and two prosulae without concordances in the other two Nonantolan manuscripts: no. 18, *Dilectus iste domini;* no. 20, *Hodie te domine suggentes;* no. 41, *Hodie rex gloriae Christus* (v. [1]); Alleluia prosulae no. 20, *Pentecosten advenisse* (without neumes); and no. 34, *Semper sonet nostra lingua.* By comparison, the most extensive Nonantolan troper, Rc 1741, preserves only two Proper trope complexes and four prosulae not found in the other two sources: tropes no. 44, *Cum essent apostoli;* and no. 52, *In iubilo vocis;* and prosulae nos. 13, 16–18. Rn 1343 contains no Proper items not found in the other Nonantolan tropers.

To understand how the Nonantolan repertory of Proper tropes and prosulae reached the stage that comes down to us is to confront the difficult question of the formation of northern and central Italian chant. Two general observations may be made here.[7] First, tropes in Nonantolan sources, like those collected elsewhere in northern and central Italian manuscripts, were subject to considerable variation of form and content in their transmission and local development.[8] Even in closely related sources the same trope element may be associated with different chants; it may follow different introductory elements; and its place in the order of the trope may change. The same trope texts are also found in vastly different musical settings. A comparison of the Nonantolan tropers with a related source, VEcap 107, is instructive in this regard.[9] As I have shown elsewhere, even in this case where 87% of the Introit tropes in the Nonantolan manuscripts also appear in VEcap 107, the arrangement of the elements is often different.[10]

The second observation, which concerns the origins of the Nonantolan repertory, is that local compositions account for a smaller percentage here than in the repertory sung, say, at important Aquitanian monasteries or those in East Frankland. Indeed, compared with other central and northern Italian centers, the dependence of the Nonantolan abbey upon imported chants was pronounced: only three Introit trope elements of a total of 171 in the sources under consideration here are *unica.* Broadening the base of comparison to include the closely related VEcap 107, the number of what are probably local compositions increases to twenty-one elements. Yet this represents only 12% of the total. Thus it becomes clear that the majority of tropes sung in Nonantola have concordances in manuscripts beyond the immediate locale.

Where did these tropes come from? The largest group comprises elements found in sources from all parts of medieval Italy, known as pan-Italian tropes. A little over one quarter of the Nonantolan repertory of Introit trope elements (28%) have Italian concordances, including those parallels with southern manuscripts. Adding to these the apparent *unica* and Introit trope elements found exclusively in the three Nonantolan tropers and VEcap 107, the Italian component of the Nonantolan repertory increases to 42%. These figures correlate roughly to the percentage of Italian sequences in VEcap 107. According to Lance Brunner's research, approximately 30% of the sequences in this manuscript are of Italian composition.[11]

Outside Italy, studies of concordances referred to in the commentaries and elsewhere[12] indicate that the strongest affinity was with northern and central France. The connections between readings in the Nonantolan manuscripts and Pa 1169, for example, are close. The closeness of this connection contrasts with the relationship between Nonantolan and East Frankish tropers, where one would expect more affinity than what is actually found.

It remains difficult to account for this set of relationships. As explained in the "General Introduction," the Franco-Roman chant repertory that came to the abbey of Nonantola in the wake of the Carolingian reform of Roman liturgy was probably not pure, that is, it contained among other things accretions to the standard items that we call tropes and prosulae.[13] Because Nonantola's cultural ties with certain French centers were traditionally closer than those with East Frankish monasteries, it makes sense that such connections would be reflected in the Nonantolans' choice of repertory.

A Note on Performance Practice

Because directions for liturgical performance, known as ordinals (*ordines*), have not survived from the medieval abbey of Nonantola, reconstructing the performance there is a matter of conjecture. Evidence from other Italian centers, however, does shed some light on this matter. The eleventh-century ordinal of the cathedral of Verona (VEcap 94), for example, indicates that Proper tropes were performed by two or three soloists who alternated with a larger contingent of singers that performed the Proper items.[14] Thus one might think of the trope elements as soloistic interpolations inserted into choral chants. Prosulae and the verses which they elaborate were likewise performed by small groups of experienced singers.

Notes

1. The most recent of these is David Hiley, *Western Plainchant: A Handbook* (Oxford, 1993), 196–223.

2. Alejandro Planchart, "Italian Tropes," *Mosaic* 18 (1985): 11–31, has observed that Italian tropists were not always concerned with keeping a close connection between trope element and standard chant phrase. This is true in certain cases in the Nonantolan sources, but since about half the trope repertory was imported, it might be better characterized as international rather than strictly Italian.

3. This is suggested not only by the lack of a rubric, but also by the cue to the lesser doxology (*Gloria patri*) following v. [3].

4. An impression of the variability in use may be gained by consulting Olof Marcusson, ed., *Corpus Troporum II: Prosules de la messe, 1, Tropes de l'Alleluia*, Studia Latina Stockholmiensia, vol. 21 (Stockholm, 1976). Marcusson's identification of distinct prosulae forms the basis for the numeration of these pieces in this edition.

5. These are the four Sundays of Advent, the three Masses on Christmas Day, Epiphany, Sexagesima Sunday, the Fourth Sunday of Lent, Palm Sunday, Easter Sunday, Monday, Tuesday, and the Octave, First Sunday after Easter, Ascension, Pentecost, Trinity Sunday, and five Sundays after Pentecost.

6. St. Stephen, St. John Evangelist, St. Silvester, Purification, Ss. Senesius and Theopontius, St. John the Baptist, St. Peter, Translation of St. Benedict, St. Lawrence, Assumption, Birth of the Blessed Virgin, Michael Archangel, Ss. Simon and Jude, All Saints, St. Martin, and St. Andrew.

7. See James Borders, "The Northern and Central Italian Trope Repertoire and Its Transmission," *Atti del XIV Congresso della Società internazionale di Musicologia*, ed. Lorenzo Bianconi, 3 vols. (Turin, 1990), 3:546. For a further discussion of the transmission of tropes in Italy, see Planchart, "Italian Tropes," 11–31, and idem, "On the Nature and Transmission and Change in Trope Repertories," *JAMS* 41 (1988): 215–49. See also Planchart's seminal early study, *The Repertory of Tropes at Winchester*, 2 vols. (Princeton, 1977).

8. Planchart, "Italian Tropes," 11, describes the local conditions which, in part, governed the preservation of the Italian trope repertory. He observes that most Italian tropes come down to us in Gradual books, the format of which effectively limited the number of pieces preserved. See also James Borders, "Tropes and the New Philology," *Cantus Planus I: Papers Read at the Fourth Meeting, International Musical Society Study Group* (Budapest, 1992), 393–94.

9. The similarity of repertory among these manuscripts extends to the melodic readings, to the extent that this can be determined since the Verona manuscript is notated in staffless neumes.

10. Borders, "Northern," 544–45, 550.

11. Brunner, "The Sequences of Verona, Biblioteca capitolare CVII and the Italian Sequence Tradition," 2 vols. (Ph.D. diss., University of North Carolina, 1977), 1:162.

12. The different historical and geographical influences to which the entire Introit trope repertory was subject are discussed in David Hiley, "Some Observations on the Interrelationships between Trope Repertories," in *Research on Tropes*, ed. Gunilla Iversen (Stockholm, 1983), 29–37.

13. This conjecture is an extension of Richard Crocker's research on Latin Kyries summarized in "Troping Hypothesis," *MQ* 52 (1966): 183–203. See also Andrew Hughes, *Style and Symbol, Medieval Music: 800–1453*, Institute of Mediaeval Music, Musicological Studies, vol. 51 (Ottawa, 1989), 13–15.

14. James Borders, "The Cathedral of Verona as a Musical Center in the Middle Ages: Its History, Manuscripts, and Liturgical Practice," 2 vols. (Ph.D. diss., University of Chicago, 1983), 1:93–94.

Critical Apparatus

List of Manuscript Sigla

APT 17	Apt, Basilique de Ste. Anne, MS 17
APT 18	Apt, Basilique de Ste. Anne, MS 18
Bu 7	Bologna, Biblioteca Universitaria, MS Q 7
Bu 2824	Bologna, Biblioteca Universitaria, MS 2824
BAs 5	Bamberg, Staatliche Bibliothek, MS Lit. 5
BAs 6	Bamberg, Staatliche Bibliothek, MS Lit. 6
BV 34	Benevento, Biblioteca Capitolare, MS 34
BV 35	Benevento, Biblioteca Capitolare, MS 35
BV 39	Benevento, Biblioteca Capitolare, MS 39
Ccc 473	Cambridge, Corpus Christi College, MS 473
CA 60	Cambrai, Bibliothèque Municipale, MS 60
CA 75	Cambrai, Bibliothèque Municipale, MS 75
IV 60	Ivrea, Biblioteca Capitolare, MS 91 (Bollati LX)
Kl 15	Kassel, Murhardsche Bibliothek, MS 4° MS theol. 25
Lbm 14	London, British Library, Cotton MS Caligula A. xiv
Lbm 19768	London, British Library, Additional MS 19768
Mah 288	Madrid, Biblioteca Nacional, MS 288
Mah 289	Madrid, Biblioteca Nacional, MS 289
Mbs 14083	Munich, Bayerische Staatsbibliothek, MS clm. 14083
Mbs 14322	Munich, Bayerische Staatsbibliothek, MS clm. 14322
Mza 75	Monza, Biblioteca Capitolare, MS C 12/75
Mza 76	Monza, Biblioteca Capitolare, MS C 13/76
MOd 7	Modena, Biblioteca Capitolare (Duomo), MS O.I.7
MZ 452	Metz, Bibliothèque Municipale, MS 452
Ob 27	Oxford, Bodleian Library, MS Selden supra 27
Ob 222	Oxford, Bodleian Library, MS Douce 222
Ob 775	Oxford, Bodleian Library, MS Bodley 77
Pa 1169	Paris, Bibliothèque de l'Arsenal, MS 1169
Pn 778	Paris, Bibliothèque Nationale, fonds latin, MS 778
Pn 903	Paris, Bibliothèque Nationale, fonds latin, MS 903
Pn 909	Paris, Bibliothèque Nationale, fonds latin, MS 909
Pn 1084	Paris, Bibliothèque Nationale, fonds latin, MS 1084
Pn 1118	Paris, Bibliothèque Nationale, fonds latin, MS 1118
Pn 1119	Paris, Bibliothèque Nationale, fonds latin, MS 1119
Pn 1235	Paris, Bibliothèque Nationale, fonds latin, MS 1235
Pn 1240	Paris, Bibliothèque Nationale, fonds latin, MS 1240
Pn 9448	Paris, Bibliothèque Nationale, fonds latin, MS 9448
Pn 9449	Paris, Bibliothèque Nationale, fonds latin, MS 9449
Pn 10508	Paris, Bibliothèque Nationale, fonds latin, MS 10508
Pn 10510	Paris, Bibliothèque Nationale, fonds latin, MS 10510
Pn 13252	Paris, Bibliothèque Nationale, fonds latin, MS 13252
PAc 20	Padua, Biblioteca Capitolare, MS A 20
PAc 47	Padua, Biblioteca Capitolare, MS A 47
PAs 697	Padua, Biblioteca del Seminario Vescovile, MS 697
PCsa 65	Piacenza, Biblioteca e Archivio di San Antonio, MS 65
PS 119	Pistoia, Biblioteca Capitolare (Cattedrale), MS C 119
PS 120	Pistoia, Biblioteca Capitolare (Cattedrale), MS C 120

PS 121	Pistoia, Biblioteca Capitolare (Cattedrale), MS C 121
Ra 123	Rome, Biblioteca Angelica, MS 123
Rc 1741	Rome, Biblioteca Casanatense, MS 1741
Rn 1343	Rome, Biblioteca Nationale Centrale Vittorio Emanuele III, MS 1343 (olim Sessoriano 62)
Rv 52	Rome, Biblioteca Valliceliana, MS C 52
Rvat 602	Rome, Biblioteca Apostolica Vaticana, Urb. lat. 602
SGs 381	Saint Gall, Stiftsbibliothek, MS 381
SGs 484	Saint Gall, Stiftsbibliothek, MS 484
Tn 18	Turin, Biblioteca Nazionale Universitaria, MS F.IV.18
Tn 20	Turin, Biblioteca Nazionale Universitaria, MS G.V.20
VCd 146	Vercelli, Biblioteca Capitolare (Duomo), MS 146
VCd 161	Vercelli, Biblioteca Capitolare (Duomo), MS 161
VCd 162	Vercelli, Biblioteca Capitolare (Duomo), MS 162
VEcap 90	Verona, Biblioteca Capitolare, MS XC
VEcap 105	Verona, Biblioteca Capitolare, MS CV
VEcap 107	Verona, Biblioteca Capitolare, MS CVII
VO 39	Volterra, Biblioteca Guarnacci, MS L.3.39
Wn 1609	Vienna, Österreichische Nationalbibliothek, MS 1609

List of Works Cited

Benoit-Castelli, "L'Antienne" = Benoit-Castelli, Georges. "L'Antienne 'Jam fulget oriens'." *Études grégoriennes* 4 (1961): 55–61.

Borders, "The Cathedral" = Borders, James. "The Cathedral of Verona as a Musical Center in the Middle Ages: Its History, Manuscripts, and Liturgical Practice." 2 vols. Ph.D. diss., University of Chicago, 1983.

Borders, "Northern" = Borders, James. "The Northern and Central Italian Trope Repertoire and Its Transmission." In *Atti del XIV Congresso della Società internazionale di Musicologia*. 3 vols. Edited by Lorenzo Bianconi et al., 3:543–53. Turin, 1990.

Borders, "Tropes" = Borders, James. "Tropes and the New Philology." In *Cantus Planus I: Papers Read at the Fourth Meeting, International Musical Society Study Group*. Budapest, 1992. Pp. 393–406.

Brunner, "Sequences" = Brunner, Lance. "The Sequences of Verona, Biblioteca capitolare CVII and the Italian Sequence Tradition." Ph.D. diss., University of North Carolina, 1977.

CT 1/1 = Jonsson, Ritva, et al., eds. *Corpus Troporum I: Tropes du propre de la messe. 1, Cycle de Noël*. Studia Latina Stockholmiensia, vol. 21. Stockholm, 1975.

CT 2/1 = Marcusson, Olof, ed. *Corpus Troporum II: Prosules de la messe. 1, Tropes de l'Alleluia*. Studia Latina Stockholmiensia, vol. 22. Stockholm, 1976.

CT 3/2 = Björkvall, Gunilla, Gunilla Iversen, and Ritva Jonsson, eds. *Corpus Troporum III: Tropes du propre de la messe. 2, Cycle de Paques*. Studia Latina Stockholmiensia, vol. 25. Stockholm, 1982.

CT 5 = Björkvall, Gunilla, ed. *Corpus Troporum V: Les deux tropaires d'Apt mss. 17 et 18: Inventaire, édition et analyse*. Studia Latina Stockholmiensia, vol. 37. Stockholm, 1986.

De Boor, *Die Textgeschichte* = De Boor, Helmut. *Die Textgeschichte der lateinischen Osterfeiern*. Hermanea germanistische Forschungen, n.s., 22 (1967): 68–80.

Evans, *Early Trope Repertory* = Evans, Paul. *The Early Trope Repertory of Saint Martial de Limoges*. Princeton, 1970.

Gautier, *Les Tropes* = Gautier, Léon. *Histoire de la poésie liturgique au moyen âge: Les Tropes*. 1886. Reprint, Ridgewood, N.J., 1966.

Hiley, "Some Observations" = Hiley, David. "Some Observations on the Interrelationships between Trope Repertories." In *Research On Tropes*. Edited by Gunilla Iversen, 29–37. Stockholm, 1983.

Hiley, *Western Plainchant* = Hiley, David. *Western Plainchant: A Handbook*. Oxford, 1993.

Husmann, "Sinn und Wesen" = Husmann, Heinrich. "Sinn und Wesen der Tropen: Veranschaulicht an den Introitustropen des Weihnachtsfestes." *Archiv für Musikwissenschaft* 16 (1959): 135–47.

McGee, "The Liturgical Placements" = McGee, Timothy. "The Liturgical Placements of the *Quem quaeritis* Dialogue." *JAMS* 39 (1967): 1–29.

Pfaff, *Die Tropen* = Pfaff, Heinrich. "Die Tropen und Sequenzen der Handschrift Rom, Bibl. Naz. Vitt. Emm. 1343 (Sessor. 62) aus Nonantola." Inaugural-Dissertation, Ludwig-Maximillian University, Munich, 1948.

Planchart, "Italian Tropes" = Planchart, Alejandro Enrique. "Italian Tropes." *Mosaic* 18 (1985): 11–31.

Planchart, "Nature and Transmission" = Planchart, Alejandro. "On the Nature and Transmission and Change in Trope Repertories," *JAMS* 41 (1988): 215–49.

Planchart, *Repertory* = Planchart, Alejandro Enrique. *The Repertory of Tropes at Winchester.* 2 vols. Princeton, 1977.

Roederer, *Festive Troped Masses* = Roederer, Charlotte, ed. *Festive Troped Masses from the Eleventh Century: Christmas and Easter in the Aquitaine.* Collegium Musicum: Yale University, 2d ser., vol. 11. Madison, 1989.

Schlager, *Alleluia-Melodien* = Schlager, Karlheinz, ed. *Alleluia-Melodien I.* Monumenta Monodica Medii Aevi, vol. 7, Kassel, 1968.

Stäblein, *"Gregorius Praesul"* = Stäblein, Bruno. *"Gregorius Praesul,* der Prolog zum römischen Antiphonale." In *Musik und Verlag: Karl Vötterle zum 65. Geburtstag.* Edited by Richard Baum and Wolfgang Rehm, 537–61. Kassel, 1968.

Stäblein, *Hymnen* = Stäblein, Bruno, ed. *Hymnen: Die mittelalterlichen Hymnenmelodien des Abendlandes.* Monumenta Monodica Medii Aevi, vol. 1. Kassel, 1956.

Strehl, "Zum Zusammenhang" = Strehl, Reinhard. "Zum Zusammenhang von Tropus und Prosa 'Ecce iam Christus'." *Die Musikforschung* 17 (1964): 269–71.

Treitler, "Homer and Gregory" = Treitler, Leo. "Homer and Gregory: The Transmission of Epic Poetry and Plainchant." *MQ* 40 (1974): 333–72.

Van Deusen, *Music at Nevers* = Van Deusen, Nancy. *Music at Nevers Cathedral: Principal Sources of Medieval Chant.* 2 vols. Musicological Studies, vol. 30, nos. 1–2. Henryville, Ottawa, and Binningen, 1980.

Vecchi, *Troparium* = Vecchi, Giuseppe, ed. *Troparium Sequentiarium Nonantulanum: Cod. Casanat. 1741.* Monumenta Lyrica Medii Aevi Italica, I: Latina. Modena, 1955.

Weiss, *Introitus Tropen* = Weiss, Günther, ed. *Introitus-Tropen, I. Das Repertoire der südfranzösischen Tropare des 10. und 11. Jahrhunderts.* Monumenta Monodica Medii Aevi, vol. 3. Kassel, 1961.

Editorial Methods

Arrangement and Identification of Proper Tropes and Prosulae

Tropes and prosulae for the Proper of the Mass in this volume are arranged into two distinct series according to their use during the church year and their liturgical assignment, a scheme of organization that corresponds to the arrangement of the manuscript sources from the abbey of Nonantola. Thus, tropes for Christmas precede those for Pentecost, and Introit tropes for a given feast precede those for the Offertory and Communion. Individual trope elements are generally combined with one another as they were presumably performed. These groupings are referred to as trope complexes in the commentaries and they are numbered sequentially regardless of the genre of chant they accompany. For example, no. 13 identifies *Qui primus meruit,* a four-element trope complex sung with the Introit, *Etenim sederunt,* while no. 14 is the introductory Communion trope, *Magnus et felix,* for *Video caelos apertos.* All Proper chants have been transcribed from VEcap 105, a plenary missal employing Nonantolan notation, since no complete Gradual from Nonantola survives. Rubrics are reproduced as they are found in the manuscript sources, although the various abbreviations of the word *tropus* have been left standing. (For a discussion of the reasoning behind this decision, see Eva Odelman, "Comment a-t-on appelé les tropes? Observations sur les rubriques des tropes des Xe et XIe siècles," *Cahiers de civilisation médiévale* 18 [1975]: 14–36.)

Like the tropes of the Proper, the prosulae for Graduals, Tracts, Alleluias, and Offertories are presented in manuscript order, that is, in order of feast and liturgical assignment. They are numbered individually and presented as distinct pieces in the commentaries, the foundation for the editor's identification of individual prosulae being *CT* 2/1. To facilitate their musical performance, however, prosulae that were combined in the Nonantolan tropers within the same Proper chant are printed together in this edition. Thus, prosulae no. 8, *Audi nos te deprecamur,* and no. 9, *Alme caeli rex immortalis,* appear in close proximity since they were sung successively during performances of the Alleluia ℣ *Dies sanctificatus.* The same applies to prosulae nos. 14–15, 17–18, 21–22, 23–25, and 31–33.

Text incipits of introductory tropes, trope complexes, and prosulae are included in the headings to individual pieces in the commentaries and in the music where applicable. Because these incipits also serve as uniform titles in the edition, their spelling has been standardized for ease of access and recognition according to normal classical grammar and spellings as reported in Lewis and Short, *A Latin Dictionary.* Thus *Aeterno genitus genitore* is the uniform title of the Introit trope for St. John Evangelist (no. 15) despite the fact that Nonantolan scribes rendered the first word as *Eterne.* Proper names, including *Deus* but not *dominus,* are also capitalized in the uniform titles but nowhere else unless indicated in the typical manuscript readings. Finally, the manuscript source of the chant selected as the typical reading, along with inclusive folio numbers, is signaled by boldface type in the commentaries; the source is also provided at the beginning of the first line of the music.

Selection and Presentation of Versions and Variants

In most cases, the versions of chants in this edition come from Rn 1343. The decision to treat this manuscript as the typical source rests on two observations concerning the three Nonantolan tropers and their relationships. First, Rn 1343 is earlier and thus closer to the presumed original source than Rc 1741, which is otherwise comparable to Rn 1343 in its scope and contents. Second, the text and melodic readings in Bu 2824, which is perhaps the earliest Nonantolan source but the one containing the fewest items, generally agree with Rn 1343 but not as frequently with Rc 1741. One should note, however, that the versions of chants in Rn 1343 and Bu 2824 are not necessarily more correct textually or musically than Rc 1741. As a practical consideration, the editor also notes that a facsimile edition of Rc 1741 (Vecchi, *Troparium*) is widely available for comparison with this edition.

In certain cases, however, a version of a chant other than that in Rn 1343 has been selected for inclusion in the edition. This applies if the Rn 1343 text or music is marred by extensive lacunae or obvious mistakes. Regardless of which source has been judged typical, all the available Nonantolan readings may be reassembled from the variants listed in the commentary. Of course, pieces not found in Rn 1343 but in one or both of the other tropers are identified as such.

Typical Texts and Translations

Proper chant texts are centered in the commentary; trope elements, verses, and prosulae are printed flush to the left margin and provided with arabic numerals enclosed in square brackets based on their sequence in a complex. The Latin trope and Proper chant texts are always printed in roman type. For prosulae, however, italic and boldface types are employed to clarify the relationship between these texts and the standard chant texts, following the practice of CT 2/1. Proper texts printed in *italic* form an integral part of a prosula's structure; **boldface** indicates a Proper text that stands outside of that structure, such as an incipit.

Typical texts in the edition are rendered diplomatically. In exceptional cases, however, editorial emendations have been made to clarify meaning. These are always given in square brackets. The incipits of Psalms and the lesser doxology (*Gloria patri*) are given as they appear in the manuscripts. Ellipses have been added in the translations to indicate the continuation of the Psalm verse or lesser doxology. The Nonantolan tropers exclude nearly all punctuation, but the scribes did use capital letters to mark the beginnings of new periods and, for this reason, the capitalization of the typical readings has been scrupulously retained. The resultant long lines are divided into sense units in the text edition to clarify the structure of the chants and to render syntax understandable without added punctuation. The musical settings of these texts, however, are printed as through-composed.

Spellings have also been retained from the manuscript sources in both the commentary and the music. Hence the letters *i* and *j* are treated as the same letter (*i*), following the practice of the Nonantolan scribes. Only text variants that have a bearing on meaning, syntax, or pronunciation are reported in the commentary. Thus variants of orthography, such as differences in the use of *c* and *t* in words like *gratias*, are not indicated. Moreover, although the *ae* ligature (in Rn 1343 and Bu 2824) or *e-caudata* (in Rc 1741) are presented in the typical readings as in the manuscript source, the differing practices of the scribes with respect to their use are not reported, nor are variants noted. Errors in a single word or letter of the typical text have been corrected in translation and cued in the commentary. Oversights and errors in initial letters, to which the rubricating scribe of Rn 1343 was unfortunately prone, have been corrected based on concordant readings.

Standard contractions and suspension found in the texts—such as ℊ for *per*, ℊ for *pro*, ℊ for *qui*, ℊ for *-bus*, and the *nomina sacra* including *Xpistus* for *Christus*—have been resolved in the texts of the edition and commentary without comment. Truncated or heavily abbreviated phrases of the base chant texts, however, have been reproduced as they are found in the typical source, with abbreviations expanded within angle brackets. All other editorial additions are placed within square brackets.

English translations are provided for all the Latin texts. These translations employ modern liturgical English in the style of the New American Catholic Edition of the Bible (New York, 1961) and *The Saint Andrew Daily Missal* (Bruges, 1962). Literary sources for the tropes in Holy Scripture, the writings of the Fathers, and in the liturgy are traced in the appropriate *Corpus Troporum* volumes. In the present edition, no consistent attempt has been made to duplicate these references, although they are sometimes discussed in the commentaries. Similarly, certain irregularities in the standard Latin meters are alluded to but not discussed.

The Notation of Music in the Edition

Following modern scholarly custom, chants in this edition are notated in stemless black noteheads on five-line staves with either bass or treble clef transposed down an octave. In addition to stemless noteheads, two special signs are also employed in the commentary and the music. The first is the oriscus, which signals a prolongation of the preceding note or a note repetition. In the commentaries an oriscus is indicated as a tilde (~) printed next to the letter name designating its pitch; in the music the oriscus appears as an italic *n*. The second special sign is the liquescent, which is transcribed as two slurred notes, the second being smaller and in parentheses as in Roederer, *Festive Troped Masses;* the slurs are placed under the notes with a verticule. Nonantolan scribes used liquescent neumes in connection with most diphthongs and liquid consonants. The singing of B-flat is also occasionally indicated in Rc 1741 by an additional green line (besides the yellow and red ones). Where B-flat is clearly called for in a chant melody, a flat sign has been placed on the staff. In all other cases nothing has been added.

All notes sung to a single syllable are printed under a slur. Slurs within slurs indicate ligated notes; gapped slurs show subgroupings of notes within aggregate neumes. The manuscript readings generally correspond in the subgrouping of neumes; the few variants that do occur are not reported in the critical apparatus because they have not been judged to affect performance significantly. Although bar lines were obviously not notated by the Nonantolan scribes, single bars are employed in the edition to distinguish the trope elements from the phrases of the Proper texts and to close certain other sections of music. Double bars are found at the ends of pieces. But since the prosulae are to be inserted into whole compositions, these are marked with single barlines.

All music not found in the typical source is given in square brackets, particularly the portions of standard chants which the scribe left unnotated. Single hyphens have been inserted between syllables in the text indicating the division according to the rules of syllabification in Latin classical verse. Thus *Chris-te* is preferred over *Chri-ste,* and *Be-ne-dic-tus* over *Be-ne-di-ctus.*

Pitch is designated in the commentary according to the medieval gamut, beginning on the lowest line of the bass clef:

Γ A B C D E F G a b-flat b c d e f g

The notation for Psalm verses and the lesser doxology (*Gloria patri*) appended to some antiphons in the manuscript sources has been rendered diplomatically. No attempt has been made in such cases to supply the missing portions of the melodic formulae, called *toni,* where the Nonantolan versions have not survived. Should the performance of these simple formulaic verses be desired, the user is directed to the appropriate pages of *GR, GT,* and Terence Bailey, *The Intonation Formulas of Western Chant,* Pontifical Institute of Mediaeval Studies, Studies and Texts, vol. 28 (Toronto, 1974).

Commentaries

Each commentary includes:

- SOURCE of text and music gives the location of each chant in the Nonantolan manuscripts. The main source of the text and music in the edition is indicated in **boldface.**
- REFERENCES to books, editions, periodical articles, and dissertations in which information about the chant and its text may be found. (See the lists of abbreviations and works cited.)
- A TEXT COMMENTARY which describes the structure of the text (those in standard meters are designated as such) and briefly surveys other aspects, such as its meaning and liturgical or historical background.
- The TEXT AND TRANSLATION of the main source.
- An overview of the DISTINCTIVE VARIANTS that differentiate the Nonantolan readings from those found in other sources. Here, special attention has been devoted to concordances in northern and central Italian manuscripts—to treat more fully the range of European concordances for all the chants discussed would have represented a project well beyond the scope of this edition. (The sigla for manuscripts cited in the commentaries are generally those employed in RISM.) As is the case with MELODIC VARIANTS, the manuscript source of the variant is indicated in **boldface** type. When multiple trope elements or verses are involved, the portion of the text in which the variant appears is identified by its verse number in square brackets. Thereafter follow the variant words or phrases and the readings from the typical text. Individual variants are separated by a semicolon; variants in the different manuscript sources are separated by a period.
- A listing of MELODIC VARIANTS in the Nonantolan tropers based on the approaches of Stäblein, *Hymnen,* and Schlager, *Alleluia-Melodien.* The manuscript source of the melodic variants is indicated in boldface type. Thereafter follow individual words in italics, with the unaffected syllables in parentheses. When multiple trope elements or verses are involved, the portion of the text in which the variant appears is identified by its verse number in square brackets. The letter of the medieval gamut represent the pitches of the scale (see above). Liquescent notes are indicated in parentheses and the oriscus is represented by a tilde (~) placed next to the letter name designating its pitch. Letters are grouped in two ways, either with a space between groups of letters to indicate groupings of neumes over the same syllable or with an apostrophe to indicate a syllable break. Individual variants are separated by a semicolon; variants in the different manuscript sources are separated by a period.

Proper Chants and Tropes

1. Introit: Ad te levavi

TROPE: *Sanctissimus namque Gregorius*

SOURCES

Rn 1343 fols. 18r–v Tropus in dom<inic>a de Adventu (addn.)
Rc 1741 fols. 46v–47r Trop Dom<inica> De adven<u>.
Bu 2824 fols. 15v–16v TRophe i<n> adventu<m> d<omi>ni

REFERENCES

AH 49, no. 3 (see also pp. 19–24); *CT* 1/1, 195, 69, 209; *AMS*, xxxiv–xxxv; *New Grove*, s.v. "Gregory the Great," by Helmut Hucke; Planchart, "Italian Tropes," 29, n. 1; Stäblein, "*Gregorius Praesul*," 537–61; Treitler, "Homer and Gregory," 333–72.

TEXT COMMENTARY

In prose; v. [1] may be divided into two sections, each comprising five lines of similar length but different patterns of accentuation. Also note the inexact parallelism between vv. [2] and [3], which is echoed in the musical setting.

Sanctissimus namque Gregorius is among a number of medieval texts that treat the central legend of chant composition literally. In v. [1] Pope Gregory prays for inspiration and the Lord responds by sending the Holy Spirit in the form of a dove. The introduction ends dramatically, that is, at the very moment when the saint begins to dictate the opening Introit of the church year. (The Gregory myth and its significance to the music history of the Carolingian period are discussed in Treitler, "Homer and Gregory," 334–44.) Vv. [2–3] lack a clear connection to the introduction, but together comprise a petition for faith in the common form of a prayer.

TEXT AND TRANSLATION

[1] Sanctissimus namque gregorius
cum preces effunderet ad dominum
ut musicum tonum ei
desuper in carminibus
dedisset
Tunc descendit spiritus sanctus
super eum in specie columbæ
et illustravit cor eius
et sic demum exorsus est canere
ita dicendo
    Ad te levavi [animam meam]
[2] Creator cæli et terræ
institutor et rector
adimple in nobis fidem
et dilectionem tuam
    Deus [meus in te confido
    non erubescam]
[3] Ut possimus contrariæ
virtuti resistere
ac tibi fideliter
servire
    neque [irrideant me inimici mei
    etenim universi
    qui te exspectant non confundentur]
    [Ps.] Vias tuas domine

*

[1] For most holy Gregory
prayed to the Lord
that, from above,
He would impart to him
musical sound in songs.
Then the Holy Spirit descended
upon him in the form of a dove
and lit up his heart,
and so he began to sing,
singing thus:
    To You I have lifted up my soul.
[2] Creator of heaven and earth,
Founder and Ruler,
increase in us faith and love:
    O my God, in You I put my trust,
    let me not be put to shame.
[3] So that we may resist temptation
and serve You faithfully:
    Let not my enemies ridicule me,
    for none who waits for You shall be confounded.
    Ps. Your Way, O Lord . . .

DISTINCTIVE VARIANTS

Rc 1741 [1] *inlustravit* for *illustravit*. **Bu 2824** [1] *corda* for *cor*. All northern Italian sources of v. [1] preserve basically the same melody, although Tn 18 is somewhat more elaborate than the other versions. Vv. [2–3] are found only in the Nonantolan tropers and VEcap 107, which resemble one another closely in their neumations.

MELODIC VARIANTS

Rc 1741 [1] *(Sanc)tis(simus)* FE; *(nam)que* GG~F; *(musi)cum* a(G); *et (sic)* GFD Fa F(G); [2] (Transposed) Creator C'DC'D (etc.); *(ad)im(ple)* E(D); [3] (Transposed) *Ut possimus* C'CD'DE'DC (etc.). **Bu 2824** [1] *(sanc)tis(simus)* FE; *(grego)ri(us)* aG; *et (sic)* GFD Fa F(G); *(cor)da* lacking notation.

2. Introit: Ad te levavi

TROPE: *Almipotens verus Deus*

SOURCES

Rn 1343 fol. 18v (no rubric)
Rc 1741 fols. 47r–v alius ton<us>
Bu 2824, fol. 16v (no rubric)

REFERENCE
CT 1/1, 57.

TEXT COMMENTARY
Although written in prose, the beginning of this trope of introduction resembles hexameter verse ("Almipotens . . . succure"). The mode of expression is similar to that of numerous prayers of the Mass and Office.

TEXT AND TRANSLATION
Almipotens verus deus immensus
succurre nobis hodie
per adventum tuum
nobis tuis famulis indignis
    Ad te levavi [animam meam
    Deus meus in te confido non erubescam
    neque irrideant me inimici mei etenim universi
        qui te exspectant non confundentur]
        Gl<ori>a pa<tr>i
          *

Gracious in might, true, boundless God,
help us, Your unworthy servants, today
by Your coming:
    To You I have lifted up my soul.
    O my God, in You I put my trust, let me not be
        put to shame.
    Let not my enemies ridicule me,
    for none who waits for You shall be confounded.
        Glory be to the Father . . .

DISTINCTIVE VARIANTS
Bu 2824 cue *Gloria patri* lacking. The Nonantolan tropers and VEcap 107, the only known sources of the trope, correspond in their text and music. In VEcap 107, however, "Almipotens verus deus" is followed by two internal elements, "Creator caeli" and "Ut possimus," sung at Nonantola in connection with *Sanctissimus namque Gregorius* (no. 1). Noteworthy in the relationship between words and music in *Sanctissimus* is the form a a' b, which corresponds to the rhetorical division of the text.

MELODIC VARIANTS
    Rc 1741 *(im)men(sus)* c(b); *tu(um)* cdca; *(in)dig(nis)* a(G). **Bu 2824** *(im)men(sus)* c(b).

3. Introit: Ad te levavi

TROPE: *Ecce iam Christus*

SOURCES
Rn 1343 fol. 18v (no rubric)
Rc 1741 fols. 47v–48r (no rubric)
Bu 2824, fols. 17r–v al<ius> [tonus]

REFERENCES
AH 37, no. 14; Brunner, "Sequences," 170–71; *CT* 1/1, 84, 201, 72, 191; Strehl, "Zum Zusammenhang," 269–71.

TEXT COMMENTARY
The four elements of this prose trope are related to the Italian sequence *Ecce iam Christus* (*AH* 37, no. 14). As was the case with *Almipotens verus Deus*, the resemblance to prayer formulas is noteworthy, particularly in vv. [1–3].

TEXT AND TRANSLATION
[1] Ecce iam christus
     quem sancti patres prophetarunt
     advenit nobis
        Ad te [levavi animam meam]
[2] Suam nos salvet per nativitatem gloriosam
        Deus [meus in te confido
          non erubescam]
[3] Cui omnes occurrentes clamemus
     salva nos deus rex israhel
        Neque [irrideant me inimici mei]
[4] Rex christe deus abraham deus isaac
     deus iacob miserere nobis
     Quia tu es salvator et misericors
     verax pius et sanctissimus amen
        Etenim [universi qui te exspectant
          non confundentur]
        *

[1] Lo! At this very time Christ,
     whom the holy prophets foretold, comes to us:
        To You I have lifted up my soul.
[2] May He save us by His glorious nativity:
        O my God, in You I put my trust,
        let me not be put to shame.
[3] As we all run to meet You, let us cry out:
     "Save us, God, King of Israel!"
        Let not my enemies ridicule me.
[4] Christ the King, God of Abraham, God of Isaac,
     God of Jacob, have mercy on us!
     For You are the Savior and the merciful One,
     truthful, benevolent, and most holy One:
        For none who waits for You
          shall be confounded.

DISTINCTIVE VARIANTS
Bu 2824 [1] *prophetarum* for *prophetarunt*. Italian manuscripts yield four versions of *Ecce iam Christus*, discussed in Brunner, "Sequences." These include a sequence, the text of which corresponds closely to the above Introit trope (see esp. Tn 18, fol. 2v). It is not certain whether the sequence or the trope originated first. Strehl argues for the primacy of the former, but his reasoning is based on an incomplete survey of the sources.

MELODIC VARIANTS
   Rc 1741 [1] *Chris(tus)* G; [3] *om(nes)* aa(G); [4] *(a)bra-(ham)* cbaG.

4. Introit: Dominus dixit

TROPE: *Verbo altissimi patris*

SOURCES
Rn 1343 fols. 19r–v Troph. IN NOC<te>. In N<atale>. D<omi>ni
Rc 1741 fols. 49v–50r trop In nocte [in] nat<ale> d<omini>.
Bu 2824 fols. 18r–v Ton<us> in nat<ale> d<omi>ni ad missa de noc<te>

REFERENCES
CT 1/1, 212, 176, 99; Pfaff, *Die Tropen*, 139.

TEXT COMMENTARY
   This prose trope was probably transmitted from southern France to northern Italy, where it is found in the Nonantolan tropers and VEcap 107.

TEXT AND TRANSLATION
[1]   Verbum altissimi patris genitoque regis
         prophetica laude psallendo
                  Dominus [dixit ad me]
[2]   Quia veni vitam largire regiamque gloria recitare
                  Filius [meus es tu]
[3]   Venerante filium
         vaticinando prophetando atque dicendo
                  Ego ho[die genui te]
                         *
[1]   By the word of the Father most high and with
         the birth of the King,
      with the prophet's praise to be sung in the
         Psalm:
                  The Lord said to me:
[2]   Because You came to bestow life and proclaim
         the King's glory,
                  "You are my Son."
[3]   The begetting Son,
      by predicting, prophesying, and saying:
                  "This day I have begotten You."

DISTINCTIVE VARIANTS
   Rc 1741 [1] *Verbo* for *Verbum*; [2] *largiri regiamque gloriam* for *largire regiamque gloria*; [3] *Generante* for *Venerante*. **Bu 2824** [1] *Verbo* for *Verbum* (corrected); [3] *Generantem* for *Venerante*. The Nonantolan tropers and VEcap 107 are the sole Italian sources of this trope; it also survives in three Aquitanian tropers and APT 18. Regarding regional differences, the non-Italian sources of v. [1] agree in their texts, transmitting *patri* for *patris*, *regi* for *regis*, and *proficiat* for *prophetica*; APT 18 corresponds to the Nonantolan MSS and VEcap 107 in this case. Likewise for vv. [2–3], the Italian texts agree against the Aquitanian reading.
   Aquitanian manuscripts transmit two different melodies for these elements, neither of which corresponds exactly to that found in the Nonantolan tropers. With respect to overall shape, however, the Nonantolan version more closely resembles Pn 887 than Pn 1871.

MELODIC VARIANTS
   Rc 1741 [2] *(ve)ni* Ga; [3] *at(que)* FGFE E(D). **Bu 2824** [2] *(ve)nit* FG.

5. Introit: Lux fulgebit

TROPE: *Hora est iam nos*

SOURCES
Rn 1343 fol. 19v Troph ad mis<sa> de luce.
Rc 1741 fols. 50r–v Trop de Luce.
Bu 2824 fols. 20v–21r Troph

REFERENCE
CT 1/1, 113.

TEXT COMMENTARY
   The prose trope of introduction *Hora est iam nos* is found exclusively in northern and central Italian sources, that is, the Nonantolan tropers, VEcap 107, Ob 222, IV 60, and Ra 123. It opens with a verbatim passage from Rom. 13.11 ("hora est . . . surgere"), and continues with imagery and words drawn from Jer. 32.19 ("cuius occuli aperti sunt") and John 1.9 ("lux vera") amplifying the theme of the Introit, *Lux fulgebit* (Isa. 9.2, 6, 7).

TEXT AND TRANSLATION
Hora est iam nos de somno surgere
et aperti sunt oculi nostri surgere ad lucem
quia lux vera fulget in cælo
         Lux fulgeb<it> [hodie super nos
         quia natus est nobis dominus
         et vocabitur admirabilis
               deus princeps pacis
               pater futuri seculi
         cuius regni non erit finis]
[Ps.] D<omi>n<u>s reg<navit> dec<orem>
                  *
It is now the hour for us to rise from sleep
and open our eyes, lifting (them) to the light,
for the True Light shines forth in heaven:
   A light shall shine upon us this day:
      for the Lord is born to us:
      and He shall be called Wonderful,

God, the Prince of Peace,
the Father of the world to come:
of whose reign there shall be no end.
Ps. The Lord has reigned . . .

DISTINCTIVE VARIANTS
Rc 1741 *cęlis* for *cælo*. **Bu 2824** *sonno* for *somno*; *cælis* for *cælo*. The exclusively Italian sources of *Hora est iam nos* display considerable variation in the text toward the end of the line (see *CT* 1/1, 113), but correspond in their musical settings. Ob 222 shows the greatest independence from the other readings.

MELODIC VARIANTS
None.

6. Introit: Lux fulgebit

TROPE: *Ecce iam venit hora*

SOURCES
Rn 1343 fol. 19v (no rubric)
Rc 1741 fol. 50v Alius ton<us>
Bu 2824 fol. 21r (no rubric)

REFERENCE
CT 1/1, 84.

TEXT COMMENTARY
This prose introduction to *Lux fulgebit* alludes to the fulfillment of the prophesy on Christmas. It refers specifically to "all things that were announced by the angel" to the shepherds, a scene described in gospel for the Mass at Dawn (Luke 2.17). The trope survives exclusively in the Nonantolan tropers and VEcap 107.

TEXT AND TRANSLATION
Ecce iam venit hora illa ut procedat dominus
quem prophetæ predixerunt
impleta sunt omnia per mariam virginem
adnunciante angelo
    Lux ful<gebit> [hodie super nos
    quia natus est nobis dominus
    et vocabitur admirabilis
    deus princeps pacis
    pater futuri seculi
    cuius regni non erit finis]
    Gl<ori>a patri
*
Lo! The hour is at hand in which the Lord,
whom the prophets foretold, is born;
all things that were announced by the angel were
    fulfilled by the Virgin Mary:
    A light shall shine upon us this day:
    for the Lord is born to us:
    and He shall be called Wonderful,
    God, the Prince of Peace,
    the Father of the world to come:
    of whose reign there shall be no end.
    Glory be to the Father . . .

DISTINCTIVE VARIANTS
Bu 2824 *Gloria patri* incipit lacking. The melodic readings in the Nonantolan MSS and VEcap 107, the only sources of the trope, are very similar.

MELODIC VARIANTS
Rc 1741 *(proce)dat* c(b); *(im)ple(ta)* F; *an(gelo)* abaG G(F).

7. Introit: Lux fulgebit

TROPE: *Iam surgens aurora*

SOURCES
Rn 1343 fol. 19v (no rubric)
Rc 1741 fol. 50v (no rubric)
Bu 2824 fol. 21v (no rubric)

REFERENCES
Benoit-Castelli, "L'Antienne," 55–63; *CT* 1/1, 115; Planchart, *Repertory*, 1:223, 2:117–19.

TEXT COMMENTARY
Iam surgens aurora, which comes down to us in the Nonantolan tropers, VEcap 107, and VO 39, is an adaptation of the Christmas trope, *Iam fulget oriens* (*CT* 1/1, 115). The latter survived into modern times as a processional antiphon for the Fourth Sunday of Advent and the Vigil of Christmas (*Processional monastique* [Solesmes, 1893], 26).

TEXT AND TRANSLATION
Iam surgens aurora
iam veniet dies
iam venit dominus
illuminare nobis lumen vitæ
    Lux fulg<ebit> [hodie super nos
    quia natus est nobis dominus
    et vocabitur admirabilis
    deus princeps pacis
    pater futuri seculi
    cuius regni non erit finis]
*
Now the dawn is breaking,
and now the day shall come;
now the Lord comes
to illuminate in us the light of life:
    A light shall shine upon us this day:
    for the Lord is born to us:
    and He shall be called Wonderful,
    God, the Prince of Peace,
    the Father of the world to come:
    of whose reign there shall be no end.

DISTINCTIVE VARIANTS

Rc 1741 *venit et* for *veniet*. The readings in the Nonantolan tropers and VEcap 107 are nearly identical. For a comparison of the text and melodies of *Iam surgens aurora* and the more widely transmitted *Iam fulget oriens*, from which the Nonantolan trope stems, see Benoit-Castelli, "L'Antienne."

MELODIC VARIANTS
None.

8. Introit: *Puer natus est nobis*

TROPE: *Hodie salvator mundi per virginem*

SOURCES
Rn 1343 fol. 20r Tropi in die ad missam.
Rc 1741 fols. 51v–52r Trop ad missa<m>.
Bu 2824 fols. 22v–23r Troph

REFERENCES
CT 1/1, 112, 175, 144, 134; Husmann, "Sinn und Wesen," 135–36; Planchart, *Repertory*, 2:138–41.

TEXT COMMENTARY
Vv. [3–4] are drawn from the same biblical source as the Introit text they elaborate, namely, Isa. 7.14 and 9.6 respectively. Note that imbedded within v. [4] is the text of the preceding verse, suggesting that the lines may have been composed at different times.

The introduction *Hodie salvator mundi*, which is non-scriptural, resembles certain *Hodie* Office chants (cf. *CAO* 4: 6848, 6856, 6858). Like this trope, many of these antiphons were composed in the East Frankish region.

TEXT AND TRANSLATION

[1] Hodie salvator mundi per virginem nasci dignatus est
    gaudeamus omnes de christo domino
    qui natus est nobis eia et eia
        Puer natus [est nobis
        et filius datus est nobis]
[2] Quem virgo maria genuit
    Cuius imp<eriu>m [super humerum eius]
[3] Nomen eius hemmanuhel vocabitur
    Et vocabi<tur> [nomen eius]
[4] Magni conscilii angelus
    eia iste vocabitur nomen hemmanuhel
    psallite domino iubilate dicentes
        Magni [consilii angelus]
            *

[1] Today the Savior of the world deigned to be born of the virgin!
    Let us all rejoice because of Christ the Lord, who is born to us, yea and yea!
    A Child is born to us,
    and a Son is given to us.
[2] Whom the virgin Mary bore:
    Whose government is upon His shoulder.
[3] His name shall be called Emmanuel:
    And His name shall be called:
[4] The angel of good counsel, aye!
    His name shall be called Emmanuel!
    Sing to the Lord! Make a joyful noise, singing:
        The Angel of good counsel.

DISTINCTIVE VARIANTS
Rn 1343 [3] cue *Et vocabitur* [Ps.] *Cant<ate> d<omino>* for cue *Et vocabit<ur> nomen eius*; [4] lacking. **Rc 1741** [4] cue *Magni [consilii angelus]* P<s.> *Cantate [domino canticum novum]* for cue *Magni [consilii angelus]*. The four elements of the Nonantolan trope have different patterns of transmission. Vv. [2] and [3] circulated widely, but v. [1] has only two concordances outside northern Italy: one in the early Rhenish troper Lbm 19768, the other in a MS from Regensburg, Kl 15.

All northern and central Italian readings of *Hodie salvator mundi* correspond in their musical settings. In comparing the Nonantolan version with melodies transmitted outside Italy, one notes a similarity to Pn 1235 (Nevers) and to other French readings that circulated outside Aquitaine.

MELODIC VARIANTS
Rn 1343 [1] *qui natus* a'a'G; *e(ia et)* a; [2] *(ge)nu(it)* abaa~. **Rc 1741** [1] *sal(vator)* aa(G); *mundi* c(b)'aGa; *gau(deamus)* aa~; *om(nes)* c(b).

9. Introit: *Puer natus est nobis*

TROPE: *Hodie exultent iusti natus est*

SOURCES
Rn 1343 fol. 20r Alius tonus
Rc 1741 fols. 52r–v alius ton<us>
Bu 2824 fols. 23r–v (no rubric)

REFERENCES
CT 1/1, 108, 78–79, 100, 121; Pfaff, *Die Tropen*, 140; Planchart, *Repertory*, 2:136–38.

TEXT COMMENTARY
The opening of v. [1] was adapted in a trope for the feast of St. John the Baptist. V. [1] of this text (trope no. 45 in this edition) reads: "Hodie exultent iusti natus est sanctus iohannes deo gracias dicite eia." The Christmas trope is found in East Frankish sources predating those with the trope for St. John the Baptist, suggesting that the former is the original version.

TEXT AND TRANSLATION

[1] Hodie exultent iusti
  natus est filius dei
  deo gracias dicite eia
    Puer [natus est nobis
    et filius datus est nobis
    cuius imperium super humerum eius
    et vocabitur nomen eius]
[2] Deus pater filium suum misit in mundum
  de quo gratulantes dicamus cum propheta
    Magni [consilii angelus]
[3] Glorietur pater in filio suo unigenito
    Gl<ori>a patri [et filio
    et spiritui sancto]
[4] In principio erat et est in seculorum secula
    Sicut erat [in principio
    et nunc et semper
    et in secula seculorum amen]

*

[1] Let the just rejoice today!
  The Son of God is born,
  thanks be to God, sing, yea:
    A Child is born to us,
    and a Son is given to us:
    whose government is upon His shoulder:
    and His name shall be called.
[2] God the Father sent His Son into the world,
  of whom we sing joyfully with the prophet:
    The Angel of good counsel.
[3] May the Father glory in His only begotten Son:
    Glory be to the Father, and to the Son,
    and to the Holy Spirit.
[4] He was in the beginning and is forever:
    As it was in the beginning,
    is now, and ever shall be,
    world without end. Amen.

DISTINCTIVE VARIANTS

Bu 2824 [2] cue *magni con<silii>* P *Cantate domino* for cue *Magni [consilii angelus]*. Like the preceding trope complex, *Hodie salvator mundi,* the elements of *Hodie exultent iusti* have different patterns of transmission. V. [1] was known in Saint Gall, Reichenau (BAs 5), the Rhineland, and Autun (Pa 1169), though not in combination with the more widely disseminated v. [2]. Vv. [3–4], whose only Italian witnesses are the Nonantola MSS and VEcap 107, have mostly French concordances.

MELODIC VARIANTS

Rc 1741 [1] *Ho(die)* aa~; *exultent* aa~'G'a(G); *(na)tus* cb; *(fili)us* cb; [2] *(pa)ter* dd~; *(di)ca(mus)* cb; [3] (Transposed) *Glorietur* D'Da'a'Gfa (etc.). **Bu 2824** [1] *Ho(die)* aa~.

10. Introit: *Puer natus est nobis*

TROPE: *Hic enim est de quo prophetae*

SOURCES
Rn 1343 fols. 20r–v (no rubric)
Rc 1741 fols. 52v–53r (no rubric)
Bu 2824 fol. 23v (no rubric)

REFERENCES
CT 1/1, 82–83, 110; Pfaff, *Die Tropen,* 140; Planchart, *Repertory,* 2:138–41.

TEXT COMMENTARY

V. [1] is found in numerous French, Aquitanian, Italian, and a few East Frankish sources; the Nonantolan tropers preserve a variant form. V. [2], which survives only in Nonantola and VEcap 107, is apparently either a parody of a *Hodie* antiphon or responsory text (cf. *CAO* 3:3111; 4:6855–56), or another Proper trope.

TEXT AND TRANSLATION

[1] Hic enim est de quo prophetæ cecinerunt dicentes
    Puer natus [est nobis
    et filius datus est nobis
    cuius imperium super humerum eius
    et vocabitur nomen eius]
[2] Hodie natus est salvator mundi
  cantemus illi voce precelsa ovantes
    Magni [consilii angelus]

*

[1] This is indeed the one of whom the prophets sang, singing:
    A Child is born to us,
    and a Son is given to us:
    whose government is upon His shoulder:
    and His name shall be called.
[2] Today the Savior of the world is born!
  Let us sing to Him in loud voices, exulting:
    The Angel of good counsel.

DISTINCTIVE VARIANTS

The Nonantolan tropers, PS 121, and Be 11 are the only MSS among many to transmit the variant form of v. [1], "Ecce adest de quo." This variant may relate to the widely transmitted Christmas III Introit trope, *Hodie cantandus est* (*CT* 1/1, 107), which includes the words: "Hic enim est quem praesagus. . . ." (*Hodie cantandus est,* though not found in Nonantolan sources, was copied into VEcap 107, which has close ties to the Nonantolan repertory.) Despite the difference in text between "Hic enim est" and "Ecce adest," all sources transmit reasonably similar melodies. V. [2] is found as an introductory element in VEcap 107.

MELODIC VARIANTS

Rc 1741 [2] (transposed) *Hodie natus est salvator mundi* aa~'G'a'c'cd'd'de'd'cdef' fee(d)'d; *cantemus illi voce precelsa ovantes* de'd'c'd(e)'e'e'd' e'd(c)'baa~'G'bcd(c)'aG cc~a.

11. Introit: Etenim sederunt principes

TROPE: *Hodie inclitus martyr Stephanus*

SOURCES

Rn 1343 fol. 21v TROPI IN NAT<ivitate>. S<ancti>. Stephani.
Rc 1741 fols. 56r-v Trop. In. n<ativitate>. S<ancti>. Steph<ani>
Bu 2824 fols. 26v-27r TRO i<n> [nativitate] S<ancti> Steph<a>ni

REFERENCES

CT 1/1, 109, 122, 124, 203; Evans, *The Early Trope Repertory*, 56–58; Planchart, *Repertory*, 2:77–78.

TEXT COMMENTARY

This widely transmitted prose trope is one of the most poignant and dramatic pieces in the repertory. (For an extended discussion of this text and others like it, see Evans, *The Early Trope Repertory*.) As it was known in Nonantola and other centers, *Hodie inclitus martyr* opens with a short but vivid description of St. Stephen's triumph in heaven; the related Aquitanian v. [1] is longer but more prosaic than the Italian version ("Hodie Stephanus martyr caelos ascendit, quem propheta dudum intuens eius voce dicebat"). The remaining lines, which were themselves adapted from scripture (see *CT* 1/1), transform the psalmodic text of the Introit (Ps. 118.23, 86) into the words of the protomartyr at the moment of his martyrdom.

TEXT AND TRANSLATION

[1] Hodie inclytus martyr stephanus paradisum laureatus ascendit
    Etenim [sederunt principes
    et adversum me loquebantur]
[2] Insurrexerunt contra me iudeorum populi iniqui
    Et iniq<ui> [persecuti sunt me]
[3] Invidiosæ lapidibus oppresserunt me
    Adiuva [me domine deus meus]
[4] Suscipe meum in pace spiritum
    Quia servus [tuus exercebatur
    in tuis iustificationibus]
    [Ps.] Beati [immaculati]
    *
[1] Today the illustrious martyr Stephen went up to heaven crowned with laurels:
    For the princes sat,
    and spoke against me.

[2] The wicked Jewish people rose up against me:
    And the wicked persecuted me.
[3] Out of envy they threw stones at me:
    Help me, Lord my God!
[4] Receive my spirit in peace
    Because Your servant was severely tried
    in Your justifications.
    Ps. Blessed are the undefiled . . .

DISTINCTIVE VARIANTS

Rc 1741 [3] *Invidiose* for *Invidiosæ*. **Bu 2824** [3] *Invidiose* for *Invidiosæ*. Except for PS 121, all other northern Italian versions of this trope lack v. [4]. This means that at some centers the trope element *Grandine lapidum* (Introit trope no. 12) could conceivably have been sung as part of the complex that would have included vv. [1–3] of *Hodie inclitus martyr*.

MELODIC VARIANTS

Rc 1741 [1] (*Stepha*)*nus* DD~C; *lau*(*reatus*) a(G). **Bu 2824** [3] (*Invi*)*di*(*osae*) aGE.

12. Introit: Etenim sederunt principes

TROPE: *Grandine lapidum*

SOURCES

Rn 1343 fol. 21v (no rubric)
Rc 1741 fol. 56v AL<ius> [tonus]
Bu 2824 fol. 27v (no rubric)

REFERENCES

CT 1/1, 101; *CT* 5, 199; Planchart, *Repertory*, 2: 77–78, 235–37.

TEXT COMMENTARY

This independent prose trope, which at Nonantola was evidently sung as an internal line upon the repetition of the Introit antiphon (following the Psalm), concludes the narration begun in the preceding trope complex. At the moment of his death, St. Stephen appeals for God's help with the same psalmodic text he uttered when his torment began ("adiuva me, domine Deus meus").

TEXT AND TRANSLATION

Grandine lapidum mox moriturus
sanctus stephanus spe vitæ manentis
lætabundus ita dicebat
    Adiuva me [domine deus meus
    quia servus tuus exercebatur
    in tuis iustificationibus]
    Gloria patri
    *
In a shower of stones joyful St. Stephen,
who was about to die with hope of everlasting life,
spoke thus:

Help me, Lord my God!
Because Your servant was severely tried
in Your justifications.
Glory be to the Father . . .

DISTINCTIVE VARIANTS

Bu 2824 *Grandines* for *Grandine*; cue *Gloria patri* lacking. In the Nonantolan MSS, Ra 123, and MOd 7, *Grandine lapidum* is intercalated into the Introit antiphon as indicated here, but in northern France, Aquitaine, and England it was an internal trope of the Communion, *Video caelos*, or an Offertory trope (APT 18). The arrangement of elements in Ra 123 suggests that *Grandine lapidum* could have been sung in connection with vv. [1–3] of *Hodie inclitus martyr*.

MELODIC VARIANTS
None.

13. Introit: Etenim sederunt principes

TROPE: *Qui primus meruit*

SOURCE
Bu 2824 fols. 27r–v al<ius> to<nus>

REFERENCES
CT 1/1, 181, 145–46, 65, 143; Planchart, *Repertory*, 1:214, 2:79–81.

TEXT COMMENTARY

Hexameters. Like the preceding tropes of *Etenim sederunt principes, Qui primus meruit* opens with a narration in v. [1]. Subsequent elements place the psalmodic Introit text into a dramatic context. Here, though, the focus is on the unjustness of the accusation against Stephen rather than his stoning. Moreover, the later elements here are not drawn from scripture, unlike Introit tropes nos. 12 and 13.

TEXT AND TRANSLATION

[1] Qui primus meruit post cristum ocurrere martir
iure suo tali testatur voce labore
Etenim [sederunt principes
et adversum me loquebantur]
[2] Non nullum nocui nec legum iura resolvi
Et iniq<ui> [persecuti sunt me]
[3] Christe tuus fueram tantum quia rite minister
Adiuva [me domine deus meus]
[4] Ne tuus in dubio frangar certamine miles
Quia serv<us> [tuus exercebatur
in tuis iustificationibus]
Gl<ori>a pat<ri>
Eteni<m>
*

[1] He who first, after Christ, was worthy to offer himself as martyr
in his own right, bore witness in word and deed:
For the princes sat,
and spoke against me.
[2] I have not harmed anyone,
nor have I broken any law:
And the wicked persecuted me.
[3] O Christ, because I have been your faithful servant:
Help me, Lord my God!
[4] Let not Your soldier be crushed
in uncertain combat:
Because Your servant was severely tried
in Your justifications.

DISTINCTIVE VARIANTS

The text of *Qui primus meruit* found in Bu 2824 was consistently transmitted in many sources, but set to two different melodies. The Nonantolan version corresponds to that found in the majority of northern Italian and Aquitanian manuscripts.

14. Communion: Video caelos apertos

TROPE: *Magnus et felix*

SOURCES
Rn 1343 fol. 22v P<ro>sa de co<mmunione>.
Rc 1741 fols. 58r–v p<ro>sa de co<mmunione> Video.

REFERENCE
CT 1/1, 135.

TEXT COMMENTARY

This prose introduction to the Communion combines narrative and drama, placing into context the heavenly scene recounted in Acts 7.56, 59–60. The trope probably originated in East Frankland.

TEXT AND TRANSLATION

Magnus et felix fuerat nimium ordine primus martyrum
qui dum imbres lapidum sustinuit
christum stantem vidit et ait
Video [caelos apertos
et hiesum stantem a dextris virtutis dei
domine hiesu accipe spiritum meum
et ne statuas illis hoc peccatum
quia nesciunt quid faciunt]
*

Great and happy has been the first in rank among the countless martyrs!
He who endured the rain of stones
sees Christ standing before him and says:

xxvi

I see the heavens opened,
and Jesus standing on the right hand
of the power of God:
Lord Jesus, receive my spirit,
and lay not this sin to their charge
for they know not what they do.

DISTINCTIVE VARIANTS

The only Italian sources of *Magnus et felix* are Rn 1343 and Rc 1741. The latter yields a single text variant at the end of the line: *dixit* for *ait*. The Nonantolan melody was apparently similar to that sung north of the Alps (compare with Mbs 14083 and Ob 27).

MELODIC VARIANTS

Rc 1741 (ni)mi(um) aa~G; mar(tyrum) a; sus(tinuit) ed; stan(tem) ded.

15. Introit: *In medio ecclesiae*

TROPE: *Aeterno genitus genitore*

SOURCES

Rn 1343 fol. 22v TROPI. IN NAT<ivitate> s<an>c-<t>i ioh<anni>s.
Rc 1741 fols. 58v–59r Trop In. N<ativitate>. S<ancti>. Ioh<ann>is.
Bu 2824 fols. 29v–30r TROh i<n> [nativitate] S<ancti> ioh<anni>s

REFERENCES

CT 1/1, 56, 156, 137, 149; cf. Planchart, *Repertory*, 2:108–9.

TEXT COMMENTARY

Hexameters. The four verses of *Aeterno genitus genitore* divide equally between narration in vv. [1–2] and exhortation in vv. [3–4]. The trope is found in its present form in Ra 123; MOd 7 contains only the first three elements.

TEXT AND TRANSLATION

[1] Eterno genitus genitore ex tempore christus
        In medio [ecclesiae aperuit os eius]
[2] Pectoris atque sacri pandit mysteria sancta
        Et im[plevit eum dominus spiritu sapientiae
                et intellectus]
[3] Mentibus ergo piis cantemus queso deo qui
        Stolam [gloriae induit eum]
[4] Omnes voce deo cantate et psallite corde
        [Ps.] Bonum est [confiteri domino
                et psallere nomini tuo altissime]
                *
[1] Christ, begotten before time from the eternal Father:
        In the midst of the Church
        he opened his mouth.
[2] He discloses the holy mysteries of the sacred soul
        And the Lord filled him with the spirit
        of wisdom and understanding.
[3] I beseech you, therefore, let us sing with grateful hearts to God, who
        Clothed him in a robe of glory
[4] Sing and chant all to God with voice and heart:
        Ps. It is good to give praise to the Lord,
        and to sing Your name, Most High.

DISTINCTIVE VARIANTS

Vv. [1–3] are found with a different set of verses in MOd 7 and PAc 47. The arrangement of trope elements given in Planchart, *Repertory*, as Version B of *Gratia celsa dei*, corresponds to the reading in MOd 7. In PAc 47, vv. [2] and [3] are combined into a single element which precedes the repeat of the Introit antiphon.

The Nonantolan melody agrees in most details with the neumation in Ra 123. The greatest difference between the readings occurs at the end of v. [3], *corde*, for which Ra 123 preserves an epiphonus (liquescent pes) rather than the more elaborate cadence found in the Nonantolan version. Despite the differences in text between MOd 7 and PAc 47, their musical readings resemble one another more closely than they do the Nonantolan version.

MELODIC VARIANTS

Rc 1741 [1] tem(pore) a(G); [4] canta(te) EFG(F)'FE.
Bu 2824 [3] que(so) dc.

16. Introit: *In medio ecclesiae*

TROPE: *Ille qui dixit*

SOURCES

Rn 1343 fol. 22v Alius tonus
Rc 1741 fol. 59r AL<ius> [tonus]
Bu 2824 fol. 30r al<ius> to<nus>

REFERENCES

CT 1/1, 117, 67, 200.

TEXT COMMENTARY

Two of the three brief elements of *Ille qui dixit* come from Eccles. 15.3 (v. [2]) and 45.8 (v. [3]), the same source as the Introit that they ornament (Eccles. 15.5).

TEXT AND TRANSLATION

[1] Ille qui dixit aperi os tuum
        In me[dio ecclesiae aperuit os eius]
[2] Cibavit illum panem vitæ
        Et imple[vit eum dominus spiritu sapientiae
                et intellectus]

[3] Statuit illi testamentum sempiternum
Stolam [gloriae induit eum]
Gloria patri

*

[1] He who said, "Open your mouth":
In the midst of the Church (the Lord) opened his mouth.
[2] He nourished him with the bread of life:
And the Lord filled him with the spirit of wisdom and understanding.
[3] He made an eternal covenant:
He clothed him in a robe of glory.
Glory be to the Father . . .

DISTINCTIVE VARIANTS

Outside Nonantola the same three-line version of *Ille qui dixit* is found in PCsa 65 and two Aquitanian tropers, Pn 909 and Pn 1119. Perhaps because vv. [2–3] are scriptural, text variants are few. Versions of v. [2] in PCsa 65 and some French sources, however, read: "Cibavit illum dominus pane vitae."

MELODIC VARIANTS

Rc 1741 [1] *di(xit)* dd~; [3] *il(li)* e(d).

17. Introit: In medio ecclesiae

TROPE: *Amor angelorum et gaudium*

SOURCES
Rn 1343 fols. 22v–23r (no rubric)
Rc 1741 fols. 59r–v AL<ius> [tonus]

REFERENCES
CT 1/1, 58, 187, 89; Planchart, *Repertory*, 1:183, 194, 2:104.

TEXT COMMENTARY

Although in prose, the influence of accentual meter is apparent in *Amor angelorum*. V. [1], for example, divides and closes with proparoxytones (*gaudium/diligens*). In addition, the beginning of v. [2] ("Quo panderetur omnibus") has the same pattern of accents (8pp) as the close of v. [1] ("Christus iohannes diligens").

TEXT AND TRANSLATION

[1] Amor angelorum et gaudium
christus iohannem diligens
In me[dio ecclesiae aperuit os eius]
[2] Quo panderetur omnibus
lux gentibus verbi dei
Et imple[vit eum dominus spiritu sapientiae et intellectus]
[3] Et hunc ad æternum suum hodie vocans convivium
Stolam [gloriae induit eum]

*

[1] Object of the angels' love and joy,
John, esteemed of Christ,
In the midst of the Church He opened his mouth.
[2] Through whom the light of God's word would be spread to all peoples:
And the Lord filled him with the spirit of wisdom and understanding.
[3] And calling him today to His eternal company:
He clothed him in a robe of glory.

DISTINCTIVE VARIANTS

Amor angelorum survives only in Nonantolan and English sources (Winchester tropers and Lbl 14). Since it is unlikely that the piece was transmitted directly from one of these places to the other, Planchart (*Repertory*, 1:194) suspects that it may have come from northern France—the transmission of a northern French trope to both England and northern Italy was a typical pattern—though the northern French source is apparently lost.

MELODIC VARIANTS

Rc 1741 [1] *(io)han(nem)* ef(e); [2] *lux* abc aa~G; *de(i)* cdc; [3] *ho(die)* efgf; *(convi)vium* cba'a.

18. Introit: In medio ecclesiae

TROPE: *Dilectus iste domini*

SOURCE
Bu 2824 fols. 30r–v Al<io> tono

REFERENCES
AH 49, no. 47; *CT* 1/1, 81, 153; *CT* 5, 168; Gautier, *Les Tropes*, 3.

TEXT COMMENTARY

V. [1] of *Dilectus iste domini* is in the so-called Ambrosian meter, iambic dimeter; v. [2] is in prose. Blume discusses the introductory element only, passing over in silence the fact that v. [2] is generally found in connection with it and sometimes two additional elements.

TEXT AND TRANSLATION

[1] Dilectus iste dominus
iohannes est apostolus
scriptis eius et monitis
pollet decus ecclesie
Gloria pa[tri]
[2] Os tuum inquiens aperi
meque illud ipsum pro certo s[c]ias implere
Et imple[vit eum dominus
spiritu sapientiae et intellectus
stolam gloriae induit eum]

*

[1] John is the apostle beloved of the Lord;
the glory of the Church is powerful in your writings and admonitions.
Glory be to the Father . . .
[2] Open Your mouth in reply,
and kindly fill me also with the self-same:
And the Lord filled him with the spirit of wisdom and understanding.
He clothed him in a robe of glory.

DISTINCTIVE VARIANTS

Text variants in both elements isolate the two Italian and one southeastern French readings (Bu 2824, PS 121, and APT 18) from the East Frankish sources. Bu 2824 is the only one to preserve a two-line version of what was normally a four- or five-element trope (cf. *CT* 1/1, 236–38). Perhaps the transmission of the piece to Nonantola was garbled. Although v. [1] in Bu 2824 introduces the doxology, not the Introit, v. [2] precedes a line within the Introit, "et implevit."

Despite the differences between the Nonantolan trope complex and all the others, the musical reading of vv. [1–2] corresponds to the neumations preserved in the East Frankish sources, including Wn 1609.

19. *Offertory: Iustus ut palma*

TROPE: *Florebit iustus ut palma*

SOURCES
Rn 1343 fol. 23v (no rubric)
Rc 1741 fol. 61r P<ro>sa de of<fertorio>
Bu 2824 fol. 32r P<ro>s<a> ante of<fertorium>

REFERENCE
CT 1/1, 95.

TEXT COMMENTARY

This prose trope of introduction draws on the same scriptural source as the Offertory it ornaments, namely, Ps 91.13. The textual content and word order of the trope differs, however, from both the Offertory and the psalm. Note the subtle interlocking of trope and Proper texts despite the repetition of the same words. That is, by placing "Iohannes" at the end of the introduction, the first word of the Offertory chant, "Justus," is placed into apposition. It should be noted, however, that a longer version of the trope, whose text continues beyond the word "Iohannes," comes down to us in Pn 1240 (without notation).

TEXT AND TRANSLATION
Florebit iustus ut palma multiplicabitur
ut cedrus iohannes
Justus [ut palma florebit
sicut cedrus quae in libano est multiplicabitur]
*

The just man shall flourish like the palm tree;
he shall grow like the cedar. John,
The just man, shall flourish like the palm tree:
he shall be multiplied like the cedar that is in Lebanon.

DISTINCTIVE VARIANTS

The Nonantolan MSS and Ra 123 are the only readings of *Florebit iustus ut palma* to come down to us in notated form. Comparison reveals only a few differences in melodic detail.

MELODIC VARIANTS
Rc 1741 *ut* aa~DD(C); *ce(drus)* DD~C.

20. *Introit: Ex ore infantium*

TROPE: *Hodie te domine suggentes*

SOURCE
Bu 2824 fol. 32r-v Ton<us> i<n>nocentor<um>

REFERENCE
CT 1/1, 113, 204, 211.

TEXT COMMENTARY

In prose; vv. [2–3] are reminiscent of numerous prayer formulae. These elements are always found together regardless of the introductory line (*CT* 1/1, 241–42).

TEXT AND TRANSLATION
[1] Hodie te domine suggentes ubera matribus clamant nosque laudibus eia
Ex ore [infantium deus]
[2] Teneri exercitus preconia
sparsisti orbis circula miranda
Et lacten[tium perfecisti laudem]
[3] Ut tua gloria in minimis fulgeret alta
Propter [inimicos tuos]
*
[1] Babes at their mothers' breasts cry out to You today, O Lord, and we (call out) in praise, yea:
Out of the mouths of infants, O God,
[2] You have spread the news of the tender army throughout this admiring world:
And of sucklings, you have perfected praise.
[3] That Your glory may shine on high
upon the lowly:
Because of Your enemies.

DISTINCTIVE VARIANTS

The same three-element form of this trope complex is found in VEcap 107, BAs 5 (Reichenau), and Pn 10510 (Echternach) (cf. *CT* 1/1, 241–42). V. [1] was used as a single-element introduction at Saint Gall.

21. Introit: *Statuit ei dominus*

TROPE: *Venite populi ad conlaudandum*

SOURCES
Rn 1343 fol. 23v TROP. In. [nativitate] S<ancti>. Silv<est>ri.
Rc 1741 fols. 61v–62r Trop
Bu 2824 fols. 34r–v Troh i<n> [nativitate] s<ancti> silv<est>ri

REFERENCES
Pfaff, *Die Tropen*, 139–40, 143; Planchart, "Italian Tropes," 25–27; Planchart, *Repertory*, 2:166.

TEXT COMMENTARY
In prose; the length and hortatory character of the first two elements of *Venite populi* contrast with vv. [3–4], which are considerably shorter and relate more closely to the Introit text (Eccles. 45.30). Unlike the next Introit trope, no. 22, *Hic est Silvester* does not refer to the events in the life of the abbey's patron, Pope Sylvester.

TEXT AND TRANSLATION

[1] Venite populi ad collaudandum regem regum dominum
    qui triumphat in confessore suo Silvestro agite
        Statuit [ei dominus testamentum pacis]
[2] Celsa nunc rutila[n]t festa beati silvestri
    dicamus omnes voce precelsa ovantes
        Et prin[cipem fecit eum]
[3] Quo uniti sumus fide
    Ut sit [illi sacerdoti dignitas]
[4] Manet indeficiens
    In æt[ernum]
    [Ps.] Mi<sericordi>as tuas
        *

[1] Come, ye people, to praise the King of kings, the Lord,
    who triumphs in his confessor Sylvester, sing ye:
        The Lord made to him a covenant of peace.
[2] The high holidays of blessed Sylvester now shine forth;
    let us all sing in loud voices, rejoicing:
        And made him a prince.
[3] By whom we are united in faith:
    That the dignity of the priesthood should be to Him.
[4] He remains unfailing
    Forever.
    Ps. Have mercy on us . . .

DISTINCTIVE VARIANTS
Rc 1741 [1] *conlaudanum* for *collaudandum*; [2] *rutilant* for *rutilat*. *Venite populi* comes down to us solely in the Nonantolan tropers and VEcap 107, the latter without musical notation and assigned to the Common of Confessors. This fact of transmission led Planchart to conjecture that the trope was composed at Nonantola in honor of the abbey's patron. VEcap 107 contains the following variants: in v. [1], *Rufino* for *Silvestro*; in v. [2], *illi* for *Silvestri*.

V. [4] was known outside northern Italy and sung in connection with *Statuit ei*, but with a different set of tropes for St. Martin (Planchart, *Repertory*, 1:166).

MELODIC VARIANTS
Rc 1741 [1] *(conlau)dan(dum)* FDE; [2] *nunc rutilant* D'F'FG'G; *(sil)ves(tri)* ac; *(o)van(tes)* EFG(F); [3] *(fi)de* FED. **Bu 2824** [1] *(conlau)dan(dum)* FDE; [2] *(sil)ves(tri)* ac.

22. Introit: *Statuit ei dominus*

TROPE: *Hic est Silvester*

SOURCES
Rn 1343 fol. 23v–24r Alius tonus
Rc 1741 fol. 62r AL<ius> [tonus]
Bu 2824 fols. 34v–35r al<ius> to<nus>

REFERENCES
Pfaff, *Die Tropen*, 139–40; Planchart, "Italian Tropes," 25–27.

TEXT COMMENTARY
In prose; following the introductory element, vv. [2–3] refer to one of the main achievements of Pope Sylvester's pontificate, namely, the founding of several important churches in Rome. These include the basilica and baptistry of St. John Lateran and Santa Croce.

TEXT AND TRANSLATION

[1] Hic est silvester papa
    de quo propheta cecinit dicens
        Statuit [ei dominus testamentum pacis]
[2] Quem augustus constantinus
    statuit summum esse
    sacerdotem dei secundum
    ordinem melchisedech
        Et princi[pem fecit eum
        ut sit illi sacerdoti dignitas]
[3] Per ipsum illuminata est omnis æcclesia sancta dei
        In aeter[num]
        Gloria patri
        *

[1] This is Pope Sylvester,
    of whom the prophet sang, saying:
        The Lord made to him a covenant of peace.

[2] Whom the venerable Constantine
established to be
the highest priest of God according to
the order of Melchisedech:
And made him a prince
that the dignity of priesthood
should be to him.
[3] Through him all the holy Church of God is illuminated
Forever.
Glory be to the Father . . .

DISTINCTIVE VARIANTS

Rc 1741 [2] *christi* for *dei*. **Bu 2824** [2] *constantinum* for *constantinus*; *christi* for *dei*. Outside the Nonantolan tropers, *Hic est Silvester* is found in IV 60 and VEcap 107, the latter without notation. The neumation in IV 60 agrees with the Nonantolan version in most details. Like the preceding trope and other such items sung in honor of St. Sylvester at Nonantola, this chant may have been composed at the abbey.

MELODIC VARIANTS

Rc 1741 [1] *(Silves)ter* a(G); [2] *chris(ti secundum)* G; [3] *om(nis)* E.

23. Offertory: *Veritas mea*

TROPE: *Usque in saeculum saeculi*

SOURCES

Rn 1343 fol. 24v P<ro>sa de off<ertorio> Veritas
Rc 1741 fols. 64r–v P<ro>sa de off<ertorio>. Ver<itas>
Bu 2824 fols. 36v–37r P<ro>S<a> d<e> of<fertorio>.

REFERENCE

Planchart, "Italian Tropes," 25–27.

TEXT COMMENTARY

This text is exceptional in that it would appear to have been spoken by God. Although scriptural authority is lacking, biblical language is employed. "Usque in saeculum saeculi," for example, was centonized from Isa. 45.17, and v. [3] is a reworking of Eccles. 45.30 ("Statuit ei Dominus testamentum pacis").

Usque in saeculum is one of a small number of Offertory tropes in the Nonantolan repertory. This, and the fact that it was part of a cycle of pieces for the monastery's patron, tend to support Planchart's view that the trope was composed at Nonantola.

TEXT AND TRANSLATION

[1] Usque in seculum seculi conservabo sanctum meum
Veritas [mea]
[2] Non derelinquam eum sed in perpetuum cum eo permanebo
Et mi<sericordi>a [mea cum ipso]
[3] Statuam testamentum cum eo et stabiliam usque in æternum thronum eius
Et in nomi[ne meo exaltabitur cornu eius]

*

[1] For all eternity I shall protect my saint,
My truth.
[2] I shall not abandon Him, but shall remain with Him forever
And my mercy (shall be) with him.
[3] I shall make with Him a covenant and fortify His throne forever:
And in my name shall his horn be exalted.

DISTINCTIVE VARIANTS

According to Planchart ("Italian Tropes," 25), *Usque in saeculum* is found in two Italian sources outside Nonantola. In VEcap 107 it was copied in the prosulary without a rubric but probably assigned to the feast of St. Sylvester. This reading preserves a single text variant in v. [2] (*relinquam* for *derelinquam*, which does not alter the meaning); vv. [2–3] lack notation. *Usque in saeculum* is also found in IV 60, in this case for St. Felix, whose feast day (14 Jan.) is close enough to Sylvester's to account for its migration. The IV 60 neumation is similar to the Nonantolan version, but would seem more neumatic; precise comparison is precluded by the unheighted notation in the former source.

MELODIC VARIANT

Rc 1741 [3] *Sta(tuam)* DD~.

24. Introit: *Ecce advenit*

TROPE: *Hodie descendit Christus*

SOURCES

Rn 1343 fol. 25v TROP IN ep<ip>h<ania> d<omi>ni.
Rc 1741 fols. 66r–v Trop In epiphania d<omini>.
Bu 2824 fols. 37r–v Troph i<n> epyph<ani>a d<omi>ni.

REFERENCES

CT 1/1, 108, 148, 133, 190; *CT* 5, 160–62; Pfaff, *Die Tropen*, 139.

TEXT COMMENTARY

In prose; following the setting of the scene of Christ's baptism in v. [1], the internal elements expand on the Introit text and were conceived from the perspective of the omniscient observer. V. [1] would seem more appropriate for the Octave of Epiphany, on which Christ's baptism is commemorated, than Epiphany itself (though the same chant formulary was employed on both occasions). According to *CT* 1/1, however, the trope was never assigned to the Octave.

TEXT AND TRANSLATION

[1] Hodie descendit christus in iordanem
     ibi expurgat nostra facinora
     deo gracias dicite
          Ecce ad[venit]
[2] Olim promissus a[c] cupidis patribus venerandus
          D<omi>nator [dominus]
[3] Laxare vincula strictum quibus humanum detinebatur genus
          [Et regnum in manu eius]
[4] Regnum quod nullo defectu corrumpi
     umquam possit vel minui perpetim
          Et pote[stas et imperium]
          [Ps.] D<eu>s iudiciu<m>
               *

[1] Today Christ goes down to the Jordan River;
     there He cleanses our sins,
     thanks be to God, let us sing:
          Behold He comes.
[2] Promised of yore and revered by the eager fathers:
          The Ruler, the Lord.
[3] Be loosened, ye bonds with which the human race was held tight:
          And the kingdom is in His hand.
[4] Kingdom that no defect can ever corrupt or diminish:
          And power, and dominion.
          Ps. Give to the King your judgment . . .

DISTINCTIVE VARIANTS

Bu 2824 [1] *iordane* for *iordanem*. Although v. [1] was known at a number of northern Italian centers, it was generally combined with different internal elements or used as an introduction only (*CT* 1/1, 244–46). The setting of v. [1] in the Nonantolan MSS seems to resemble the East Frankish reading more than the French (APT 17 and APT 18), but all the East Frankish sources omit the words "deo gracias dicite," which are in the APT readings. For the less widely disseminated vv. [2–4], the settings in the Nonantolan sources and VEcap 107 are more neumatic than the East Frankish versions.

MELODIC VARIANTS

Rc 1741 [1] *(chris)tus* DCD; [2] *(vene)ran(dus)* F(E); [4] *pos(sit)* F; *(minu)i* DD~.

25. Introit: *Ecce advenit*

TROPE: *Forma speciosissimus*

SOURCES
Rn 1343 fol. 25v (no rubric)
Rc 1741 fols. 66v–67r alius
Bu 2824 fol. 37v (no rubric)

REFERENCES
AH 49, no. 11; *CT* 1/1, 96; Pfaff, *Die Tropen*, 83–84; Planchart, *Repertory*, 1:130, 2:70–71.

TEXT COMMENTARY

Iambic dimeters. That *Forma speciosissimus* was modeled on a hymn is suggested not only by its Ambrosian meter (8 + 8 pp), but by its mostly syllabic musical setting. Pfaff surmises that the principal objective of the trope's author was end-rhyme, but this is not achieved in the Nonantolan reading (cf. *CT* 1/1, 96).

TEXT AND TRANSLATION

Forma speciosissimus
manuque potentissimus
ex david origine
natus mariæ virginis
     Gl<ori>a patri
          *

Most beautiful in form
and most powerful in might,
come from the house of David,
born of the virgin Mary:
     Glory be to the Father . . .

DISTINCTIVE VARIANTS

Rc 1741 cue *Ecce [advenit] Gl<ori> [patri]*. **Bu 2824** cue *Ecce advenit*. Besides having been sung in connection with the Introit *Ecce advenit* and the doxology —note the difference between the cues in the Nonantolan tropers—*Forma speciosissimus* was sung at East Frankish centers in connection with the Introit, *Vultum tuum* (Planchart, *Repertory*, 1:130). The Nonantolan MSS and VEcap 107, the only Italian sources of the trope, together yield variants not found elsewhere. All the sources preserve the same melodic outline, the chief difference occurring typically in connection with one of the text variants, *David* for *Davidis*.

MELODIC VARIANTS

Rc 1741 *(po)ten(tissimus)* c(b); *(vir)gi(nis)* b.

26. Introit: *Ecce advenit*

TROPE: *Haec est praeclara dies*

SOURCES
Rn 1343 fols. 25v–26r alius ton<us>.
Rc 1741 fols. 67r–v alius ton<us>

REFERENCES
AH 49, no. 77; *CT* 1/1, 103, 172, 119–20, 141; Pfaff, *Die Tropen*, 139, 141, 143; Planchart, *Repertory*, 2: 73–74.

TEXT COMMENTARY
Like the antiphon *ante evangelium, Tribus miraculis ornatum* (*CAO* 3:5184), sung at Nonantola on Epiphany before the gospel, the text of this brief trope refers to the early miracles of Christ's public ministry. These events are recounted in the gospels of Epiphany, its Octave, and the Second Sunday after the Epiphany.

TEXT AND TRANSLATION

[1] Hæc est preclara dies
     tribus sacrata miraculis
     in qua cum propheta canamus dicentes
          Ecce [advenit]
[2] Quem magi hodie muneribus honorant
     et ut regem supernum adorant
     qui est
          D<omi>nator [dominus]
[3] In iordane a iohanne baptizatus
     paterna voce filius patris est
     hodie adclamatus
          Et reg<num> [in manu eius et potestas]
[4] Naturas limpheas hodie mutavit
     in saporiferos austus per potestatem
          Et impe[rium]
               *
[1] This is the celebrated day
     hallowed with three miracles
     on which, with the prophet, we sing, chanting:
          Behold He is come,
[2] Whom today the Magi honor with gifts,
     and while they adore the celestial King
     who is
          The Ruler, the Lord.
[3] Baptized by John in the Jordan River,
     the Son is acclaimed today by the paternal voice
     of the Father:
          And the kingdom is in His hand,
          and the power.
[4] Today in a miracle he changed ordinary water
     into wine:
          And dominion.

DISTINCTIVE VARIANTS
Rc 1741 [4] *haustus* for *austus*. Aquitanian manuscripts preserve a different version of v. [2]: "Cui magi hodie munera offerunt / et ut regem supernum adorant / qui est ubique." Of the remaining elements, v. [3] is the most variable in its text from source to source.

The melodic settings differ somewhat from region to region. Northern Italian readings, including those in the Nonantolan tropers, resemble more closely the southeastern French version (APT 18) than the Aquitanian.

MELODIC VARIANTS
Rc 1741 [2] *(su)pernum* FFE; *qui* FGF; [3] *In* DD~; *(pa)ter(na)* DD~; [4] *(hodi)e* DECC~A; *haus(tus)* FGaGFED; *(po)tes(tatem)* FE.

27. Introit: *Suscepimus*

TROPE: *Adest alma virgo*

SOURCES
Rn 1343 fol. 27r Tropi in p<u>r<i>f<icatione>. S<anctae>. MARIAE.
Rc 1741 fols. 69v–79r Trop. In pur<ificatione>. S<anctae< Marię
Bu 2824 fols. 43r–v Troh in purificatione S<anctae> mariae.

REFERENCES
AH 49, no. 27; Borders, "Northern," 166; Pfaff, *Die Tropen*, 82–83; Planchart, *Repertory*, 1:232–34, 2: 176–78.

TEXT COMMENTARY
Trochaic dimeters (8 + 8 p). The meter of *Adest alma virgo* resembles that employed in hymns popular among the Carolingians, such as *Pange lingua gloriosi/proelium certaminis* (*AH* 2, p. 44). Vv. [3–4], though in prose, employ internal rhyme: *aeternum/dominum; braciis/Simeonis*. The text of vv. [2–3], generally transmitted as a single verse preceding the Introit, may be among the oldest in the trope repertory.

TEXT AND TRANSLATION

[1] Adest alma virgo parens
     adest verbum caro factum
          Suscepim<us> [deus
          misericordiam tuam
          in medio templi tui]
[2] Proclamemus omnes laudes
     in excelso celso patri
          S<e>c<un>d<u>m [nomen tuum
          deus ita et laus tua]

[3] Lumen eternum christum dominum
   In fine[s terrae]
[4] In brachiis sancti symeonis
   Iusticia [plena est dextera tua]
   [Ps.] Magnus [dominus]

      *

[1] The loving, fruitful virgin is here;
 the Word made flesh is at hand:
   We have received, O God,
    Your mercy in the midst of Your temple.
[2] Let us all proclaim praises
 in the highest to the heavenly Father:
   According to Your name, O God,
    so also is Your praise.
[3] Eternal light, Christ, Lord:
   Unto the ends of the earth.
[4] In the arms of St. Symeon:
   Your right hand is full of justice.
   Ps. Great is the Lord . . .

Distinctive Variants

Bu 2824 [4] cue *Suscepimus* for *Iusticia*. The wide geographical distribution of this trope, its many text variants (particularly in v. [1]), and variety of musical settings have obscured its transmission. But if the scope of comparison is narrowed to West Frankish and Italian readings, distinct relationships emerge. One of these is between Pa 1169 and Nonantolan MSS and VEcap 107. The other connection is between CA 75 and northern Italian sources Ob 222, Tn 20, and Tn 18. (For a more detailed discussion of these relationships, see Borders, "Northern.")

Melodic Variant

Rc 1741 [3] *Lu(men)* a.

28. Introit: *Suscepimus*

Trope: *Psallentes legimus*

Sources
Rn 1343 fol. 27r (no rubric)
Rc 1741 fol. 70r AL<ius> [tonus]

References
AH 49, no. 169; Planchart, *Repertory*, 2:183.

Text Commentary

Hexameters (vv. [1–2]) and pentameters (v. [3]). The introductory v. [1] is so general in scope, referring only to the Psalms, that one would expect it to have been more widely transmitted than the surviving sources would indicate. The epithets in vv. [2–3], though amplifying the Proper text, add little to its meaning, suggesting that the trope elements may have been appropriated from a pre-existent source, perhaps a hymn.

Text and Translation
[1] Psallentes legimus david cecinisse propheta
   Susce[pimus deus
   misericordiam tuam in medio templi tui
   secundum nomen tuum deus
   ita et laus tua]
[2] Oblatum purum non munere purificandum
   In fine[s terrae]
[3] Arctos et esperos auster et eous
   Iusti[tia plena est dextera tua]

      *

[1] We gather together, singing the Psalm David
 the prophet sang:
   We have received, O God,
   Your mercy in the midst of Your temple
   according to Your name, O God,
    so also is Your praise.
[2] Undefiled oblation, not to be purified by works:
   Unto the ends of the earth.
[3] The North wind and the evening star;
 the South wind and the morning star:
   Your right hand is full of justice.

Distinctive Variants

Rc 1741 [1] *prophetam* for *propheta*; [3] *Artos* for *Arctos*; cue *Iusti[tia] Gl<ori>a [patri]* for *Iusti[tia plena est dextera tua]*. *Psallentes legimus* is also found in VEcap 107 in the form found in Nonantolan MSS; Ra 123 includes an extra element between vv. [1] and [2]. This element, "Verbum incarnatum legis sub lege magistrum," was also known in southern Italy and Winchester (Ccc 473). In their music, northern and central Italian readings of the trope are similar; the Nonantolan MSS and VEcap 107 are nearly identical in neumation.

29. Introit: *Domine ne longe facias*

Trope: *Ingresso Iesu*

Sources
Rn 1343 fols. 28r–v TROPI in ramis palmarum
Rc 1741 fol. 74r Trop In dom<inica> de palma.
Bu 2824 fols. 46r–v TROH i<n> dom<inica> de palma

References
CT 3/2, 125; Planchart, *Repertory*, 1:90, 2:65.

Text Commentary

The prose introduction *Ingresso Jesu* places the psalmodic Introit text (Ps. 21.20, 22) in the context of Christ's suffering. The trope is based on a free interpretation of passages in the gospels of Mark (15.13) and John (18.28–40). In these accounts, Pilate absolves Jesus of guilt while remaining unconvinced of his claim to kingship. Concerning Pilate's judgment, John 18.38 reads: "Ego nullam invenio in eo causam" ("I find no guilt in him"). In the trope, however, Pilate declares: "Regem vestrum verum non crucifigam ego" ("I shall not crucify your true king"). The trope also reverses the order of events in the gospels, that is, the crowd calls for Jesus' crucifixion before, not after, Pilate's interrogation.

TEXT AND TRANSLATION

[1] Ingresso hiesu in pretorium
 stante ante pilatum
 iudei clamabant
 crucifige crucifige eum
 pilatus respondens dixit ad illos
 regem vestrum verum non crucifigam ego
 de quo david propheta cecinit dicens
  Domine [ne longe facias
   auxilium tuum a me]
[2] Sed cæleri succurre michi pietate paterna
  Ad defen[sionem meam aspice
   libera me de ore leonis]
[3] Qui cupit insontem morsu lacerare ferino
  Et a cor[nibus unicornuorum]
[4] Vide pater
  Humilita[tem meam]
 *
[1] When Jesus, having entered into the praetorium,
 was standing before Pilate,
 the Jews cried out:
 "Crucify, crucify Him!"
 Replying, Pilate said to them:
 "I shall not crucify your true King,"
 of whom the prophet David sang, saying:
  O Lord, do not keep your help far from me,
[2] But in your fatherly concern hasten to help me:
  Look to my defense:
   deliver me from the mouth of the lion,
[3] Who longs to tear the innocent to pieces with
   savage bites,
  And from the horns of the unicorns.
[4] Behold, Father,
  My lowliness.

DISTINCTIVE VARIANTS

Rc 1741 [1] cue *Domine* P<s> *Deus [Deus meus respice in me]*. Bu 2824 [1] *stantem* for *stante*; [4] (lacking). The introduction *Ingresso Jesu* survives in the three Nonantolan tropers, VEcap 107, and MOd 7. In all these save one it is an independent introduction—in Rn 1343 it is combined with vv. [2–3] of *Suspensus ligno patri* (see no. 30; see also *CT* 3/2, 255, and Planchart, *Repertory*, 2:65). Collation of the Nonantolan text with VEcap 107 and MOd 7 yields a number of variants, mostly grammatical; a significant difference is the omission of the reference to David in MOd 7.

In their music, the Nonantolan and VEcap 107 versions of the trope resemble one another closely, whereas the MOd 7 reading is distinct with respect to melodic details.

MELODIC VARIANTS

Rc 1741 [1] *clamabant* FE'DE'DD~C; *verum* FEDC'DEE~D; *(pro)phe(ta)* FE. Bu 2824 *(prophe)ta* DC.

30. Introit: *Domine ne longe facias*

TROPE: *Suspensus ligno patri*

SOURCES
Rc 1741 fol. 74v AL<ius> [tonus]
Bu 2824 fol. 46v (no rubric)

REFERENCES
AH 49, no. 87; *CT* 3/2, 200, 193, 177, 212; Planchart, *Repertory*, 2:65.

TEXT COMMENTARY

Hexameters (vv. [1–3]). Following the narrative introduction in v. [1], the remaining trope elements place into Christ's mouth the words of the psalmodic Introit text (Ps. 21.20, 22).

TEXT AND TRANSLATION

[1] Suspensus ligno patri sic filius infit
  D<omi>ne [ne longe facias auxilium tuum a me]
[2] Sed celeri succurre michi pietate paterna
  Ad de[fensionem meam aspice
   libera me de ore leonis]
[3] Qui cupit insontem morsu lacerare ferino
  Et a cor[nibus unicornuorum]
[4] Vide pater
  Humi[litatem meam]
 *
[1] Having been hung on the cross, the Son begins
   (to speak) to the Father thus:
  O Lord, do not keep Your help far from me.
[2] But in Your fatherly concern hasten to help Me:
  Look to my defense:
   deliver me from the mouth of the lion,
[3] Who longs to tear the innocent to pieces with
   savage bites,
  And from the horns of the unicorns.
[4] Behold, Father,
  My lowliness.

DISTINCTIVE VARIANTS

Bu 2824 [4] lacking. Vv. [1–3] are stable in Italian transmission. V. [2], which was also known in England, may be based on another trope element for Palm Sunday (*CT* 3/2, 192). V. [4] is found in Ob 222, IV 60, and Tn 18 in connection with a different trope complex (*CT* 3/2, 255). The scribe of Rn 1343 combined vv. [2–4] with the introduction *Ingresso Jesu.*

Comparing the music of the Nonantolan MSS with settings copied outside Italy, some affinity with Ccc 473 is noted (vv. [1–3]). In the Italian tradition, MOd 7 yields numerous minor variants, such as the filling-in of gaps (v. [1] *patri*: gabcbag; v. [2] *pietate*: g/abc) and simpler closing formulae than those in Nonantolan MSS and VEcap 107.

MELODIC VARIANTS
Rc 1741 [2] *(pie)ta(te)* cb; [3] *(in)son(tem)* aa∼; [4] *pa(ter)* abaa∼.

31. Introit: Resurrexi

TROPE: *Hora est surgite/Quem quaeritis*

SOURCES
Rn 1343 fol. 28v TROPI In dom<inica>. De Pascha
Rc 1741 fols. 75r–v Tropi Dom<inica> in pasca
Bu 2824 fol. 47r Troh in s<an>c<ta>m pasch-<am>

REFERENCES
Boor, *Die Textgeschichte*, 68–80; *CT* 3/2, 220, 217; McGee, "The Liturgical Placements," 1–29; Planchart, *Repertory*, 1:136–37, 237–38; 2:37–42.

TEXT COMMENTARY
In prose; following the brief introductory exhortation, *Hora est surgite*, the widely disseminated *Quem quaeritis* serves as a trope of the Introit *Resurrexi*. (This liturgical function was by no means the only one known in northern Italy; see McGee, "The Liturgical Placements.") The version that comes down to us in the Nonantolan tropers, like those in many other sources, stems from accounts of the resurrection scene in the four gospels.

TEXT AND TRANSLATION
Hora est surgite
iubet domnus canere
eia dicite
Quem queritis in sepulchro christicole
Hiesum nazarenum crucifixum o celicole
Non est hic
surrexit sicut predixerat
ite nuntiate quia surrexit dicentes
    Resur[r]ex<i> [et adhuc tecum sum
        alleluia
      posuisti super me manum tuam
        alleluia
        mirabilis facta est scientia tua
        alleluia alleluia]
      [Ps.] D<omi>ne p<ro>basti

*
It is the hour! Arise!
The Lord commands to sing,
yea, saying:
Whom do you seek in the tomb,
O followers of Christ?
Jesus of Nazareth (who was) crucified,
O celestial ones.
He is not here.
He is risen as He foretold.
Go, announce that He is risen from the sepulcher:
    I arose, and am still with You,
        alleluia.
    You have laid Your hand upon me,
        alleluia.
    Your knowledge is become wonderful,
        alleluia, alleluia.
    Ps. Lord, You have searched me . . .

DISTINCTIVE VARIANTS
Rc 1741 and **Bu 2824** cue [Ps.] *Domine probasti* lacking. The introduction *Hora est surgite* is found mostly in southern French and northern Italian sources, though the Nonantolan version alone reads "surgite" for the more widely transmitted "psallite." As regards the text variants in *Quem quaeritis*, Nonantolan and most other Italian sources transmit the text "in sepulchro christicolae," rather than "in sepulchro o christicolae," found in VEcap 107, IV 60, the Vercelli MSS, as well as many Aquitanian, French, and East Frankish sources. Nonantolan and many other Italian readings (including VEcap 107 and IV 60) preserve a different version of the closing phrase than that transmitted in the West Frankish territory ("quia surrexit de sepulchro"; other text variants are collated in *CT* 3/2, 217).

Comparison of the musical settings in northern and central Italian sources yields many differences in detail, but all readings share the same basic outline. The versions are difficult to group into families. Similarities link Ra 123, PS 121, Tn 18, and PCsa 65; the Nonantolan MSS, VEcap 107, Ob 222, and MOd 7 transmit a somewhat less ornate setting.

MELODIC VARIANTS
Rc 1741 [1] *(surgi)te* BA; *(queri)tis* DD∼; *(sepul)chro* FDE; *Hiesum* DD∼; [2] *(sur)re(xit)* FE. **Bu 2824** (transposed) *Hora est* D'Da (etc.); *Quem queritis* G(D)'FE'CD'D (etc.).

32. Introit: Resurrexi

TROPE: *Christus de sepulchro resurrexit*

SOURCES
Rn 1343 fols. 28v (no rubric)
Rc 1741 fols. 75v–76r AL<ius tonus>
Bu 2824 fols. 47r–v; 47v–48r (no rubric)

REFERENCE
CT 3/2, 66, 76, 174.

TEXT COMMENTARY

In prose; like the texts of certain other Italian tropes, *Christus de sepulchro resurrexit* is not well integrated with the Proper text (see Planchart, "Italian Tropes," 28–29). Note that the narrative in v. [1] does not lead smoothly to the Psalm text (138.18), which in the present context could have been spoken by the risen Christ. Note also the lack of a connection between v. [2] and the succeeding Introit phrase. The final element is the best integrated of the three, with "mirabilis facta est scientia tua" presumably referring to what Christ revealed to Mary Magdalene ("mulier") at the scene of the resurrection (John 20.15–17).

TEXT AND TRANSLATION

[1] Christus de sepulchro resurrexit
in galilea videndum se mandavit
    Resur[rexi et adhuc tecum sum
        alleluia]
[2] Cum apostolis cito properemus
et hunc resurgentem cum eis adoremus
    Posuisti [super me manum tuam
        alleluia]
[3] Quem quęris mulier in monumento
resumpto corpore iam vivit
et est in galilea
    Mirabilis [facta est scientia tua
        alleluia alleluia]
    P<s.> D<omi>ne [probasti me]
        *

[1] Christ has risen from the sepulcher.
He commends Himself to be seen in Galilee:
    I arose, and I am still with you,
        alleluia.
[2] Let us hasten quickly with the apostles,
and with them honor the resurrection:
    You have laid your hand upon me,
        alleluia.
[3] Whom do you seek in the tomb, woman?
He lives with his body recovered,
and is in Galilee:
    Your knowledge is become wonderful,
        alleluia, alleluia.
    Ps. Lord, You have searched me . . .

DISTINCTIVE VARIANTS

Rn 1343 [3] cue *[M]irabilis Gl<ori>a patri.* **Bu 2824** [1] *videndus* for *videndum*; [3] cue *Mirabilis Gl<ori>a patri*. The three-element trope *Christus de sepulchro* is found only in northern and central Italian MSS: Rn 1343, Rc 1741, VEcap 107, PS 121, and VO 39. In Bu 2824 the introductory line *Hodie resurrexit leo fortis* (see no. 33) is combined with vv. [2] and [3]; v. [1] was copied separately (47r–v). Despite the different arrangement in Bu 2824, however, the musical setting is practically identical to the other Nonantolan readings.

MELODIC VARIANTS

Rn 1343 [1] (Transposed) *Christus de* e'dcdeaa~'G (etc.); *in* aba(G); *(vi)den(dum)* c(d); [3] *(mulier) in* e; *(est) in* cc~b. **Bu 2824** [1] (Transposed) *Christus* a'GFGa (etc.); *in* DEDD(C); [3] *(mulier) in* a; *(est) in* FF~E.

33. Introit: Resurrexi

TROPE: *Hodie resurrexit leo fortis*

SOURCES
Rn 1343 fol. 28v alius tonus
Rc 1741 fol. 76r AL<ius> [tonus]
Bu 2824 fol. 47v (no rubric)

REFERENCES
CT 3/2, 114, 166; Pfaff, *Die Tropen*, 142.

TEXT COMMENTARY

In prose; both elements are hortatory in character. Like certain other tropes beginning with the word *Hodie*, *Hodie resurrexit leo fortis* is found in an early source (Pn 9448 from Prüm) solely as an introduction without intercalated elements. (Single-line introductory tropes may be among the earliest in the repertory. See *MGG*, s.v. "Tropus," by Bruno Stäblein.) The "leo fortis" to which v. [1] refers is presumably the lion of the Apocalypse (5.5): "ecce vicit leo de tribu Iuda, radix David, aperire librum, et solvere septem signacula eius" ("behold, the lion of the tribe of Judah, the root of David, has overcome to open the scroll and its seven seals"; cf. no. 35, *Laus honor virtus*, v. [3]: "Leo fortis de tribu iuda hodie surrexit . . ."). V. [2], found only in the Nonantolan tropers, Mza 76, and Pn 1118, may stem from the *Quem quaeritis* introduction, *Hora est psallite* (*CT* 3/2, 220; see also no. 31).

TEXT AND TRANSLATION

[1] Hodie resurrexit leo fortis
christus filius dei
deo gracias dicite
    Resurre[xi et adhuc tecum sum
        alleluia
    posuisti super me manum tuam
        alleluia]
[2] Psallite fratres hora est
resurrexit dominus eia et eia
    Mirabilis [facta est scientia tua
        alleluia alleluia]

[1] Today the mighty Lion,
   Christ, the Son of God, has risen!
   Thanks be to God, sing ye:
      I arose, and I am still with you,
         alleluia.
      You have laid your hand upon me,
         alleluia.
[2] Sing brothers, it is the hour!
   The Lord has risen, yea and yea!
      Your knowledge is become wonderful,
         alleluia, alleluia.

DISTINCTIVE VARIANTS

Rc 1741 [2] cue *Mirabilis Gl<ori> [patri]*. **Bu 2824** [2] cue *Resurrexi*. All the sources of v. [1] transmit essentially the same text; the Nonantolan tropers and VEcap 107, however, omit the closing "eia" found in all other readings ("deo gratias dicite eia"). V. [2] is associated in a complex with *Hodie resurrexit* only in Nonantolan sources; in Pn 1118 it is combined with v. [1] ("eia psallite fratres mi omnes hora est eia"). In the music, the version of *Hodie resurrexit* in Nonantolan MSS and VEcap 107 resembles APT 18 most closely, though concordant sources preserve similar melodies.

MELODIC VARIANTS

Rc 1741 [1] *(resurre)xit* DCD; [2] *do(minus)* ED. **Bu 2824** [2] *do(minus)* ED.

34. Offertory: *Terra tremuit*

TROPE: *Ab increpatione et ira*

SOURCES
Rn 1343 fols. 29v–30r P<ro>sa de off<ertorio>
Rc 1741 fol. 79r P<ro>sa de of<fertorio> T<er>ra [tremuit]
Bu 2824 fols. 50v–51r P<ro>S[a] D<e> of<fertorio>

REFERENCES
CT 3/2, 53, 68, 69, 139; Evans, *The Early Trope Repertory*, 161–62; Planchart, *Repertory*, 1:171, 2:214–18.

TEXT COMMENTARY

In prose; despite the range of scriptural and non-scriptural sources from which the trope elements were drawn—v. [2], for example, was borrowed practically verbatim from Matt. 27.52, while v. [3] resembles the Credo ("Et iterum venturus est . . . judicare vivos et mortuos")—the text of *Ab increpatione* is well integrated with the Offertory text. In vv. [1–3] Christ's resurrection is interpreted as a foreshadowing of the Last Judgment, to which the Proper chant alludes. V. [4], which precedes the common expression of joy in the liturgy ("alleluia"), shifts the focus back to the day's events.

TEXT AND TRANSLATION

[1] Ab increpacione et ira furoris domini
      Terra [tremuit et quievit]
[2] Monumenta aperta sunt
   et multa corpora sanctorum surrexerunt
      Dum [resurgeret]
[3] Christus iudicaturus est vivos et mortuos
   quando venerit
      In iudic<io> [deus]
[4] Christus surrexit a mortuis
   venite adoremus eum omnes
   una voce proclamantes
      Allelu[ia]

*

[1] At the Lord's rebuke and furious anger:
      The earth trembled and was still.
[2] The tombs were opened,
   and many bodies of the saints arose:
      When (God) arose.
[3] Christ will be the one to judge
   the living and the dead
   when He comes:
      God (arose) in judgment.
[4] Christ has risen from the dead!
   Come, let us all adore Him,
   crying out in one voice:
      Alleluia.

DISTINCTIVE VARIANTS

The elements of this widely disseminated Offertory trope are variously combined, as may be seen in CT 3/2, 260–61. Most northern and central Italian sources preserve the same order of elements as the Nonantolan tropers; this arrangement is found outside Italy in Pn 9449, Pn 1235, Pa 1169, APT 17 and APT 18, and Pn 903.

All sources of the trope yield similar melodies, though the chant appears to have been reworked at some Italian centers in the latter half of the twelfth century. The melody in PAc 47 in particular is simpler and more direct in its motion than Nonantolan readings. Compare the settings of v. [1] (see example 1). Note that the leap from D to a, commonplace among Mode I melodies, is delayed in PAc 47, permitting a direct scalar descent on "increpat*ione et ira*."

MELODIC VARIANTS

Rc 1741 [1] *i(ra)* ED; [2] *(Monu)men(ta)* a(G); *sanc(torum)* G(F). **Bu 2824** [1] *i(ra)* ED; [3] *ve(nerit)* acc~a.

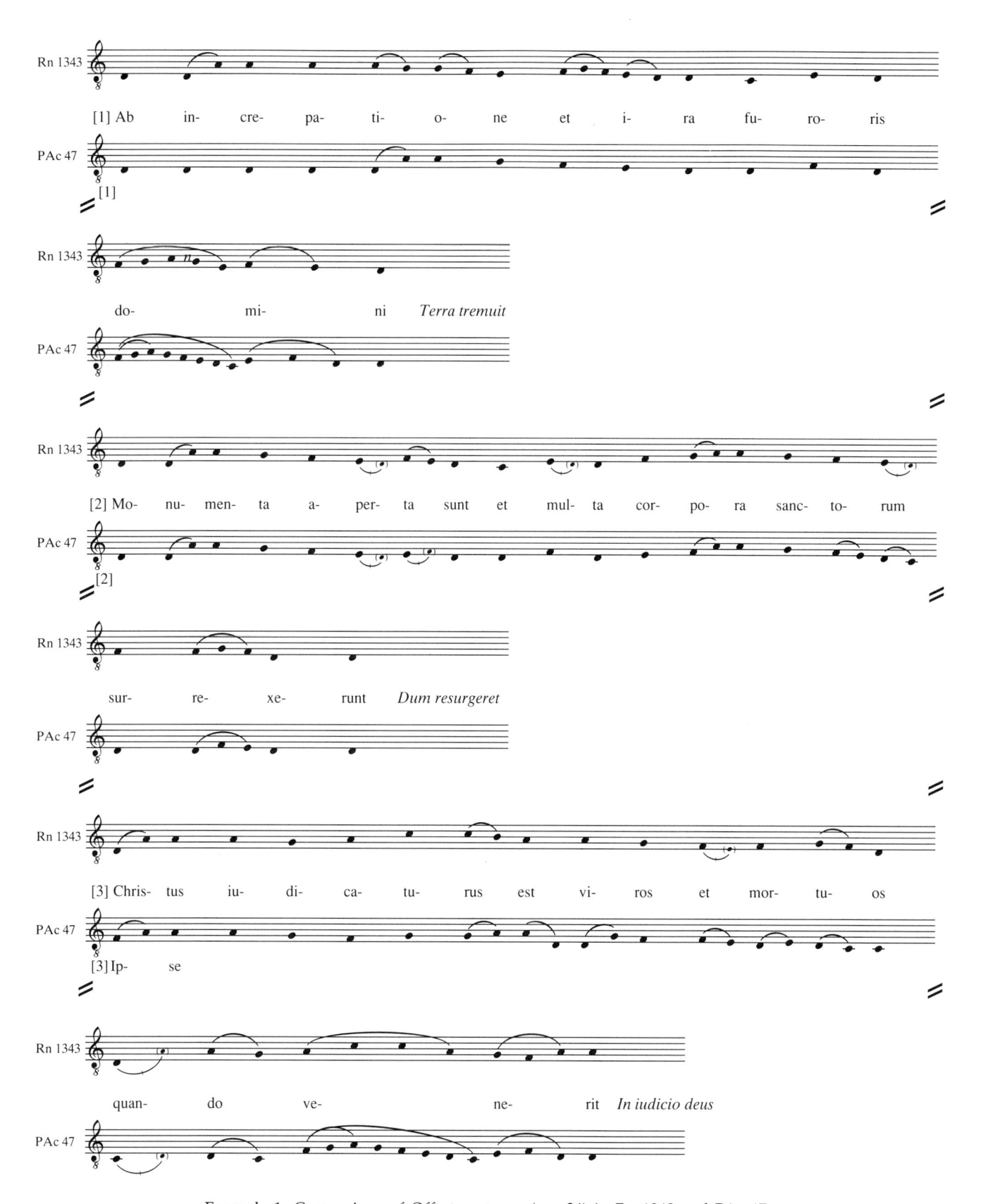

Example 1. Comparison of Offertory trope (no. 34) in Rn 1343 and PAc 47

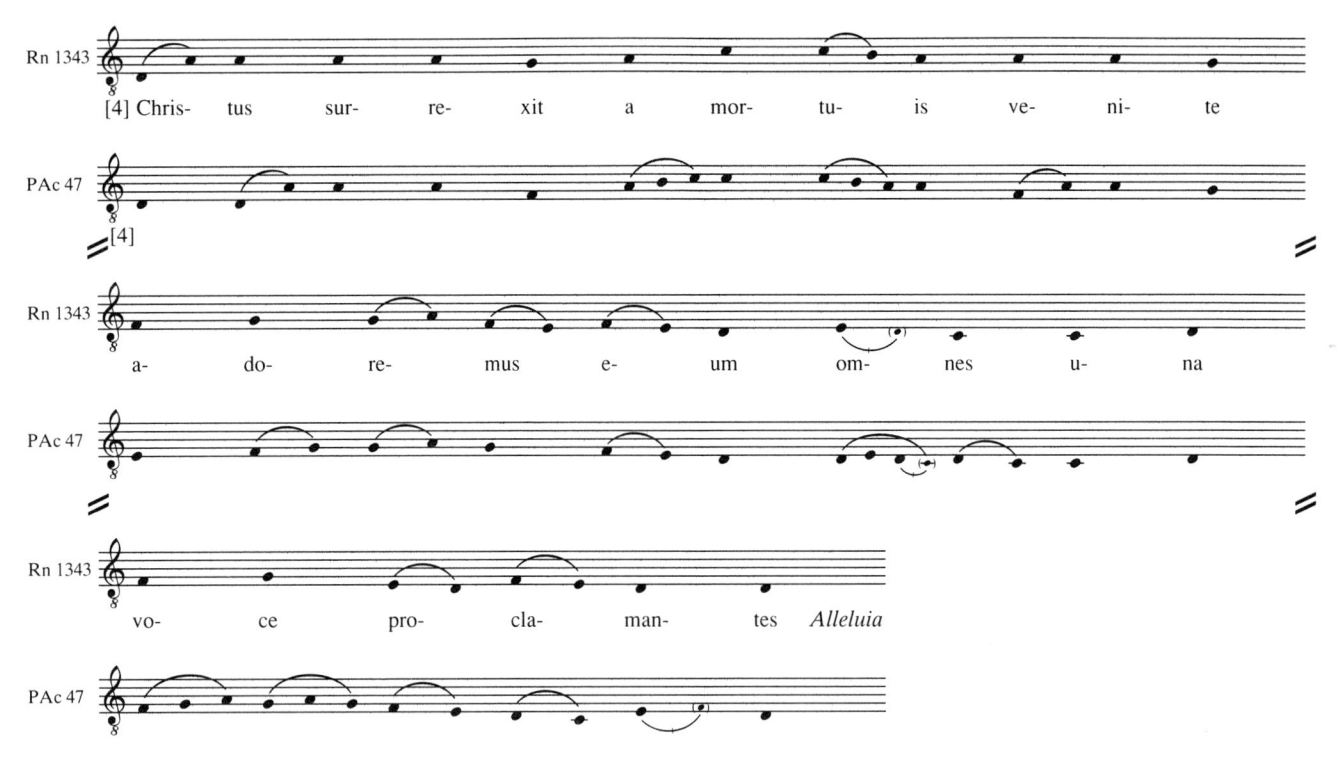

```
Rn 1343   [4] Chris- tus  sur- re- xit  a   mor- tu-  is  ve-  ni- te
PAc 47    [4]

Rn 1343   a-  do-  re-  mus  e-  um  om-  nes  u-  na
PAc 47

Rn 1343   vo-  ce  pro-  cla-  man-  tes  Alleluia
PAc 47
```

Example 1. *Continued*

35. Communion: *Pascha nostrum*

TROPE: *Laus honor virtus*

SOURCES
Rn 1343 fol. 30r P<ro>sa de co<mmunione>
Rc 1741 fol. 79v P<ro>sa de com<munione>
Bu 2824 fols. 51r–v P<ro>S[a] d<e> co<munione>

REFERENCES
  AH 49, no. 403; CT 3/2, 133, 158, 134; Evans, *The Early Trope Repertory*, 164–65; Planchart, *Repertory*, 2:228–30.

TEXT COMMENTARY
  In prose; widely transmitted as a three-element trope, *Laus honor virtus* is one of the oldest pieces in the repertory (Planchart, *Repertory*, 2:230). Following the expression of exultation in v. [1], the remaining lines complement the Communion text (1 Cor. 5.7–8). The division in Italian sources of a single line ("Leo fortis de tribu iuda . . . in cuius laude . . .") into two distinct elements detracts from the sense of integration. In v. [3] there is an allusion to Apoc. 5.5 (see also *Hodie resurrexit leo fortis*, no. 33).

TEXT AND TRANSLATION

[1]   Laus honor virtus deo nostro
      decus et imperium regi nostro
      qui precio redemptionis nostræ
            Pascha [nostrum immolatus est]

[2]   Peccata nostra ipse portavit
      et propter scelera nostra oblatus est
            Christus [alleluia]

[3]   Leo fortis de tribu iuda
      hodie surrexit a mortuis alleluia
            Itaque [epulemur in azymis sinceritatis
                et veritatis]

[4]   In cuius laude celsa voce pertonate
            Alle[luia alleluia alleluia]

                    *

[1]   Praise, honor, and power to our God!
      Glory and dominion to our King,
      who as the price of our redemption:
            Our Pasch was immolated.

[2]   He bore our sins Himself,
      and was sacrificed for our wickedness:
            Christ, alleluia.

[3]   The strong Lion of the tribe of Juda
      has risen this day from the dead, alleluia!
      Therefore let us feast with the
            unleavened bread of sincerity
            and truth.

[4]   In whose praise sing ye in a loud voice:
            Alleluia, alleluia, alleluia.

DISTINCTIVE VARIANTS
  Bu 2824 [3] *resurrexit* for *surrexit*. Bu 2824 preserves the same four-element form as the other Nonantolan tropers (cf. Planchart, *Repertory*, 2:229). Numerous sources of v. [3], including Tn 20, Tn 18, Ra 123, PS 119 and PS 120, omit "fortis."

Despite the division of the line "Leo fortis de tribu iuda . . . in cuius laude . . ." into two distinct elements, the surviving sources preserve similar melodies.

MELODIC VARIANTS

Rc 1741 [1] *(nos)tro* DFFD; *(redemp)ti(onis)* FG: [2] *nos(tra)* G; *ip(se)* aG; [3] *(mor)tu(is)* cd; *lau(de)* a(G); *cel(sa)* a(G). **Bu 2824** [1] *(redemp)ti(onis)* FG; [3] *resur(rexit)* F'F; *(mor)tu(is)* cd.

36. Introit: Gaudeamus . . . Senesii

TROPE: *Cuncti fideles Christi*

SOURCES

Rc 1343 fols. 32v–33r In nat<ivitatibus> s<an>c-<t>orum senesii. et theopontii. TROPI.
Rn 1741 fols. 86v–87r In .N<ativitatibus>. S<an>c-<t>orum Senesii. et Theop[ontii].
Bu 2824 fols. 55v–56r al<ius> ton<us>

REFERENCES
AH 49, no. 369; Planchart, *Repertory*, 2:119.

TEXT COMMENTARY

In prose; given the limited transmission of *Cuncti fideles Christi*, not to mention its assignment to the feast of two of the monastery's patrons, it is possible that the trope was composed at Nonantola. The evidence, however, is inconclusive. The text does not refer to the legends of these martyrs, but relates generally to the Proper text. Since the Introit *Gaudeamus* was also assigned traditionally to feasts of virgin martyrs, as well as All Saints and the Ascension, it is equally possible that the trope was transmitted to Nonantola and reworked into its present form. (*Cuncti fideles Christi* is assigned to All Saints in VEcap 107, the only other source of the trope known to me.) V. [5] was sung to the same music as part of the trope complex *Admirans vates*, Introit *Mihi autem* (see no. 62).

TEXT AND TRANSLATION

[1] Cuncti fideles christi venite
 ad hanc solle<m>pnitatem beatorum martyrum
 Senesii et theopontii
 de qua in cælis gaudent angeli
 et nos in terris
  Gaudea[mus omnes in domino]
[2] Agentes gracias illi
 qui triumphat in sanctis suis atque
  Diem [festum celebrantes]
[3] Debitis laudibus venerantes
  Sub ho[nore sanctorum Senesii
   et Theopontii]
[4] Quo etherea pecierunt regna
  De quorum [solemnitate gaudent angeli]
[5] Consortes suorum effectos atque socios
  Et conlaud[ant filium dei]
   Gaudeamus

*

[1] Come, all the faithful of Christ,
 to this commemoration of the blessed martyrs
 Senesius and Theopompus,
 about whom the angels in heaven
 and we on earth rejoice:
  Let us all rejoice in the Lord
[2] Give thanks to Him who triumphs in His saints,
 and:
  Celebrating a festal day,
[3] Venerating with due praises:
  In honor of blessed Senesius
   and Theopompus,
[4] On whose (feast) the heavenly dominions prayed:
  On whose solemnity rejoice the angels,
[5] His partners, accomplished and sharing:
  And give praise to the Son of God.
   Let us all rejoice . . .

DISTINCTIVE VARIANTS

Rc 1741 [1] *solemnitatem* for *solle<m>pnitatem*; [5] cue lacking. **Bu 2824** [1] *theopunti* for *theopontii*; *de quo* for *de qua*; [5] cue lacking. VEcap 107 preserves a variant form of v. [1]: "ad hanc solemnitate *sanctorum omnium* de qua in caelis." Aside from this difference—the result of the assignment of the trope to All Saints—VEcap 107 and the Nonantolan MSS are nearly identical in their texts and neumations.

MELODIC VARIANTS

Rc 1741 [1] *(ve)ni(te)* DEFF~E; *(so)lem(nitatem)* FE; [2] *(illi) qui* aaGE; *(tri)um(phat)* EE~; [3] *(vene)ran(tes)* aGaGFG. **Bu 2824** [1] *(ve)ni(te)* DEFF~E.

37a. Introit: Gaudeamus . . . Senesii

TROPE: *Sanguine sacrati Christi*

SOURCES

Rn 1343 fol. 33r Alius ton<us>.
Rc 1741 fols. 87r–v AL<ius> [tonus]
Bu 2824 fols. 55r–v Troph in [nativitatibus] s<an>c-<t>orum Senesii et theopu[ntii]

REFERENCE
Pfaff, *Die Tropen*, 81, 140.

TEXT COMMENTARY

Leonine hexameters. The verses of *Sanguine sacrati Christi* would have been appropriate for a number of saints who died at the hands of the Roman state. The trope is found outside Nonantola in Pa 1169 and Pn 1235. V. [1] suggests that Christ, whose suffering and death made possible man's redemption, was the model for the Christian martyrs. In v. [2], the awarding of the palm branch to the champions of heaven transforms this pagan symbol of Olympic victory into a sign of the martyrs' triumph over death. This transformation is reinforced in v. [3] with the mention of the *stadium,* the site of both athletic contests and the persecution of early Christians.

TEXT AND TRANSLATION

[1] Sanguine sacrati christi quoque morte redempti
    Gaude[amus omnes in domino]
[2] Dante suis palma post aspera bella superna
    Diem festu<m> [celebrantes
      sub honore sanctorum Senesii
      et Theopontii]
[3] Qui in stadio cælebri meruerunt premia cæli
    De quorum [solemnitate gaudent angeli
      et conlaudant filium dei]

*

[1] Having been redeemed by the blood and death of Christ consecrated:
    Let us all rejoice in the Lord.
[2] Giving the palm-branch to His followers after desperate spiritual struggles:
    Celebrating a festal day
      in honor of Saints Senesius
      and Theopontius,
[3] Who in the crowded stadium merited the rewards of heaven,
    On whose solemnity the angels rejoice,
      and give praise to the Son of God.

DISTINCTIVE VARIANTS

Rc 1741 [2] *palmam . . . superna<m>* for *palma . . . superna;* [3] cue *De quor<um> Gl<ori>a [patri].* **Bu 2824** [3] cue *De quor<um> Gl<ori>a [patri].* The Nonantolan reading of *Sanguine sacrati* is virtually identical to those in French sources, except for minor grammatical differences. In v. [3], for example, Pn 1235 begins "Qui stadio," but the absence of the preposition here may simply be an omission; the line ends "premia regni." In VEcap 107, in which the trope is assigned to the feast of All Saints, v. [1] lacks musical notation beyond the incipit; the neumations of the remaining verses suggest the same melody as Nonantolan readings, but with some differences in text underlay.

MELODIC VARIANTS
    None.

37b. Introit: Gaudeamus . . . sanctorum omnium

TROPE: *Sanguine sacrati Christi*

SOURCES

Rn 1343 fol. 45r Tropi .In nat<ivitatibus> omniu<m> s<an>c<t>or<um>
Rc 1741 fol. 119v Sanguine sacrati In .N<ativitatibus>. om<n>iu<m> s<an>c<t>or<um>. Req<uire> in n<a>t<ivitibus> S<an>c<t>or<um> mar<tyrum> Senesii. et Theopon<tii>
Bu 2824 fol. 85r TRO i<n> om<n>iu<m> s<an>c<t>or<um> *Sanguinis sacrati* ut sup<ra>

COMMENTARY

All three Nonantolan tropers suggest that the three elements of the trope were sung in connection with the Introit for All Saints. In no case does a Nonantolan scribe provide more than a notated incipit.

TEXT AND TRANSLATION

[1] Sanguine sacrati [christi quoque morte redempti
    Gaudeamus omnes in domino
[2] Dante suis palma post aspera bella superna
    Diem festum celebrantes
      sub honore sanctorum omnium
[3] Qui in stadio celebri meruerunt premia caeli
    De quorum solemnitate gaudent angeli
      et conlaudant filium dei]

*

[1] Having been redeemed by the blood and death of Christ consecrated:
    Let us all rejoice in the Lord.
[2] Giving the palm-branch to His followers after desperate spiritual struggles:
    Celebrating a festal day
      in honor of all the saints
[3] Who in the crowded stadium merited the rewards of heaven,
    On whose solemnity the angels rejoice,
      and give praise to the Son of God.

VARIANTS
    Neumed incipit in Rn 1343 only.

38. Introit: Viri Galilaei

TROPE: *Quem creditis super astra*

SOURCES
Rn 1343 fol. 33v TROPI. IN ASCENSA D<omi>NI.
Rc 1741 fols. 89r–v In ascens<a> d<omi>ni
Bu 2824 fols. 57v–58r (no rubric)

REFERENCES

AH 49, no. 4; *CT* 3/2, 173; Husmann, "Sinn und Wesen," 147; Planchart, *Repertory*, 1:93–94, 220, 2:35–36, 188–90; *MGG*. s.v. "Tropus," by Bruno Stäblein.

TEXT COMMENTARY

The beginning of the trope through "Alleluia" is in prose; "Regna terrae . . ." is in iambic dimeters. The opening of *Quem creditis super astra* is a parody of the Easter dialogue, *Quem quaeritis*, in which the apostles at the Ascension are substituted for the women at Christ's tomb. Addressing them are angels ("caelicolae"), mentioned in Acts 1.10 ("duo viri"), who quote the message that Christ delivered to the apostles through Mary Magdalene (John 20.17). Following the word "Alleluia," the trope closes with an exhortation in rhymed accentual meter. This portion of the text stems either from Ps. 67.33–34 ("Regna terrae, cantate Deo; psallite Domino; psallite Deo, qui ascendit super caelum caeli"), or another trope that quotes these verses (see *CT* 3/3, 187–88).

TELXT AND TRANSLATION

Quem creditis super astra ascendisse o deicole
Christum qui surrexit de sepulchro o cælicole
Iam ascendit ut predixit
ascendo ad patrem meum et patrem vestrum
deum meum et deum vestrum
Alleluia
Regna terræ gentes linguæ
decantate domino
quem adorant cæli cives
in paterno solio
     Viri galilei
     [quid admiramini
     aspicientes in caelum
     alleluia
     quemadmodum vidistis eum
     ascendentem in caelum
     ita veniet
     alleluia alleluia alleluia]
          *

Whom do you believe to have ascended
beyond the heavens, O followers of God?
Christ, who has risen from the sepulcher,
O celestial ones.
Already He is ascending as He foretold:
"I shall ascend to My Father and your Father,
to My God and your God,"
alleluia.
Ye powers of the lands, people, tongues,
sing to the Lord
whom the citizens of heaven adore
on the paternal throne:
     Men of Galilee,
     why do you wonder,
     looking up to heaven?
     alleluia.
     He shall so come
     as you have seen Him
     going up into heaven,
     alleluia, alleluia, alleluia.

DISTINCTIVE VARIANTS

Bu 2824 *deicole* for *cælicole*; cue *Viri gal<ilaei> Omnes gen[tes] Glo<ria> patri*. The Nonantolan tropers and VEcap 107 are the only Italian sources of *Quem creditis super astra*. Bu 2824 and VEcap 107, along with some northern sources, transmit the variant "o caelicol[a]e" at the beginning of the trope (*CT* 3/2, 173). In Rc 1741 *Quem creditis* is associated with a second element, *Quem euntem angelici*, which in Rn 1343 and Bu 2824 follows the introduction *Hodie redemptor mundi ascendit* (see no. 39).

MELODIC VARIANTS

Rc 1741 [1] *(deico)le* bb~a; *(surre)xit* bb~a; *(se)pul-(chro)* de(d); *(cęlico)le* bb~a; *(as)cen(dit)* d; *(as)cen(do)* b; *ves(trum)* dd~c; *(de)canta(te)* cd'db; *ci(ves)* cb; *(pa)ter(no)* abcdee~d.

39. Introit: *Viri Galilaei*

TROPE: *Hodie redemptor mundi ascendit*

SOURCES

Rn 1343 fol. 33v Alius tonus.
Rc 1741 fols. 89v–90r; 90r–v Item alius tonus
Bu 2824 fols. 57r–v; 58r Troh in ascen<sa> d<o-mi>ni.

REFERENCES

AH 49, no. 122; *CT* 3/2, 113, 174; Planchart, *Repertory*, 2:189–90.

TEXT COMMENTARY

In prose; vv. [1–2] are narrative elaborations of the Ascension as described in Acts 1.9–11. Aside from this, there is no inherent connection between the two trope elements, which are variously combined in the surviving sources.

TEXT AND TRANSLATION

[1] Hodie redemptor mundi ascendit cælos
mirantur apostoli angelique ei locuti sunt dicentes
     Viri ga[lilaei
     quid admiramini
     aspicientes in caelum
     alleluia]
[2] Quem euntem angelici gratulantes ordines
intuentibus hinc clama~n]t apostoli[s]

Quemad[modum vidistis eum
 ascendentem in caelum
  ita veniet
   alleluia alleluia alleluia]
            *

[1] Today the Redeemer of the world ascends
into heaven.
 The apostles are amazed, and the angels
 were speaking to them, saying:
  Men of Galilee,
   why do you wonder,
    looking up to heaven?
     alleluia.
[2] Upon His ascending the angelic ranks,
 manifesting their joy on this account,
 cried out to the apostles, who were looking on:
  He shall so come
   as you have seen Him
    going up into heaven,
     alleluia, alleluia, alleluia.

DISTINCTIVE VARIANTS

Rc 1741 [1] *eis* for *ei*; [2] *clamant apostolis* for *clamat apostoli*. **Bu 2824** [2] *euntes* for *euntem*; [2] *clamant* for *clamat*. *Hodie redemptor mundi ascendit* appears without an accompanying element in Rc 1741 and Bu 2824 (*CT* 3/2, 269–71). V. [2] is found in these manuscripts, but in connection with the introductory lines "Hodie rex gloriae Christus" in Bu 2824 (no. 41) and "Quem creditis super astra" in Rc 1741 (no. 38).

MELODIC VARIANTS

Rc 1741 *redemptor mun(di)* aa~'G'a(G)'c; *e(is)* cb.

40. Introit: Viri Galilaei

TROPE: *Terrigenas summos affatur*

SOURCES
Rn 1343 fol. 34r (no rubric)
Rc 1741 fol. 90r alius ton\<us\>

REFERENCES
AH 49, no. 21; *CT* 3/2, 204, 109, 209; Planchart, *Repertory*, 2:190–91.

TEXT COMMENTARY

Hexameters. Following the introductory v. [1], which sets the stage for the words spoken at the scene of the ascension and recalled in the Proper chant (text from Acts 1.11), v. [2] confirms Christ's dual nature as God and man. V. [3] reminds the listeners of the rationale for the ascension, which permitted Christ to bestow on man the benefits of His death and resurrection.

TEXT AND TRANSLATION

[1] Terrigenas summos affatur celicus ordo
  Viri [galilaei
   quid admiramini
    aspicientes in caelum
     alleluia]
[2] Hic deus et homo cęlorum compos et orbis
  Quemadmo[dum vidistis eum
   ascendentem in caelum]
[3] Ut reddat cunctis gestorum dona suorum
  Ita veni[et
   alleluia alleluia alleluia]
            *

[1] The heavenly rank speaks to the foremost inhabitants of earth:
  Men of Galilee,
   why do you wonder,
    looking up to heaven?
     alleluia.
[2] As God and man, Master of the heavens and the earth:
   As you have seen Him
    going up into heaven,
[3] That He may render to all the gifts of His deeds:
   He shall so come,
    alleluia, alleluia, alleluia.

DISTINCTIVE VARIANTS

Rn 1343 [1] *Terriginas* for *Terrigenas*; [2] *Sic* for *Hic*; [3] *Et* for *Ut*. The collation in *CT* 3/2 indicates that neither text variant in Rn 1343 was widely transmitted. Besides this Nonantolan source, the first is found only in Pn 1121; the second is an *unicum*.

Comparison of the musical settings reveals an abundance of minor differences among versions of the same basic melody.

MELODIC VARIANTS

Rn 1343 [1] *sum(mos)* bba(G); *or(do)* baa(G); [2] *(cælo)rum* cc(b); *or(bis)* Gabcc~ba(b); [3] *(ges)to(rum)* edcc~ba bcd; *(do)na* cc~b; *(su)o(rum)* abcc~b.

41. Introit: Viri Galilaei

TROPE: *Hodie rex gloriae Christus*

SOURCE
Bu 2824 fol. 58r (no rubric)

REFERENCE
CT 3/2, 114, 174, 236.

TEXT COMMENTARY

In prose; unlike the other introductions to *Viri Galilaei* (nos. 38–40), this description of Christ's entrance into heaven does not focus on the earthly scene, but

xliv

relates the ascension to man's ultimate salvation. Like many trope texts thought to represent an early stage of the repertory, v. [1] begins with the word "Hodie." It survives as an introduction only in VEcap 107 and PS 121 (CT 3/2, 270–71).

TEXT AND TRANSLATION

[1] Hodie rex glorie christus
    cælum patenter scandens patefecit ingressum
        Viri ga[lilaei
        quid admiramini
        aspicientes in caelum
        alleluia]
[2] Quem euntes angelici gratulantes ordines
    intuentibus hinc clamant apostoli
        Quemad[modum vidistis eum
        ascendentem in caelum
        ita veniet
        alleluia alleluia alleluia]

*

[1] Today the King of glory, Christ,
    ascending into heaven, mightily threw open
    the entrance: (Read *potenter . . . ingressum*)
        Men of Galilee,
        why do you wonder,
        looking up to heaven?
        alleluia.
[2] Upon His ascending the angelic ranks,
    manifesting their joy on this account,
    cried out to the apostles, who were looking on:
        He shall so come
        as you have seen Him
        going up into heaven,
        alleluia, alleluia, alleluia.

DISTINCTIVE VARIANTS

The arrangement of elements in Bu 2824—the only Nonantolan troper that preserves v. [1] *Hodie rex gloriae Christus*—is also found in VEcap 107, Ob 222, and Ra 123 among others (CT 3/2, 270–71). Bu 2824 and VEcap 107 omit two words from the commonly transmitted version of v. [1]: "scandens vitae nobis patefecit." In some sources, including Ob 222, vv. [1] and [2] are combined into a single element (CT 3/2, 236).

42. Introit: *Spiritus domini*

TROPE: *Hodie spiritus sanctus procedens*

SOURCES
Rn 1343 fols. 34v–35r (no rubric)
Rc 1741 fols. 92v–93r Trop. In pent<ecostes>.
Bu 2824 fols. 60v–61r Tro i<n> pentecost<es>

REFERENCES
    AH 49, no. 132; CT 3/2, 116, 106, 107, 196; Pfaff, *Die Tropen*, 73; Planchart, *Repertory*, 2:158–59, 164–65.

TEXT COMMENTARY
    V. [2] is in dactylic hexameters; vv. [1, 3, 4] are in prose, the latter conceived in hexameter-like periods. The Nonantolan version comprises four elements of diverse provenance (see CT 3/2, 273–76). V. [1], sung extensively throughout Italy as an introductory trope, concerns the miraculous workings of the Holy Spirit. The remaining elements differ in character and refer alternately to Christ, the Trinity, and the Holy Spirit.

TEXT AND TRANSLATION

[1] Hodie spiritus sanctus procedens a throno
    apostolorum pectora invisibiliter penetravit
    deo gracias eia
        Sp<iritu>s [domini
        replevit orbem terrarum
        alleluia]
[2] Gloria pangatur mundi hiesu christe redemptor
        Et hoc [quod continet]
[3] Gracias agimus semper trinitatis alme
        Omnia [scientiam habet vocis]
[4] Spiritus alme nostra semper tu pectora reple
        All<eluia> all<eluia> [alleluia]

*

[1] Today the Holy Spirit, coming forth
    from the throne,
    entered the souls of the apostles unseen,
    thanks be to God, yea:
        The spirit of the Lord
        has filled the whole world,
        alleluia.
[2] May glory be sung, Jesus Christ, Redeemer
    of the world:
        And that which contains
[3] Let us always give thanks to the Holy Trinity:
        All things has knowledge of the voice.
[4] Reviving Spirit, forever fill our souls:
        Alleluia, alleluia, alleluia.

DISTINCTIVE VARIANTS
    Rc 1741 [3] *trinitati* for *trinitatis*. Although v. [1] was known throughout Italy, the present four-element version of the trope is found only in Nonantola and Mantua (in VEcap 107). IV 60 preserves the same lines in a different order [4-2-3-1]; v. [3], which reads "Gratias agamus sanctae trinitatis semper," was known outside Italy as an introduction to the Introit *Spiritus Domini*.

MELODIC VARIANTS
    Rc 1741 [1] *(spi)ri(tus)* cb; *(invisi)bi(liter)* cb; *deo gra-(cias)* aa~G'ac'cb; [3] *(trinita)ti* a; [4] *(pecto)ra* a. **Bu 2824** [2] *(redemp)tor* G(a).

43. Introit: *Spiritus domini*

TROPE: *Hodie spiritus sanctus processit*

SOURCES
Rn 1343 fol. 35r Tropi in pentecostes
Rc 1741 fol. 93v Ite<m> al<ia>
Bu 2824 fols. 61r–v al<ius> ton<us>

REFERENCES
CT 3/2, 116; Planchart, *Repertory*, 2:162–65.

TEXT COMMENTARY
In prose; though brief compared with other introductory tropes, *Hodie spiritus sanctus processit* combines narrative with exhortation and reflection. The Holy Spirit proceeds from the throne (as described in the words of the Credo: "qui Patre Filoque procedit") and fills not only the apostles (Acts 2.4: "et repleti sunt omnes Spiritu sancto"), but the whole world ("replevit orbem terrarum"). This introduction presumably relates to similar *Hodie* tropes found in East Frankish sources (see CT 3/2, 116).

TEXT AND TRANSLATION
Hodie spiritus sanctus processit a throno
et replevit totum mundum
deo gracias dicite pariter
    Spiritus [domini
    replevit orbem terrarum alleluia
    et hoc quod continet
    omnia scientiam habet vocis
    alleluia alleluia alleluia]
    *
Today the Holy Spirit came forth from the throne
and filled the whole world,
thanks be to God, sing in equal degree:
    The spirit of the Lord
    has filled the whole world, alleluia.
    And that which contains
    All things has knowledge of the voice.
    Alleluia, alleluia, alleluia.

DISTINCTIVE VARIANTS
In nearly all its sources *Hodie spiritus sanctus processit* is a single element trope of introduction—the one exception is VEcap 107, which has three accompanying elements (Planchart, *Repertory*, 163–64). The Nonantolan tropers and VEcap 107, the only Italian sources of the trope, transmit the variant "dicite pariter" for "dicite eia." The neumations of this trope are essentially the same.

MELODIC VARIANTS
Rc 1741 *sanc(tus)* c(b). **Bu 2824** *sanc(tus)* c(b).

44. Introit: *Spiritus domini*

TROPE: *Cum essent apostoli*

SOURCE
Rc 1741 fols. 93r–v Alius ton<us>.

REFERENCES
CT 3/2, 89, 82, 163, 203; Planchart, *Repertory*, 2:162–65.

TEXT COMMENTARY
In prose; like other tropes for Ascension and Pentecost, *Cum essent apostoli* is a prime example of the centonization process, in which elements were recombined in transmission. The order of vv. [2–4] in the Nonantolan tropers and VEcap 107 is different from most other sources. (They follow a different introduction in the latter MS; see CT 3/2, 274–75.) The connection between trope and Proper texts here is not close, particularly when compared with southern French sources, in which v. [1] is the introduction to the Communion for Pentecost, *Factus est repente*. In this version of the piece both the trope and Communion refer to a sound from heaven (Acts 2.2: "Factus est repente de caelo sonus"); no such reference to *sonus* is made in the Introit text.

TEXT AND TRANSLATION
[1] Cum essent apostoli in unum congregati
     propter metum iudeorum
     sonus repente de cęlo factus est
        Sp<iritu>s [domini]
[2] Deus immensus et excelsus
        Replevit [orbem terrarum alleluia]
[3] Prestans linguarum peritiam
        Et hoc [quod continet omnia]
[4] Terrestria atque superna
        Scientia[m habet vocis
        alleluia alleluia alleluia]
    *
[1] When the disciples were gathered together
     for fear of the Jews
     a sudden sound came from heaven:
        The spirit of the Lord,
[2] God without end and eternal:
        Has filled the whole world,
        alleluia.
[3] Manifesting the knowledge of languages:
        And that which contains
[4] All things on earth and on high:
        All things has knowledge of the voice,
        alleluia, alleluia, alleluia.

DISTINCTIVE VARIANTS
The present arrangement of elements is typical only of Nonantolan sources. Vv. [2–4] are found in

Aquitanian sources, but in a different grouping (*CT* 3/2, 273–76). V. [1] in Nonantolan MSS and VEcap 107 has a variant opening and word order. Moreover, the line that these manuscripts preserve is longer than that found in southern French sources. In Aquitaine, *Cum essent apostoli* was sung as a trope to the Pentecost Communion, *Factus est repente*. A variant in v. [2] (*excelsus* for *aeternnus*) in Nonantolan MSS and VEcap 107 places these close to northern French readings. Similarities between northern Italian and northern French musical settings provide further evidence for a connection between these repertories.

MELODIC VARIANTS
None.

45. Introit: *De ventre matris meae*

TROPE: *Hodie exultent iusti . . . Iohannes*

SOURCES
Rn 1343 fol. 36r Tropi in n<ativite>. s<an>c<t>i ioh<ann>is baptistae
Rc 1741 fols. 96r–v trop in .N<ativitate>. S<an>c-<t>i ioh<ann>is bap<tistae>.
Bu 2824 fols. 65r–v troh in [nativivitate] s<an>c<t>i ioh<ann>is baptistę

REFERENCE
Planchart, *Repertory*, 2:61–62.

TEXT COMMENTARY
In prose; v. [1] was apparently modeled on the Christmas III trope, *Hodie exultent iusti natus est Christus* (no. 9), with which it shares the same musical setting. The Nonantolan tropers and VEcap 107 are the only Italian sources for the latter. Like the related Christmas trope, the introduction *Hodie exultent iusti . . . Iohannes* establishes the theme of the day's liturgy. The remaining elements, which are found in other MSS with different introductory verses, are well integrated with the Introit text. Noteworthy is the imitation of biblical language in vv. [3–4]; compare v. [3], "Prophetare in nomine ipsius," with Jer. 14.15, 26.9, 27.15, and v. [4], "et parare sibi plebem perfectam," with Luke 1.17 ("parare domino plebem perfectam").

TEXT AND TRANSLATION
[1] Hodie exultent iusti
   natus est sanctus iohannes
   deo gracias dicite eia
      De ventre [matris mea
      vocavit me dominus nomine meo]

[2] Servum sibi iohanne me vocans zacharie filium
      Et posuit [os meum
      ut gladium acutum]
[3] Prophetare in nomine ipsius
   credentes consequi baptisma
      Sub te[gumento manus sue
         protexit me]
[4] Dedit me testem veritatis
   et parare sibi plebem perfectam
      Posuit [me quasi sagittam electam]
      [Ps.] Bonum est [confiteri domino]
         *

[1] Let the just rejoice today;
   Saint John is born,
   thanks be to God, sing, yea:
      The Lord has called me by my name
      from my mother's womb.
[2] Calling me, John, son of Zachary, His servant:
      And made my mouth like a sharp sword.
[3] To prophesy in His name,
   conferring baptism on (His) followers:
      In the shadow of His hand
      He has protected me, and
[4] He permitted me (to be) a witness for the truth
   and to prepare for Him a perfect people:
      He has made me as a chosen arrow.
      Ps. It is good to give praise to the Lord . . .

DISTINCTIVE VARIANTS
   Rc 1741 [2] *iohannem* for *iohannes*. The four-element form of *Hodie exultent iusti . . . Iohannes* is found outside Nonantola in Ra 123 and PAc 47. In VEcap 107, vv. [2–3] follow the introduction *Audite insulae et attendite* (no. 47), and in MOd 7, *Clara iam nobis* (no. 46, v. [2]). V. [1] is found as a single element introduction in Ob 222, MOd 7, and PS 121 and other Italian sources; in BV 39 it is the fourth element of the *Audite insulae* trope complex (Planchart, *Repertory*, 2:62). Differences between the texts are limited to endings: v. [1], "Hodie exult*ant*" (Ob 222, MOd 7, PS 121a, and PAc 47); v. [2] "Iohannem me *vocat*" (MOd 7 and PAc 47). All surviving sources preserve basically the same melody.

MELODIC VARIANTS
   Rc 1741 [1] (*ius*)*ti* DCD; *io*(*hannes*) FE; [3] (*nomi*)*ne* FE; (*con*)*se*(*qui*) FE; *ve*(*ritatis*) FE. **Bu 2824** [2] (*fi*)*li*(*um*) D.

46. Introit: *De ventre matris meae*

TROPE: *Deus pater clamat Iohannem*

SOURCES
Rn 1343 fols. 36r–v Alius ton<us>
Rc 1741 fols. 96v–97r al<ius> [tonus]
Bu 2824 fol. 65v al<ius> [tonus]

REFERENCES
Pfaff, *Die Tropen*, 140–41; Planchart, *Repertory*, 2:54–56, 61–62.

TEXT COMMENTARY
In prose; v. [1] anticipates the beginning of the Introit to the extent of repeating the key words, "ventre matris." V. [2], which was used as an introductory element in other sources, has no inherent connection with the Introit phrase it precedes.

TEXT AND TRANSLATION

[1] Deus pater clamat iohannem in ventre matris
 de quo gratulantes dicamus cum propheta
  De ventre [matris mea
   vocavit me dominus nomine meo
   et posuit os meum
   ut gladium acutum]
[2] Clara iam nobis adest hodierna refulget iohannis nativitas dicentis
  Sub tegu[mento manus sue protexit me
   et posuit me quasi sagittam electam]
   Gl<ori>a patri
    *

[1] God the Father called on John in his mother's womb,
 about whom we gratefully sing with the prophet:
  The Lord has called me by my name
   from my mother's womb:
   and made my mouth like a sharp sword.
[2] John's birth, commemorated today, shines ever bright, as we sing:
  In the shadow of His hand
   He has protected me,
   and He has made me as a chosen arrow.
   Glory be to the Father . . .

DISTINCTIVE VARIANTS
Rc 1741 [2] *nobis hodierna* for *nobis adest hodierna*. Bu 2824 [2] *dicentes* for *dicentis*. The two lines of *Deus pater clamat Iohannem* are found in a variety of different arrangements in Italian MSS. In VEcap 107, for example, v. [1] was copied after the trope complex *Angelo prenunciate magnus* and probably performed *ad repetendum*, while v. [2] was used as the introductory line of a four-element complex. In PAc 47, *Deus pater* is a Psalm trope; *Clara iam nobis* introduces the Introit. In Rc 1741 the absence of the word "adest" in v. [2] apparently is not a scribal error since the same reading is transmitted in Ra 123.

MELODIC VARIANTS
Rc 1741 [1] *ma(tris)* D; *(di)ca(mus)* FE; [2] *(hodi)er(na)* GG(F); *(re)ful(get)* E. Bu 2824 [1] *ma(tris)* D; [2] *ad(est)* FFE.

47. Introit: *De ventre matris meae*

TROPE: *Audite insulae*

SOURCES
Rn 1343 fol. 36v (no rubric)
Rc 1741 fol. 97r *alius tonus*
Bu 2824 fol. 66r (no rubric)

REFERENCES
CT 5, 169, 171, 353–54; Pfaff, *Die Tropen*, 141; Planchart, *Repertory*, 2:54–56.

TEXT COMMENTARY
In prose; the text of this introductory trope is drawn verbatim from Isa. 49.1, which immediately precedes the words of the Introit, *De ventre* (Isa. 49.1–2).

TEXT AND TRANSLATION

Audite insule et adtendite populi de longe
dominus ab utero vocavit me
 De ventre [matris mea
  vocavit me dominus nomine meo
  et posuit os meum
  ut gladium acutum
  sub tegumento manus sue protexit me
  et posuit me quasi sagittam electam]
  Gl<ori>a patri
   *

Hear, oh islands, and give heed, oh distant people:
the Lord has called me from the womb:
 The Lord has called me by my name
  from my mother's womb:
  and made my mouth like a sharp sword:
  in the shadow of His hand
  He has protected me,
  and He has made me as a chosen arrow.
  Glory be to the Father . . .

DISTINCTIVE VARIANTS
Perhaps because the text of *Audite insulae* is drawn directly from scripture, there are no significant text variants. The musical settings of the trope in northern Italian MSS resemble APT 18 more closely than the version that circulated in Aquitaine.

MELODIC VARIANTS
Rc 1741 *(Audi)te* FE; *(adtendi)te* EE~D.

48. Introit: *Nunc scio vere*

TROPE: *Beatissimus Petrus catenis*

SOURCES
Rn 1343 fol. 37r Tropi.In.N<ativitate>.s<an>c<t>i petri
Rc 1741 fol. 98v Trop In.N<ativitate>.S<ancti> petri
Bu 2824 fols. 68r–v TRO i<n> [nativitate] s<ancti> petri

REFERENCES
Pfaff, *Die Tropen*, 139–40; Planchart, "Italian Tropes," 21–24; Planchart, *Repertory*, 2:319.

TEXT COMMENTARY
In prose; the introductory element, which sets the scene of Peter's imprisonment, was widely transmitted in northern Italy and may have originated there. By contrast, vv. [2–3] were sung with *Nunc scio vere* only in Nonantola and were borrowed from the Aquitanian Sanctus trope, *Sanctus Deus omnipotens pater*. Noting the lack of connection between these borrowed trope elements and the Introit they accompany, Planchart remarks: "[W]hat seems to have been important to [the Italian trope composer] was not the connection with what followed, but the burst of 'personal' emotion that the trope verse brings into the Introit antiphon at the point where it is inserted. In other words, neither theology nor narration matter to him quite as much as emotion" ("Italian Tropes," 23).

TEXT AND TRANSLATION
[1] Beatissimus petrus
catenis in carcere vinctus cum fuisset
ab angelo potenter solutus
et de manu herodis liberatus ait
    Nunc scio [vere
    quia misit dominus angelum suum]
[2] Deus exercituum et miliciarum rex
    Et eripu[it me
    de manu herodis]
[3] O admirabiles clemenciæ plene sunt in petro
de quo gratulantes dicamus cum illo
    Et de om<n>i [exspectatione
    plebis iudaeorum]
        *
[1] When most blessed Peter,
(who had been) shackled in prison,
(was) mightily released by the angel
and freed from Herod's grasp, he said:
    Now I know for certain
    that the Lord has sent His angel.
[2] God of hosts and the King of armies:
    And He has rescued me
    from the power of Herod.
[3] O admirable graces that are full in Peter!
Let us joyfully say with him:
    And from all that the Jewish
    people were expecting.

DISTINCTIVE VARIANTS
V. [1] is found in numerous Italian sources either as a single-element trope of introduction or with different sets of internal lines; vv. [2–3] are associated with *Nunc scio vere* only in Nonantolan sources. (For an inventory of the Italian sources, see Planchart, "Italian Tropes," 24.)

The musical settings of v. [1] differ from one another in certain details. The version in MOd 7, for example, was apparently reworked into an *aab* form. (Planchart does not collate this source, perhaps because it has a variant text or was grafted onto *Divina beatus Petrus* [no. 50].) The setting in PAc 47 closely resembles MOd 7 (see example 2).

MELODIC VARIANTS
Rc 1741 [1] *(Beatissi)mus* FE; *(Pet)rus* DD~C; *(li)be-(ratus)* DEFGF; [2] *(milicia)rum* C(E); [3] *(ple)ne* E; *(gratu)lan(tes)* FE(D). **Bu 2824** [1] *(li)be(ratus)* DEFGF; [2] *(milicia)rum* C(E).

49. Introit: *Nunc scio vere*

TROPE: *Hodie sanctissimi patroni nostri Petri*

SOURCES
Rn 1343 fol. 37r (no rubric)
Rc 1741 fols. 99r–v AL<ius> [tonus]
Bu 2824 fol. 68v al<ius> to<nus>

REFERENCE
Planchart, "Italian Tropes," 31.

TEXT COMMENTARY
In prose; *Hodie sanctissimi patroni nostri Petri*, which survives in the Nonantolan tropers as a single-element introduction to *Nunc scio vere*, marks the commemoration of the feast of a monastic patron. The text is essentially a description of the saint's triumph in heaven.

TEXT AND TRANSLATION
Hodie sanctissimi patroni nostri petri
anima choris supernis iuncta iubilat
quapropter et nos exultemus canentes
    Nunc scio [vere
    quia misit dominus angelum suum
    et eripuit me de manu herodis
    et de omni exspectatione
    plebis iudaeorum]
        *
Today the soul of our most holy patron, Peter,
joined with the choirs of heaven, shouts for joy,
on account of which we ourselves rejoice, singing:
    Now I know for certain
    that the Lord has sent His angel.

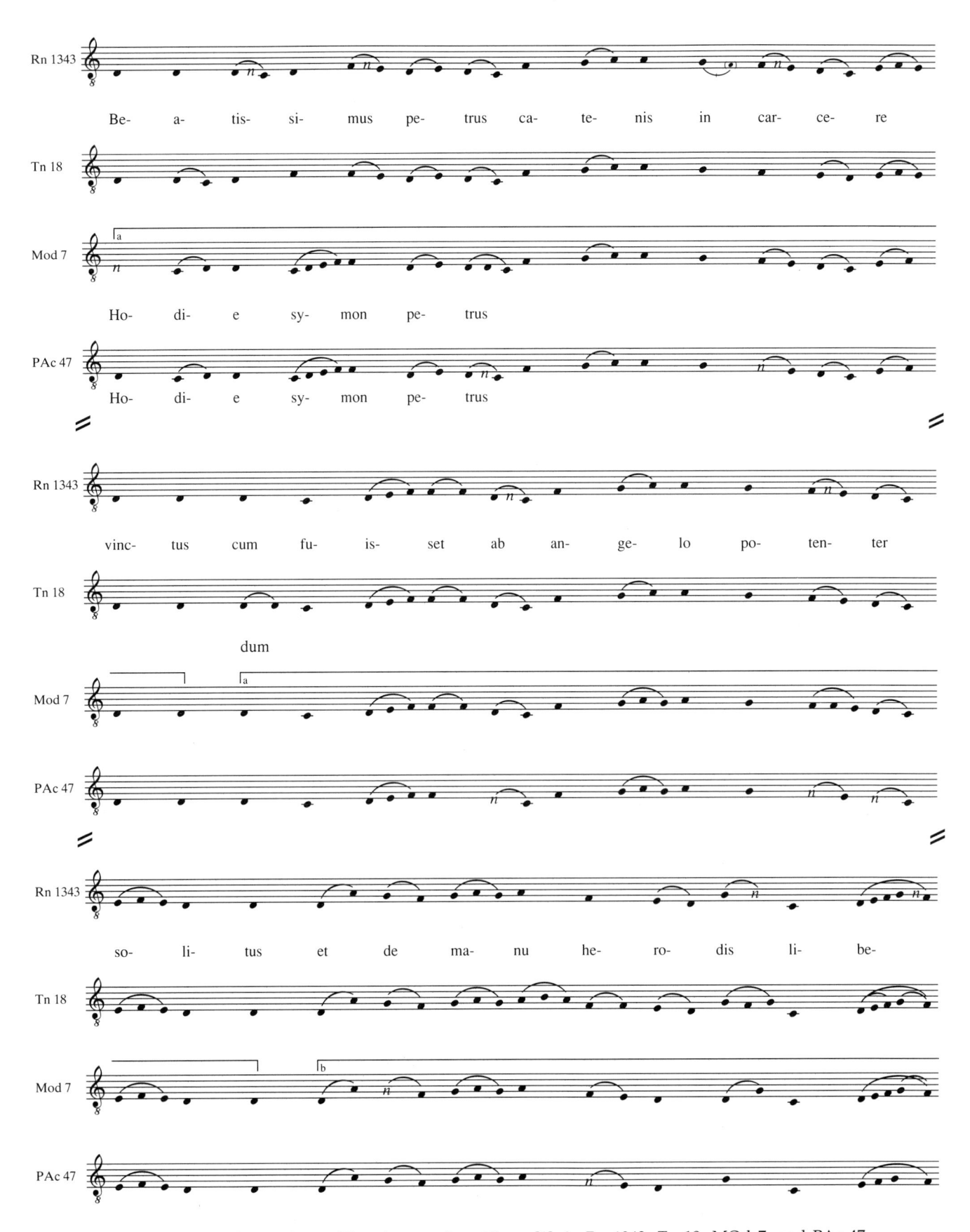

Example 2. Comparison of Introit trope (no. 48), v. [1], in Rn 1343, Tn 18, MOd 7, and PAc 47

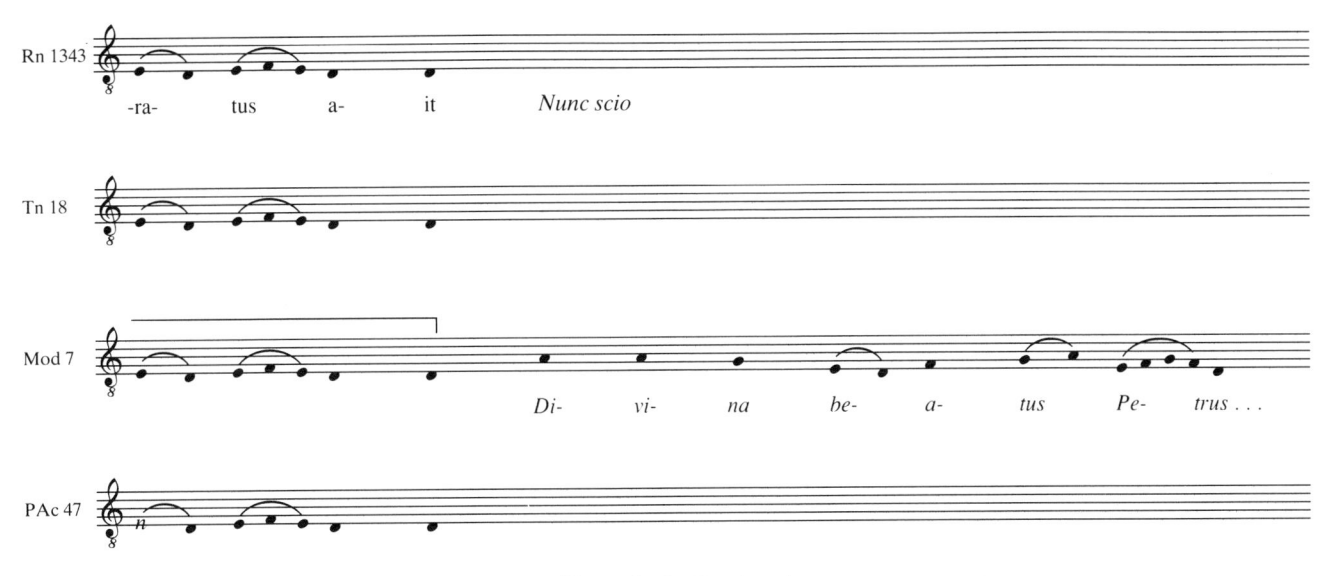

Example 2. *Continued*

And He has rescued me from the power of Herod.
And from all that the Jewish
people were expecting.

DISTINCTIVE VARIANTS

Bu 2824 *chori superni* for *choris supernis*. As Planchart has pointed out, *Hodie sanctissimi patroni nostri Petri* ultimately descends from an East Frankish trope honoring St. Gall, the patron of the famous monastery ("Italian Tropes," 31, n. 32). There, *Hodie sanctissimi patroni nostri Galli* and its internal elements were sung in connection with the Introit, *Sacerdotes tui domini*. (The same holds true for Ob 27, in which the trope was assigned to the feast of St. Martin.) How and in what form the trope reached northern Italy is an interesting matter for speculation. Outside Nonantola, *Hodie . . . Petri* is associated with *Nunc scio vere* in VEcap 107, Ob 222 (with a text variant found nowhere else: *ovantes* for *canentes*), and BV 39. Since the latter MSS once belonged to the convent of St. Peter, it is possible that the St. Gall trope was first reworked in Benevento. BV 39 also yields three internal lines found in VO 39 with *Nunc scio vere*, but with a different introductory element. Yet it should be noted that the musical settings of the trope in the Nonantolan tropers and other northern Italian sources more closely resembles East Frankish neumations than the Beneventan melody.

MELODIC VARIANTS

Rc 1741 *Ho(die)* D; *nostri Pe(tri)* Ga'a'aG; *iunc(ta)* a(G).

50. Introit: *Nunc scio vere*

TROPE: *Divina beatus Petrus*

SOURCES
Rn 1343 fols. 37r–v Alius ton<us>
Rc 1741 fols. 98v–99r Alius Tonus
Bu 2824 fols. 68v–69r (no rubric)

REFERENCES
CT 5, 169; Planchart, *Repertory*, 1:216–18, 2:126–28.

TEXT COMMENTARY

In prose; the diverse sources and complex transmission of the trope elements are not apparent in the Nonantolan version of *Divina beatus Petrus*. V. [1] resembles the passage of Acts 12.11 (the source of the Introit text) in which the tale of Peter's miraculous escape from Herod Agrippa's prison is described ("Et Petrus ad se reversus, dixit: Nunc scio vere . . ."). V. [2] incorporates the New Testament motif "lux in tenebris" (cf. Luke 1.79, 12.3; John 1.5), which is contrasted with the darkness of the prison cell. The two closing elements refer respectively to Herod himself and his attempts to placate the Jews by persecuting the early Church (cf. Acts 12.1–3).

TEXT AND TRANSLATION

[1] Divina beatus petrus erectus clemencia
in se rediens dicit
Nunc scio [vere
quia misit dominus angelum suum]

[2] Lux iusticiæ in tenebris me illuminavit
et de carcere eduxit
Et eripuit [me
de manu herodis]

[3] Liberavit me salvator meus
de manu cruenti predonis
Et de om<n>i [exspectatione]

[4] Qui me circumdedit consilio iniquo
    Plebis [iudeaeorum]

*

[1] Blessed Peter, released by divine clemency,
    (read *ereptus*)
    coming to himself, says:
        Now I know for certain
        that the Lord has sent His angel.
[2] The light of righteousness has illuminated me
    and summoned me from prison:
        And He has rescued me
        from the power of Herod.
[3] My Savior has freed me
    from the bloody hand of the plunderer:
        And from all the expectation.
[4] Which has trapped me in the evil conspiracy:
        Of the Jewish people.

DISTINCTIVE VARIANTS

Bu 2824 [3] *cruentis* for *cruenti*. Nonantolan sources transmit textual variants found in few other sources: in v. [1], "erectu" for the more common "ereptus" (PAc 47 reads "electus") and "dicit" for "dixit"; in v. [4], the masculine relative pronoun "qui," instead of "quae" or "quem." (The complex transmission of this widely known trope is summarized in Planchart, *Repertory*, 1:216–18.)

Regional differences among the musical settings are evident. The Nonantolan reading is distinct from other Italian ones in being notated a fifth higher than usual.

MELODIC VARIANTS

Rc 1741 [2] *(ius)ti(cię)* fe; *in* f; [3] *(Libera)vit* cb; *meus* cb'aa~G; *(cru)enti* ded'cb. **Bu 2824** [1] *Pet(rus)* dd~; *ius(ticiae)* cef; *e(duxit)* ac; [3] *(cru)en(ti)* ded(c).

51. Introit: *Os iusti*

TROPE: *A domino impletum*

SOURCES

Rn 1343 fol. 38v Trop .in [translatione] .S<ancti>.benedicto.
Rc 1741 fol. 102v Trop in Trans<latione> .S<ancti>.Benedicti

REFERENCES

AH 49, no. 216; Pfaff, *Die Tropen*, 82, 139; Planchart, *Repertory*, 1:222, 2:131–32.

TEXT COMMENTARY

Leonine hexameters in which vv. [2–4] do not rhyme, but correspond in vowel sound. The text of *A domino impletum* is well integrated with the Introit text, *Os iusti* (Ps. 36.30–31), a particularly appropriate chant for the founder of the Benedictine order. (On the assignment in Italy of a different Introit for the feast of St. Benedict, see Planchart, "Italian Tropes," 23.) The four verses allude respectively to Benedict's holiness, fairness, leadership, and common sense; each pairing of trope and Proper text brings the saint's life and work into ever sharper focus.

TEXT AND TRANSLATION

[1] A domino impletum sacro quoque dogmate pleno
    Os iusti [meditabitur sapientiam]
[2] Personas omnes equo discrimine pendens
    Et lingua [eius loquetur iudicium]
[3] Ut iugiter tra[c]tet quæ sunt moderamina vitæ
    Lex d<e>i [eius in corde ipsius]
[4] Unde et psalmiste versus sapienter adimplens obsequitur regi tali nos voce monendo
    [Ps.] Noli emu[lari in malignantibus]

*

[1] Made full by the Lord with sacred and complete doctrine:
    The mouth of the just shall meditate wisdom.
[2] Regarding all persons with equal fairness:
    And his tongue shall speak justice.
[3] May he guide (those things) which are the means of life:
    The law of God is in his heart.
[4] And wherefore, fulfilling prudently the verse of the Psalmist, he serves the most distinguished King, as with such a voice he warns us:
    Ps. Be not emulous of evildoers . . .

DISTINCTIVE VARIANTS

Rc 1741 [3] *tractet* for *tratet*. *A domino impletum*, a trope of northern European provenance, was not widely transmitted in northern Italy. Indeed, outside Nonantola it is found only in VEcap 107. Comparison of this MS to the Nonantolan tropers reveals few textual variants, though the small differences there are suggest that the Nonantolan version represents a later stratum of transmission than VEcap 107. For example, in v. [1] the text of VEcap 107 agrees with French and Aquitanian readings in transmitting "plenum" for "pleno." With respect to the musical setting, the Nonantolan version of the melody is notated a fifth higher than the Aquitanian one (cf. Weiss, *Introitus Tropen*, no. 258).

MELODIC VARIANTS

Rc 1741 [2] *(Perso)nas* ff~edcb; [4] *nos* cc~b; *vo(ce)* aG.

52. Introit: *Os iusti*

TROPE: *In iubilo vocis*

SOURCE
Rc 1741 fols. 102v–103r ALIUS

REFERENCES
AH 49, no. 215; Planchart, *Repertory*, 1:216, 2:133–34.

TEXT COMMENTARY
Hexameters. Compared with the preceding trope, *In iubilo vocis* is not particularly well integrated with the Introit, *Os iusti*. This is not to say, however, that connections between the trope and the Proper text are altogether lacking, if only because v. [2] and the preceding phrase of the Introit both refer to the "just man." But missing are such clever connections as between v. [4] of no. 51 ("Unde et psalmiste") and the succeeding Introit phrase, in which the admonition of the Psalmist ("Noli aemulari in malignantibus . . .") is placed into St. Benedict's mouth.

TEXT AND TRANSLATION
[1] In iubilo vocis benedicto psallite patri
    Os iusti [meditabitur sapientiam]
[2] Namque sophia struit sedem sibi pectore iusti
    Et lingua [eius loquetur iudicium]
[3] Neumate doctilogo cordis rigante secreta
    Lex dei [eius in corde ipsius]
    Gl<ori>a [patri]
    *

[1] In jubilant voices sing with Benedict to the Father:
    The mouth of the just shall meditate wisdom.
[2] For indeed wisdom establishes its place in the heart of the just man:
    And his tongue shall speak justice.
[3] With the guiding spirit of the soul speaking learnedly:
    The law of God is in his heart.
    Glory be to the Father . . .

DISTINCTIVE VARIANTS
The three verses of *In iubilo vocis* are consistently transmitted in Aquitanian, northern French, East Frankish, and northern Italian sources; Beneventan MSS have a different arrangement of elements (see Planchart, *Repertory*, 2:134–35). Rc 1741 preserves essentially the same text as the other sources. V. [3] "rigante" for "rimante" is a variant which northern Italian and Aquitanian readings share. All the melodic settings are essentially identical.

53. Introit: *Confessio*

TROPE: *Hodie beatus Laurentius levita*

SOURCES
Rn 1343 fols. 39v–40r Tropi. In N<ativitate>. S[ancti]. LAURentii.

Rc 1741 fols. 106v–107r Trop. In n<a>t<ivitate> S<an>c<t>i Laur<entii>.

Bu 2824 fols. 73v–74r Troh i<n> [nativitate] s<ancti> Laurentii

REFERENCE
AH 49, no. 280.

TEXT COMMENTARY
Hexameters, vv. [2–3]; v. [1] in prose. *Hodie beatus Laurentius levita* honors St. Lawrence, a deacon of the Roman Church who was martyred during the reign of Emperor Valerian in 258 A.D. Like no. 37, *Sanguine sacrati Christi*, this trope equates martyrdom with triumph and adapts pagan symbols of victory to Christian purposes (e.g., "palmam sertamque" in v. [3]).

TEXT AND TRANSLATION
[1] Hodie beatus laurentius
    levita pariterque christi martyr
    triumphat in cælis
    gaudent angeli et archangeli
    et nos in terris laudes deo canamus eia
    Confes[sio et pulchritudo
    in conspectu eius]
[2] Astra cæli dum conscendit iam morte de victa
    Sancti[tas et magnificentia]
[3] Vitricem meruit palmam sertamque micantem
    In s<an>c<t>i[ficatione eius]
    [Ps.] Cant<ate> [domino canticum novum]
    *

[1] Today blessed Lawrence,
    Levite and also martyr of Christ,
    triumphs in heaven;
    the angels and archangels rejoice,
    and let us on earth sing praises to God, yea:
    Praises and beauty are before Him.
[2] While, with death overcome, he ascends to the stars of the heavens:
    Holiness and majesty.
[3] He merited the beautiful palm-branch and the bright garland:
    In His sanctuary.
    Ps. Sing to the Lord a new song . . .

DISTINCTIVE VARIANTS
Rc 1741 [2] *poli* for *cæli*. **Bu 2824** [3] *sertaque* for *sertamque*. *Hodie beatus Laurentius levita* comes down to us in the Nonantolan tropers and VEcap 107, which are practically identical in their readings of the text. As regards neumation, VEcap 107 is somewhat less elaborate than the Nonantolan version, which includes more liquescence and lengthier melismas. (Compare the settings of "triumphat" and "canamus" in v. [1].)

MELODIC VARIANTS

Rc 1741 [1] (transposed) *Hodie* aa~'Ga'a (etc.); *le-(vita)* cb; *(pari)ter(que)* de; *(chris)ti* cb; *(an)ge(li)* cb; *(arch)an(geli)* aba; *(ca)na(mus)* aG cdee~d; [2] (transposed) *Astra poli* c'cb'ab'b (etc.); [3] *me(ruit)* cb.

54. Introit: *Confessio*

TROPE: *Prunas extensa*

SOURCES
Rn 1343 fol. 40r Aliu<s> ton<us>
Rc 1741 fol. 107r AL<ius>
Bu 2824 fol. 74r (no rubric)

REFERENCES
Borders, "Tropes," 403–5; Pfaff, *Die Tropen,* 139.

TEXT COMMENTARY
In prose; *Prunas extensa* relates, in an almost impressionistic fashion, the legend of St. Lawrence's martyrdom described in the *De officiis* of Ambrose of Milan. In Ambrose's account, and in later hymns and legends dependent upon oral tradition, Lawrence was said to have been burned to death on a red-hot gridiron. The gridiron also figures strongly in the iconography of the saint.

TEXT AND TRANSLATION
[1] Prunas extensa super craticulam menbra vivencia
    delicata caro crudelem extinxit ignem
    anima spirituque cum angelis cæli ianuas ingreditur
    ubi fulget sine fine
        Confes[sio et pulchritudo in conspectu eius
            sanctitas et magnificentia]
[2] Laurenti post menbra soluta calore prunarum
        In s<an>c<t>i[ficatione eius]
        Gl<ori>a patri

*

[1] Coals, living members stretched over the gridiron,
    the dripping flesh extinguished the fire;
    soul and spirit enter the gates of heaven with the angels,
    where he is forever resplendent:
        Praise and beauty are before Him:
        holiness and majesty
[2] After Lawrence's limbs were burnt by the heat of the coals:
        In His sanctuary.
        Glory be to the Father . . .

DISTINCTIVE VARIANTS
Rc 1741 [1] *spiritusque* for *spirituque*; [2] *Laurentii* for *Laurenti*; cue *Gloria patri* lacking. **Bu 2824** [1] *extensas* for *extensa*; *animas* for *anima*; *fulgens* for *fulget*; [2] cue *Confessio*. Outside Nonantola, VEcap 107 is the only source of *Prunas extensa* known to me. The texts are practically identical, save the variants *ardentes* for *extensa* in v. [1] and *penarum* for *prunarum* in v. [2]. The neumation of VEcap 107 matches the Nonantolan version.

MELODIC VARIANTS
Rc 1741 [1] (transposed) *Prunas* a'G (etc.); *(vi)ven(tia)* a; *(ex)tin(xit)* cb; *ig(nem)* aa~; *(in)gredi(tur)* aG'G; [2] *Laurentii* G(D)'G'ac'c; *post* cb; *so(luta)* GD. **Bu 2824** [1] *(vi)ven(tia)* D; *(in)gredi(tur)* DC'C.

55. Introit: *Confessio*

TROPE: *Qui tibi dedit Laurenti*

SOURCES
Rn 1343 fols. 40r–v (no rubric)
Rc 1741 fols. 107r–v alius
Bu 2824 fol. 74v (no rubric)

TEXT COMMENTARY
In prose; following the exhortation in v. [1], vv. [2–3] are rhetorically connected with the Introit text, *Confessio*. The resemblance between v. [3] and the preceding phrase of the Introit ("Sanctitas et magnificentia: Laus et iubilacio") is particularly close.

TEXT AND TRANSLATION
[1] Qui tibi dedit laurenti tormenta vincere seva liquida preconia
    nostra illi canunt hodierna caterva
        Confessio [et pulchritudo
            in conspectu eius]
[2] Simulque conson[i]s addatur hymnis
        S<an>c<t>itas [et magnificentia]
[3] Laus et iubilacio per cuncta tempora ac secla
        In s<an>c<t>i[ficatione eius]

*

[1] To You who helped Lawrence overcome savage torments,
    our company today sings flowing praises:
        Praise and beauty are before Him:
[2] And to our hymns let there also be added:
        Holiness and majesty.
[3] Praise and jubilation for all time and forever:
        In His sanctuary.

DISTINCTIVE VARIANTS
Comparing the text of *Qui tibi dedit* in six Italian MSS outside Nonantola—VEcap 107, Tn 18, Tn 20, Ob 222, IV 60, and PCsa 65—the most significant difference occurs in v. [2], for which the latter five sources transmit *consentibus* for *consonis*. Similarities

of music also link these five readings. In v. [3], for example, all have a melisma on "et" (edcde in Tn 18), in contrast with the Nonantolan reading and VEcap 107.

MELODIC VARIANTS
Rc 1741 [2] *hym(nis)* abcd; [3] (transposed) *Laus et b(e)'e* (etc.); *(cunc)ta* edcabaG. Bu 2824 [3] *(cunc)ta* aGFDEDC.

56. Introit: Gaudeamus . . . Mariae . . . assumptione

TROPE: *Exaudi virgo virginum*

SOURCES
Rn 1343 fol. 41r Trop in assu<m>p<tione>. S[anctae].Mariae.
Rc 1741 fols. 109r–v Trop In assu<m>pt<tione>. S[anctae].marię.
Bu 2824 fols. 76r–v Troph in asumpcione S<anctae> mariae

REFERENCES
AH 49, no. 183; Pfaff, *Die Tropen*, 82; Weiss, *Introitus Tropen*, xix–xx.

TEXT COMMENTARY
Iambic dimeters with rhyme in vv. [1–2]. *Exaudi virgo virginum* is noteworthy for its supplicatory tone, particularly in vv. [1] and [3]. V. [2] maintains the iambic meter of the outer verses despite its derivation from the description of the annunciation in Luke 1.28.

TEXT AND TRANSLATION
[1] Exaudi virgo virginum
 hymnum laudis et canticum
 exaudi voces supplicum
 laudentes te in perpetuum
  Gaudeamus [omnes in domino
   diem festum celebrantes]
[2] Ave beata Maria
 predixit gabrihel angelus
 benedicta pre omnibus
 feminis et virginibus
  Sub honor<e> [mariae virginis
   de cuius assumptione gaudent angeli]
[3] Nunc vivamus cum filio
 et matre sancta maria
  Et c<on>lau[dant filium dei]
   [Ps.] Eructav<it>
    *

[1] Hear, O virgin of virgins,
 the hymn of praise and the canticle;
 hear the voices of the suppliants
 praising you forever:
  Let us all rejoice in the Lord,
   celebrating a festival day.
[2] "Hail, holy Mary,"
 the angel Gabriel proclaimed,
 "blessed before all women and virgins":
  In honor of the blessed virgin Mary,
   on whose Assumption the angels rejoice.
[3] That now we may dwell with the Son
 and holy Mother Mary:
  And give praise to the Son of God.
   Ps. [My heart] overflows . . .

DISTINCTIVE VARIANTS
Rc 1741 [1] *laudantis* for *laudentes*. Bu 2824 [1] *laudantis* for *laudentes*. Outside Nonantola, the only source of *Exaudi virgo virginum* known to me is VEcap 107, the text of which is practically identical to the Nonantolan version. As with no. 53, *Hodie beatus Laurentius levita*, the Nonantolan setting of the melody employs more liquescent neumes than VEcap 107. (Compare, for example, the settings of "virgo" and "laudis" in v. [1], and "et" in v. [2].)

MELODIC VARIANTS
Rc 1741 [1] *vir(go)* a; *vir(ginum)* aG; *(can)ti(cum)* ED; [2] *ma(ria)* aG. Bu 2824 [1] *(can)ti(cum)* ED.

57. Introit: Gaudeamus . . . Mariae . . . assumptione

TROPE: *Ave beata Maria*

SOURCES
Rn 1343 fols. 41r–v al<ius> ton<us>
Rc 1741 fol. 110r AL<ius> [tonus]
Bu 2824 fol. 76v (no rubric)

REFERENCES
Pfaff, *Die Tropen*, 82; Planchart, *Repertory*, 2:100–1.

TEXT COMMENTARY
Rhymed iambic dimeters. As with no. 56, *Exaudi virgo virginum*, *Ave beata Maria* is marked by its supplicatory tone and hymn-like verse structure. Similarities of text and music between the two tropes (compare the openings of the melodies) suggest not only that one was modeled on the other, but that they were performed successively, with *Ave beata Maria* being sung *ad repetendum*. Two of the three Nonantolan tropers have a cue to the doxology following the Introit incipit.

TEXT AND TRANSLATION
Ave beata maria
ave gloriosissima
te clamant mille millia
adiuva sancta maria

Gaudeamus [omnes in domino
diem festum celebrantes
sub honore Mariae virginis
de cuius assumptione gaudent angeli
et conlaudant filium dei]
Gl<ori>a patri

*

Hail, blessed Mary,
Hail, most glorious one;
a thousand-thousand attendants call
out to you:
"Sustain (us), holy Mary!"
Let us all rejoice in the Lord,
celebrating a festival day.
In honor of the blessed virgin Mary,
on whose Assumption the angels rejoice.
And give praise to the Son of God.
Glory be to the Father . . .

DISTINCTIVE VARIANTS

Rc 1741 *milia* for *mille*; cue *Gloria patri* lacking. **Bu 2824** *milia* for *mille*. *Ave beata Maria*, which in Nonantola served solely as an introduction, was provided with three internal elements in VEcap 107. Comparisons of the available readings yields no significant variants of text or music.

MELODIC VARIANTS

Rc 1741 *ma(ria)* aG; *(gloriosis)si(ma)* E(D).

58. Introit: Gaudeamus . . . Mariae . . . assumptione

TROPE: *Nos sinus ecclesiae*

SOURCES
Rn 1343 fol. 41v (no rubric)
Rc 1741 fols. 109v–110r alius tonus

REFERENCES
AH 49, no. 180; Planchart, *Repertory*, 2:100–1.

TEXT COMMENTARY

Leonine hexameters in which vv. [2–3] do not rhyme, but correspond in vowel sound. Despite regional differences in the form of *Nos sinus ecclesiae*, the Nonantolan version of the trope was well integrated into the Introit text. The supplicatory tone of the preceding Marian tropes is lacking, having been replaced here by the musical depiction of a coronation scene.

TEXT AND TRANSLATION

[1] Nos sinus æcclesiæ matris quos enutrit alme eia
Gaudeam<us> [omnes in domino
diem festum celebrantes]

[2] In quo rex cæli reddit quoque gaudia terris
Sub hon<ore> [Mariae virginis]

[3] Esse dei genitrix que creditur omnipotenti[s]
De cu<iu>s [assumptione gaudent angeli
et conlaudant filium dei]

*

[1] The bosom of nourishing mother Church,
we whom she has nourished, yea:
Let us all rejoice in the Lord,
celebrating a festival day.

[2] On which the King of heaven also renders joys
to (all) lands:
In honor of the blessed virgin Mary.

[3] Who is believed to be the mother of the all-powerful God:
On whose Assumption the angels rejoice,
and give praise to the Son of God.

DISTINCTIVE VARIANTS

Rc 1741 [3] *quę . . . omnipotentis* for *que . . . omnipotenti*. This three-verse form of the trope is found in six northern Italian MSS, including Rn 1343, Rc 1741, Ra 123, PS 121, MOd 7, and PAc 47; Tn 20 and Tn 18 preserve v. [1] only, mutilated in the latter. Comparison of the texts in these sources yields no significant differences. Outside northern Italy, however, a variety of regional variants have come down to us (Planchart, *Repertory*, 2:100–101). Aquitanian sources, for example, preserve *erudit* for *enutrit* in v. [1]; northern French tropers, Pn 13252 and CA 75, read *omni parentis* for *omnipotentis* in v. [3]; MZ 452 has a slightly different introductory verse: "Nos sinus aecclesiae laudes ferendo canamus." Although the melodies in all the sources are similar in general outline, the differences between them are quite numerous.

MELODIC VARIANTS

Rc 1741 [1] *(al)me* aaGFGa; *e(ia)* aG aFED F(E); [2] *quo(que)* FE.

59. Introit: Vultum tuum

TROPE: *O quam clara nitet*

SOURCES
Rn 1343 fol. 42v Trop In nat<ivitate> s<anctae> mariae
Rc 1741 fols. 112r–v Trop In nat<ivitate> S<an>c<t>e mariae.

REFERENCES
AH 49, no. 159; Pfaff, *Die Tropen*, 77, 139–40; Planchart, *Repertory*, 1:195, 2:192.

TEXT COMMENTARY

Hexameters with elision in v. [2]. Given its many Italian concordances, it is conceivable that *O quam clara nitet* was composed in Italy. The Introit *Vultum tuum* was seldom troped in French sources and only occasionally in East Frankish ones. The *topos* employed in the trope—that of Mary as the bride of Christ—relates both to the Proper chant text (Ps. 44.13, 15–16), which is a nuptual ode for the messianic king, and to the tradition of chants for the Blessed Virgin.

TEXT AND TRANSLATION

[1]   O quam clara nitet agni pulcherrima sponsa
         Vultum [tuum deprecabuntur
            omnes divites plebis]
[2]   Ut cęli in thalamo semper nova cantica psallant
         Adduc<entur> [regi virgines post eam:
            proximae eius]
[3]   Angelicisque choris iunctę lętentur in evum
         Adducentur [tibi in laetitia
            et exultatione]
                  *
[1]   O how radiant shines the most beautiful
         spouse of the Lamb:
            All the rich among the people
               shall seek your favor.
[2]   That they may ever sing new songs
         in the heavenly bedchamber:
            After her virgins will be led to the King:
               her neighbors.
[3]   And let them, joined with angelic choruses,
         be joyful in Him forever:
            They are borne in to you with gladness
               and joy.

DISTINCTIVE VARIANTS

Rn 1343 [1] *nites* for *nitet*; [2] *psallat* for *psallant*; [3] *chori iuncta læten[tur]* for *choris iunctę lętentur*. In its Italian sources, the text of *O quam clara nitet* is transmitted with no significant variants (although in VEcap 107 the trope is associated with a different Introit, *Salve sancta parens*). The Italian musical settings are quite similar, with some differences in the melismas on "cantica" and "psallant" in v. [2] and "laetentur" in v. [3].

MELODIC VARIANTS

Rn 1343 [1] *ag(ni)* DDC(B); *(pul)chrer(rima)* FF~ED GG~FED; [2] *sem(per)* F; *no(va)* CDEF FGG~F; *psal(lat)* DEE~D; [3] *iunc(ta)* CDEFGG~F; *læten(tur)* aaGFa'FF~ED; *in e(vum)* [mutil.].

60. Introit: *Benedicite dominum*

TROPE: *Qui patris in caelo*

SOURCES

Rn 1343 fol. 43r (no rubric)

Rc 1741 fol. 115r Trop. in Dedic<atione>. S[ancti]. Michahel<is>

Bu 2824 fols. 80v–81r TRO i<n> [dedicatione] s<ancti> michaelis

REFERENCE

Pfaff, *Die Tropen*, 82.

TEXT COMMENTARY

Hexameters in which half-verses rhyme in the scheme: a b / b a / c c. Like the Introit text, *Qui patris in caelo* is addressed to all the angels, not just Michael Archangel. V. [1] expresses the longing of those on earth to be close to God. The next two verses, which resemble one another in structure and grammar, outline the activities of the angelic host, namely, to praise God and inspire the saints.

TEXT AND TRANSLATION

[1]   Qui patris in cælo nostris cognoscere vultum
         Benedicite [dominum
            omnes angeli eius]
[2]   Te[r] trinus ordo deum laudantes voce perhenni
         Potentes [virtute
            qui facitis verbum eius]
[3]   Sanctos firmantes sanctorum neumate mentes
         Ad audiendam [vocem sermonum eius]
                  *
[1]   You who know the countenance of our Father in
         heaven:
            Bless the Lord,
               all you His angels.
[2]   Nine-fold rank, praising God with everlasting
         voice:
            You, mighty in strength,
               who do His bidding.
[3]   Encouraging the souls of the saints
         with blessed inspiration:
            Hearken to the voice of His orders.

DISTINCTIVE VARIANTS

Rc 1741 [2] *Ter* for *Te[r]*; [3] *Sancto* for *Sanctos*. **Bu 2824** [1] *nostis* for *nostris*; [2] *Te*; [3] *Sancto* for *Sanctos*; *firmante . . . nentes* for *firmantes . . . mentes*. The Italian readings of *Qui patris in caelo* identified thus far—the Nonantolan tropers, VEcap 107, MOd 7, and PAc 47—preserve basically the same text as the Nonantolan MSS. At the end of v. [3], however, VEcap 107 reads: "sanctorum pneuma canentes." In the music, the neumation of VEcap 107 agrees with the Nonantolan readings in most details; MOd 7 and PAc 47 share many of the same variants.

MELODIC VARIANTS

Rc 1741 [2] *(lau)dan(tes)* bc; [3] *(sancto)rum* cb; *(neuma)te* b. **Bu 2824** [3] *neu(mate)* aa(G).

61. Introit: Mihi autem nimis

TROPE: *Nobile apostolici admirans*

SOURCES
Rn 1343 fol. 44v Tropi In .N<ativitatibus>. ap<osto>lor<um> Simonis. et iudae.
Rc 1741 fols. 117v–118r Trop in nat<ivitatibus> ap<osto>lor<um> Simonis. et iude.
Bu 2824 fols. 83v–84r Tro i<n> [nativitatibus] beator<um> Simonis et iude

REFERENCES
AH 49, no. 368; *CT* 5, 102; Pfaff, *Die Tropen*, 139; Planchart, *Repertory*, 2:122–23.

TEXT COMMENTARY
Leonine hexameters. Given the general nature of references in the trope, it is not surprising that outside Nonantola it was assigned to the feasts of different apostles.

TEXT AND TRANSLATION
[1] Nobile apostolici admirans decus ordinis almi
daviticus psaltes procalmat talia dicens
Michi aut [nimis honorati
sunt amici tui deus]
[2] Quo[s] divinus amor vere tibi iuncxit amicos
Nimis [confortatus est principatus eorum]
[3] Cælica namque piis reddunt acaronta superbis
P[s.] D<omi>ne p<ro>basti me
*
[1] Marveling at the noble accomplishment of the life-giving apostolic order,
the Psalmist David proclaims these things, saying:
To me Your friends, O God, are made exceedingly honorable.
[2] Those whom divine love has truly joined to you (as) friends:
Their principality is exceedingly strengthened.
[3] For they render heaven to the pious, and hell to the proud:
Ps. Lord, You have proved me and known me . . .

DISTINCTIVE VARIANTS
Rc 1741 [2] *Quos* for *Quo*; *iunxit* for *iuncxit*. **Bu 2824** [1] *apostolicæ* for *apostolici*; *daviticos* for *daviticus*; *psaltes* (addition); [2] *Quos* for *Quo*. As indicated in the collation of texts in *AH*, the sources of *Nobile apostolici admirans* transmit quite a few regional variants, though Italian readings are fairly uniform. With respect to neumation, the Nonantolan version and Ob 222 resemble most closely those in Pa 1169 and Pn 13252. There are many melodic differences between these and the two Aquitanian versions (cf. Weiss, *Introitus Tropen*, no. 138).

MELODIC VARIANTS
Rc 1741 [1] *(al)mi* DC; [3] *(acarron)ta* ED. **Bu 2824** [1] *(admi)rans* D; *al(mi)* DE; [2] *iunc(xit)* FG.

62. Introit: Mihi autem nimis

TROPE: *Admirans vates proclamat*

SOURCES
Rn 1343 fol. 44v aliu<s> ton<us>
Rc 1741 fol. 118r AL<ius> [tonus]

REFERENCES
AH 49, no. 369; Planchart, *Repertory*, 1:119 n. 1, 198; 2:119.

TEXT COMMENTARY
Hexameters. *Admirans vates proclamat*, which is found outside Italy in only two MSS—Ob 775 and Pn 9449 (the latter without notation)—is very likely an Italian product (Planchart, *Repertory*, 1:119). Like no. 61, the text refers to the dedicatee in the most general terms. It would appear that, in tropes of this type, the emphasis was placed on a smooth connection with the Introit text rather than association with a particular saint.

TEXT AND TRANSLATION
[1] Admirans vates proclamat voce sonora
Michi aut [nimis honorati
sunt amici tui deus]
[2] Qui tibi sunt iuncti divino neumate pleni
Nimis [confortatus est principatus eorum]
*
[1] The admiring prophet proclaims in a resounding voice:
To me Your friends, O God, are made exceedingly honorable.
[2] They who are joined to you completely by the divine Spirit:
Their principality is exceedingly strengthened.

DISTINCTIVE VARIANTS
The same two-element version of *Admirans vates proclamat* is found in many Italian sources, including Beneventan ones. The Nonantolan and Beneventan melodies resemble one another closely; the main difference occurs in v. [2], *iuncti di(vino)*, for which BV 39 reads: Ga'E'GF.

MELODIC VARIANTS
Rc 1741 [1] *(Admi)rans* FE; *procla(mat)* DEFGGG~F'GaGFED; [2] *Qui* DC; *di(vino)* FGE; *ple(ni)* CDED.

63. Introit: *Mihi autem nimis*

TROPE: *Consortes tuorum effecti*

SOURCES
Rn 1343 fol. 44v (no rubric)
Rc 1741 fol. 118r (no rubric)
Bu 2824 fol. 84r (no rubric)

REFERENCES
AH 49, no. 369; Planchart, *Repertory*, 2:119.

TEXT COMMENTARY
Consortes tuorum effecti, which is very closely connected in Nonantolan MSS with *Admirans vates proclamat*, would seem to be a local product. Outside Nonantola it is found only in VEcap 107 but without neumes.

TEXT AND TRANSLATION

Consortes tuorum effecti atque socios
    Michi aut [nimis honorati
        sunt amici tui deus
    nimis confortatus est principatus eorum]
            *

Having been made Your partners and companions:
    To me Your friends, O God, are made
        exceedingly honorable.
    Their principality is exceedingly strengthened.

DISTINCTIVE VARIANTS
Rc 1741 cue *Gloria patri* for *Michi aut*. **Bu 2824** *suorum* for *tuorum*. The single element *Consortes tuorum effecti* is found outside Nonantola only in VEcap 107, where it is cued to *Nimis [confortatus est principatus eorum]*.

MELODIC VARIANTS
Rc 1741 *(Con)sor(tes)* DEFEE~. **Bu 2824** *(Con)sor(tes)* DEFE(D); *(at)que* DEFED.

64. Introit: *Statuit ei dominus*

TROPE: *Divini fuerat*

SOURCES
Rn 1343 fol. 46r IN NAT<ivitate>. S<an>c<t>i Martini. TROPI.
Rc 1741 fol. 120v Trop In .N<ativitate>. S[ancti]. martini
Bu 2824 fols. 86v–87r TRO i<n> [nativitate] s<an>c-<t>i martini

REFERENCES
AH 49, no. 376; Pfaff, *Die Tropen*, 140; Planchart, *Repertory*, 1:222, 2:167–68.

TEXT COMMENTARY
Hexameters. Like other tropes for saints discussed above, *Divini fuerat* lacks specific reference to the dedicatee.

TEXT AND TRANSLATION

[1] Divini fuer[a]t quoniam fervoris amator eia
    Statuit [ei dominus testamentum pacis]
[2] Et pactum vitæ firmum stabilivit in evum
    Et pri[ncipem fecit eum
    ut sit illi sacerdotii dignitas]
[3] Incensumque suæ condignum deferat are
    In æt<ernum>
      *

[1] Seeing that he has been a lover of divine passion, yea:
    The Lord made him a covenant of peace.
[2] And established a firm pact of life in eternity:
    And made him a prince.
    That the dignity of priesthood
    should be to him.
[3] That he may bear worthy incense to His altar:
    Forever.

DISTINCTIVE VARIANTS
Rn 1343 [1] *fuerunt* for *fuer[a]t*. **Rc 1741** [1] *fuerat*. **Bu 2824** [1] *fuerat*. The three-element version of *Divini fuerat* given here is uniformly transmitted in Italian sources, in which it is variously assigned to the feasts of St. Martin, Pope Marcellus, St. Sylvester, St. Nicholas, St. Columbanus, and the Common of Confessors. The texts are virtually identical (VEcap 107, however, preserves *sibi* for *sui* in v. [3]) as are the melodic settings.

MELODIC VARIANTS
Rc 1741 [1] *(quo)ni(am)* cb; [2] *pac(tum)* DC; [3] *con-(dignum)* abcd; *a(re)* FE. **Bu 2824** [1] *Divi(ni)* Da'a.

65. Introit: *In omnem terram*

TROPE: *Festis nunc in apostolicis*

SOURCES
Rn 1343 fols. 47r–v TROPI IN [Nativitate] S<ancti> ANDREAE.
Rc 1741 fols. 123v–124r alius ton<us>

REFERENCES
AH 49, no. 366; *CT* 5, 166; Planchart, *Repertory*, 2:119–20.

TEXT COMMENTARY
Hexameters; vv. [1–2] are Leonine. Like the preceding tropes for saints, *Festis nunc in apostolicis* is assigned to different feasts depending on the locale. Specific references to a saint are lacking.

TEXT AND TRANSLATION

[1] Festis nunc in apostolicis laus clangat erilis
         In omnem [terram exivit sonus eorum]
[2] Angelici patres clari super ethera cives
         Et in fi[nes orbis terrae verba eorum]
[3] Qui debriant evangelico sophismate quosmum
         [N]on sunt [loquelae neque sermones
         quorum non audiantur voces eorum]
                     *

[1] Now on the apostle's feastday, let the Master's
         praise resound:
         Through all the earth their voice resounds.
[2] Angelic fathers, bright citizens of heaven above:
         And the ends of the world their message.
[3] Who inspire the world with gospel wisdom:
         Not a word nor a discourse
         whose voice is not heard.

DISTINCTIVE VARIANTS

Rc 1741 [1] *herilis* for *erilis*. In all sources except the Nonantolan tropers and PCsa 65, *Festis nunc in apostolicis* accompanies the Introit, *Mihi autem*. Text variants (collated in *AH*) shed little light on the trope's transmission.

The Nonantolan melody closely resembles the settings in Tn 18, Tn 20, and VEcap 107 (where neumes for vv. [2–3] are lacking). The Aquitanian version (Weiss, *Introitus Tropen*, no. 135) would appear to be a local adaptation of a more widely disseminated melody. Unfortunately, other notated sources do not transmit the Introit *In omnem terram,* the text of which has been conjecturally reconstructed. There are no known sources for the Introit melody.

MELODIC VARIANTS

Rc 1741 [1] *(apos)to(licis)* FE; *heri(lis)* CE GFEDC'-EFD CD; [2] *(e)the(ra)* FE; [3] *sophisma(te)* aF aaGF'-G'FE.

66. Introit: *In omnem terram*

TROPE: *Hodie beatissimus Andreas*

SOURCES
Rn 1343 fol. 47v aliu<s> ton<us>
Rc 1741 fol. 123v Trop.In.n<ativitate>. S[ancti]. Andr<eae>.
Bu 2824 fols. 89v–90r TRO i<n> [nativitate] S[ancti] andree

TEXT COMMENTARY

In prose; this trope of introduction describes the triumphal entrance of St. Andrew into heaven. Not only in its text but also in its music, *Hodie beatissimus Andreas* resembles other *Hodie* tropes sung at Nonantola, such as *Hodie sanctissimi patroni nostri* (no. 49).

TEXT AND TRANSLATION

Hodie beatissimus andreas apostolus
plaudentibus angelicis agminibus cælum provectus
    est
deo gracias dicite
         In omnem [terram exivit sonus eorum
         Et in fines orbis terrae verba eorum
         Non sunt loquelae neque sermones
         quorum non audiantur voces eorum]
                     *

Today the most blessed apostle Andrew
is led to heaven by applauding angelic legions,
thanks be to God, sing:
         Through all the earth their voice resounds:
         And the ends of the world their message.
         Not a word nor a discourse
         whose voice is not heard.

DISTINCTIVE VARIANTS

Bu 2824 *angeli* for *angelici*. Outside Nonantola, the only source of *Hodie beatissimus Andreas* known to me is VEcap 107, in which it is connected with the Introit *Mihi autem*. The versions of the trope are identical in text and neumation, except for a difference of underlay at "dicite."

MELODIC VARIANTS

Rc 1741 *(bea)tis(simus)* FE; *(agmini)bus* DC; *provec-(tus)* FE'DD~. **Bu 2824** *Ho(die)* D.

67. Introit: *Benedicta sit*

TROPE: *Splendor et imago patris*

SOURCES
Rn 1343 fol. 51r DOM<inica>.De S<ancta>. Trinitate
Rc 1741 fols. 127r–v Dom<inica> de s<an>c<t>a trinitate. Tropi.

REFERENCE
CT 3/2, 198, 157, 205, 96.

TEXT COMMENTARY

In prose; like many other Italian tropes, the connection between *Splendor et imago patris* and the Introit text, *Benedicta sit*, is not close. Although the elements are unified by their reliance on epithets, in their relation to the Introit they more closely resemble Kyrie prosulae than other Proper tropes.

TEXT AND TRANSLATION

[1] Splendor et imago patris trinus et unus
         Benedic[ta sit sancta trinitas]
[2] Pater et filius et spiritus sanctus in unum sunt
         Atq<ue> [indivisa unitas]

[3] Trinitas et unitas deitas
    Confi[tebimur ei]
[4] Est unigenitus sabaoth nomen adonay
    Quia [fecit nobiscum misericordiam suam]

*

[1] Splendor and image of the Father, three and one:
    Blessed be the Holy Trinity.
[2] They are Father, Son, and Holy Spirit in one:
    And undivided Unity.
[3] Trinity and Unity, Deity:
    We give glory to Him.
[4] He is the only begotten (Lord) of Hosts,
    the Logos, the Lord of Lords:
    Because He has shown His mercy.

DISTINCTIVE VARIANTS
Splendor et imago patris is found only in the Nonantolan tropers and Ra 123. The texts are identical, and the neumations are very similar.

MELODIC VARIANT
Rc 1741 [1] *i(mago)* aG.

Prosulae

1. Gradual: *Universi qui te exspectant* ℣ *Vias tuas domine*

PROSULA: *Venturum te cuncti dixerunt*

SOURCES
Rn 1343 fol. 18v P<ro>sa de v<er>su Vias tuas
Rc 1741 fol. 48r p<ro>sa de R<esponsorium> G<raduale> Univ<er>si.
Bu 2824 fol. 17v p<ro>sa Vias Tuas

REFERENCE
GT, 16.

TEXT AND TRANSLATION
Venturum te cuncti dixerunt prophetæ
nasciturum esse de virgine
multi te expectant ex omni plebe

*

All the prophets have spoken of Your coming,
born of a virgin;
many men from every nation await You.

DISTINCTIVE VARIANTS
Bu 2824 *cunctis* for *cuncti*; *cuncti* for *multi*.

MELODIC VARIANTS
None.

2. Offertory: *Ad te domine levavi* ℣2 *Respice in me*

PROSULA: *Invocavite altissime*

SOURCES
Rn 1343 fols. 18v–19r P<ro>sa de v<ersu> Respice
Rc 1741 fols. 48r–v p<ro>sa de v<ersu> Respice

REFERENCE
OT, 5–6.

TEXT AND TRANSLATION
Invocavite
altissime venturum
quem longe cecinere prophetæ
gloria laus et honor christe
sic dicitur tibi rex pie
qui veni salvare me
et te vera fides in se blande suscipiat devote te volente

*

Bring forth, O Most High, the advent
which the prophets have so long foretold.
Glory, praise, and honor, O Christ,
thus is said to You, O benevolent King,
You who come to redeem me;
and may true faith in itself sustain You, gentle,
    devoted, and willing One.

DISTINCTIVE VARIANT
Rc 1741 *venis* for *veni*.

MELODIC VARIANTS
Rc 1741 *chris(te)* a; *(vo)len(te)* c.

3. Offertory: *Deus tu convertens* ℣2 *Misericordia et veritas*

PROSULA: *Possessor polorum Deus*

SOURCES
Rn 1343 fol. 19r P<ro>sa Mi<sericordi>a
Rc 1741 fols. 48v–49r P<ro>sa de v<ersu> Mi<sericordi>a et ver<itas>

REFERENCE
OT, 6–8.

TEXT AND TRANSLATION
Possessor polorum
deus qui nos de terra origo finxit
angelico cętui copulavit
et cohęrevit custodiendo eius pręceptionem
promereamur nos cęlesticolas mansiones

*

Possessor of the heavens,
God who fashioned us from clay,
allied us with the angelic race,
and united us by hallowed precept,
may we merit places in heaven.

DISTINCTIVE VARIANTS
 Rn 1343 *populorum* for *polorum*; *fincxit* for *finxit*; *cohesit . . . preceptione* for *coherevit . . . preceptionem*.

MELODIC VARIANTS
 Rn 1343 *populorum* c′c′c′a; *cohesit* c′c′a.

4. Gradual: *Qui sedes domine*
   ℣ *Qui regis Israel*

PROSULA: *Qui sedes in alto throno*

SOURCES
Rn 1343 fol. 19r P<ro>sa Qui regis
Rc 1741 fol. 49r P<ro>sa de v<ersu>. Qui regis.

REFERENCE
 GT, 22.

TEXT AND TRANSLATION

Qui sedes in alto throno laudabilis
et non est alius in ethera
deus fortis paciens terribilis iuste
verax optime deus
miserere quos tuos perire nolis nam petimus ac benignus intende

 *

You, praiseworthy One, who sit on the high throne,
and there is no other God in heaven,
powerful God, enduring, awesome, just,
true, greatest God,
pray for those whom You do not wish to let perish,
for we have prayed, and so, hear us graciously.

VARIANTS
 None.

5. Offertory: *Benedixisti domine*
   ℣ 2 *Ostende nobis domine*

PROSULA: *Misericors et clemens famulis*

SOURCES
Rn 1343 fol. 19r P<ro>sa Ostende
Rc 1741 fols. 49r–v P<ro>sa de v<ersu> Ostende

REFERENCE
 OT, 8–9.

TEXT AND TRANSLATION

Misericors ac clemens
famulis rogo christe tuis gloriosa premia largire
quod promisisti sanctis tuis *da nobis*

 *

Compassionate and kind One,
 I beg, O Christ: grant us Your servants the glorious rewards that You have
 promised to Your saints. (Read *quae*)

DISTINCTIVE VARIANT
 Rc 1741 *et* for *ac*.

MELODIC VARIANT
 Rc 1741 *(cle)mens* bG.

6. Offertory: *Ave Maria*
   ℣ 1 *Quomodo in me*

PROSULA: *A supernis caelorum*

SOURCES
Rn 1343 fol. 19r P<ro>sa [de] v<ersu> Quomodo
Rc 1741 fol. 49r p<ro>sa de v<ersu> Quomodo.
Bu 2824 fols. 17v–18r p<ro>s[a] de v<ersu> Quom<odo>

REFERENCE
 OT, 13–14.

TEXT AND TRANSLATION

A supernis cælorum angelus missus
veniens ad virginem hoc ait
clemens audi maria virgo et sacra
spiritus sanctus te illuminat
incorrupta virgo dubitat
[Quomodo in me fiet hoc
quae virum non congnosco?]

 *

From the highest places of heaven
the angel was sent.
Coming to the virgin, he said this:
"Hearken, Mary, kind and blessed virgin!
The Holy Spirit fills you!"
The uncorrupted virgin hesitated:
"How shall this happen,
since I do not know man?"

DISTINCTIVE VARIANTS
 Bu 2824 *superni* for *supernis*; *inluminat* for *illuminat*.

MELODIC VARIANT
 Rc 1741 *(du)bi(tat)* GF.

7. Offertory: *Deus enim fermavit*
   ℣ 2 *Mirabilis in excelsis*

PROSULA: *Dierum noctuque*

SOURCES
Rn 1343 fols. 19v–20r P<ro>sa de v<er>su Mirabilis
Rc 1741 fol. 50v–51r P<ro>sa de v<ersu> Mirabil<is>
Bu 2824 fols. 21v–22r P<ro>s[a]

REFERENCE
 OT, 16–18.

lxii

TEXT AND TRANSLATION

Dierum noctuque vigilare quoque ad te rector cælorum et maris atque terræ
qui venisti humanum genus salvare passus expolians mortem
qui tercia die surrexisti christe ascendens dexteram patris sedens
interpellans pro tua plebe
super quem tuum permanebit nomen trinum per evum

*

By day and by night we watched for You, O Ruler of the heavens, the sea, and the earth;
You who came to redeem the human race, to endure and dismantle death,
You who arose on the third day, O Christ, ascending, being seated at the right hand of the Father,
interceding on behalf of Your people,
over whom Your triune name shall endure forever.

DISTINCTIVE VARIANTS
Bu 2824 *a te* for *ad te*; *caelorum maris et aque terre* for *caelorum et maris atque terrae*; *ascensus ad dextram* for *ascendens deteram*.

MELODIC VARIANTS
Rc 1741 *(sal)va(re)* a; *chris(te)* a; *(per e)vum* caccaccca. . . . Bu 2824 *maris et aque* a'G'a'G'F; *dextram (patris)* b'a; *(per e)vum* caccaccc~a. . . .

8. Alleluia
℣ Dies sanctificatus

PROSULA: *Audi nos te deprecamur*

SOURCES
Rn 1343 fol. 20v P<ro>sa de v<er>su Die<s> s<an>c<t>ificat<us>
Rc 1741 fol. 53r p<ro>sa de all<eluia> Dies s<an>c<t>ifi<catus>.
Bu 2824 fol. 24r P<ro>sa de al<leluia> Dies sanctificatus

REFERENCES
CT 2/1, 39; GT, 49.

TEXT AND TRANSLATION

Audi nos te deprecamur
famulorum tuorum carmine resonante benigne
All<eluia>

*

Hear us, we implore You
in the resounding song of Your servants, O kind One:
Alleluia.

DISTINCTIVE VARIANT
Bu 2824 *rex alme* for *resonante*.

MELODIC VARIANTS
Bu 2824 [1] *rex alme (benigne)* F'F'E.

9. Alleluia
℣ Dies sanctificatus

PROSULA: *Alme caeli rex immortalis*

SOURCES
Rn 1343 fol. 20v (no rubric)
Rc 1741 fol. 53r (no rubric)
Bu 2824 fol. 24r–v (no rubric)

REFERENCES
CT 2/1, 39; GT, 49.

TEXT AND TRANSLATION
All<eluia>
Alme cæli rex inmortalis hiesu christe
miserere nobis quos plasmasti ex arvo

*

Alleluia.
O indulgent One, immortal King of heaven, Jesus Christ,
pray for us whom You formed from clay.

MELODIC VARIANT
Rc 1741 [2] *ar(vo)* FF~.

10. Offertory: Tui sunt caeli
℣ 3 Tu humiliasti

PROSULA: *Proles virginis matris*

SOURCES
Rn 1343 fol. 21v P<ro>sa Tu humi[liasti]
Rc 1741 fol. 56r p<ro>sa de v<ersu> Tu hum<iliasti>.

REFERENCE
OT, 18–20.

TEXT AND TRANSLATION
[exaltetur]
Proles virginis matris hiesu christe
adveni domine et glorioso tuo sanguine nos redime sauciatum superbum
quippe humilians
[dextera tua domine]

*

The Child of the virgin Mother, Jesus Christ, is exalted;
come, O Lord, and with Your glorious blood redeem us, wounded, proud yet
humbling by Your right hand, O Lord.

VARIANTS
None.

lxiii

11. Tract: *Commovisti*
℣ *Sana contritiones eius*

PROSULA: *Sana Christe rex alme*

SOURCES
Rn 1343 fol. 28r P<ro>sa de trac<tu> Commovisti
Rc 1741 fols. 73v–74r P<ro>sa de trac<tu> Co<m>movisti.
Bu 2824 fols. 45v–46r P<ro>sa de Co<m>movisti

REFERENCE
 GT, 89–90.

TEXT AND TRANSLATION

[1] *Sana* christe rex alme
     tu guberna et defende et libera et *sana*
[2] *Ut fugiat* a nobis ira tua
     ostende faciem tuam deus noster
     ne pereamus **[facie arcus]**

*

[1] Heal, O Christ, kind King,
     govern and defend and deliver and heal.
[2] That Your anger may pass from us
     show us Your face, our God;
     do not let us perish at the sight of the bow.

DISTINCTIVE VARIANTS
 Bu 2824 *iram tuam* for *ira tua*.

MELODIC VARIANTS
 Rc 1741 [1] *al(me)* c; *(de)fen(de)* c; [2] *tu(a)* c; *nos(ter)* a. **Bu 2824** [1] *(guber)na* ed; [2] *(no)bis* ed.

12. Tract: *Qui confidunt*
℣ *Montes in circuitu eius*

PROSULA: *Mons magnus est*

SOURCES
Rn 1343 fol. 28r P<ro>sa de trac<tu> Qui c<on>fidunt
Rc 1741 fol. 74r P<ro>sa de trac<tu>. Qui c<on>fid<un>t.
Bu 2824 fol. 46r (no rubric)

REFERENCE
 GT, 109–10.

TEXT AND TRANSLATION

Mons magnus est
mons terribilis est
ibidem hiesus sedebat cum discipulis suis

*

The mountain is great,
the mountain is awesome;
in that very place Jesus sat with His disciples.

MELODIC VARIANTS
 Rc 1741 and **Bu 2824** *(su)is* GaGaa~G.

13. Tract: *Deus Deus meus*
℣ *Libera me de ore*

PROSULA: *Pater unigenitum tuum*

SOURCE
Rc 1741 fol. 75r p<ro>sa

REFERENCE
 GT, 144–47.

TEXT AND TRANSLATION

[libera me]
Pater unigenitum tuum filiumque
tu me adiuva a persecutore atque defende

*

Deliver me,
Father, Your only begotten Son:
sustain and defend me from the persecutor.

14. Alleluia
℣ *Pascha nostrum*

PROSULA: *Iam redeunt gaudia*

SOURCES
Rn 1343 fols. 28v–29r P<ro>sa de v<er>su Pascha nostrum
Rc 1741 fols. 76r–v P<ro>sa de all<eluia> Pascha.
Bu 2824 fols. 48r P<rosa> de all<eluia> Pasc[h]a

REFERENCES
 CT 2/1, 118; *GT*, 197–98.

TEXT AND TRANSLATION

Iam redeunt gaudia
festa lucent clara
iam nobis paschalia
inferni rapit spolia
agnus tremunt quem omnia
qui regit dispensat semper imperia
Pascha

*

Now joys return,
once more the illustrious celebrations
of Easter shine bright on us;
the Lamb, whom all men fear,
who rules, who for an age commands the dominions,
seizes the spoils of hell,
The Pasch.

MELODIC VARIANTS
 Rc 1741 *gaudia* d'cd'dd~; *(pas)chali(a)* a'a; *(om)ni(a)* a. **Bu 2824** *gau(dia)* d.

15. Alleluia
℣ *Pascha nostrum*

PROSULA: *Christe tu vita vera*

SOURCES
Rn 1343 fols. 29r (no rubric)
Rc 1741 fols. 76v (no rubric)
Bu 2824 fols. 48r–v (no rubric)

REFERENCES
CT 2/1, 115–16, 118; GT, 197–98.

TEXT AND TRANSLATION

Pascha
Christe tu vita vera
quem pavescit ipsa
mors nimis tartarea
te vocant nostra nunc ora
ut emundes precordia
qui regis ethera
laus tibi per secula

*

The Pasch
O Christ, You, True Life,
of whom infernal death is itself
afraid beyond measure:
our voices now call upon You
to cleanse (our) hearts.
You who reign in the heavens,
praise be to You forever.

DISTINCTIVE VARIANT
Rc 1741 *per secula alleluia* for *per secula*.

MELODIC VARIANTS
Rc 1741 *(ve)ra* dd~; *(tarta)re(a)* a; *o(ra)* d; *(ethe)ra* E.

16. Offertory: *Angelus domini*
℣ 2 *Iesus stetit*

PROSULA: *Christus intravit ianuis*

SOURCE
Rc 1741 fols. 84v–85r p<ro>sa de v<ersu> I<e>s<u>s stetit

REFERENCE
OT, 57–58.

TEXT AND TRANSLATION

[Iesus] Christus intravit ianuis clausis
ubi erant eius discipuli die una sabbatorum
postquam resurrexit a morte

Ste[tit in medio eorum]
Videte et palpate manus atque latus in his potestis credere signis
quia ego ipse sum

*

Jesus Christ entered the doors of the room
where His disciples were on the day one week
after He arose from the dead.
He stood in their midst (and said):
"Look and touch ye the hand and also the side,
   believe in these powerful signs,
for it is I."

17. Alleluia
℣ *Vos estis*

PROSULA: *Rex Deus omnipotens*

SOURCE
Rc 1741 fols. 85 P<ro>sa de all<eluia> Vos estis qui p<er>man[sistis]

REFERENCE
CT 2/1, 151–52.

TEXT AND TRANSLATION

Rex deus omnipotens ne perdas nos cum iniquis
quia scimus nos pietatem tuam magnam fore nobis
si puro corde te deprecamur
te redemptor christe verus rex
Vos estis

*

King, almighty God, do not destroy us with the wicked,
for we know that Your benevolence will be great for us
if we pray to You with a pure heart,
Redeemer, Christ, true King.
You are they.

18. Alleluia
℣ *Vos estis*

PROSULA: *Sicut tu Christe*

SOURCE
Rc 1741 fols. 85r–v (no rubric)

REFERENCE
CT 2/1, 151–52.

TEXT AND TRANSLATION

Vos estis
Sicut tu christe hiesu pro nobis in cruce pependisti
rex ita succurre
deus nobis creator polorum terręque

intercessioque apostolorum tuorum
nobis proficiat domine

*

You are they.
Since You, Christ Jesus, hung on the cross for us,
so aid (us), King,
our God, Creator of the heavens and the earth:
may the intercessions of Your apostles
help us, O Lord.

19. *Alleluia*
   ℣ Dum complerentur

PROSULA: *Erant omnes nostri linguis*

SOURCES
Rc 1741 fols. 95v–96r p<ro>sa de all<eluia> Dum c<om>pler<entur>
Bu 2824 fols. 64r–v P<ro>s<a> de all<eluia> Du<m> co<m>ple[rentur]

REFERENCES
  CT 2/1, 48–49; *GT*, 250.

TEXT AND TRANSLATION
Erant omnes nostri linguis pariter prędicantes
in mundum universum
Et insimul confirmantes
iterum nunciantes
in gentem veritatem
Nosque gaudentes cum illis
trinitas sancta sit nobiscum omnes
[pariter sedentes]

*

All of us were speaking together in tongues
to the whole world,
and encouraging at the same time,
announcing once more
the truth to the people,
and we, rejoicing with them;
May the Holy Trinity be with us all,
sitting together.

VARIANTS
  None.

20. *Alleluia*
   ℣ Dum complerentur

PROSULA: *Pentecosten advenisse*

SOURCE
Bu 2824 fol. 64v–65r (no rubric; text only)

REFERENCE
  GT, 250.

TEXT AND TRANSLATION
Pentecosten advenisse noster cristus et dicens ad apostolos
omnes non reliquam orfanos vos sed vadam et revertar
et gaudebit cor vestrum et vos euntes in mundum predicantes et dicentes
omnes [pariter]

*

On Pentecost, our Christ came and said to the apostles: "I will not leave you all
orphans, but I shall go and (then) I shall return, and your heart will rejoice; and
you will go into the world, proclaiming and saying all together."

21. *Alleluia*
   ℣ Serve bone et fidelis

PROSULA: *Alme cuncti sator orbis*

SOURCE
Bu 2824 fols. 72v P<ro>s<a>

REFERENCE
  CT 2/1, 132.

TEXT AND TRANSLATION
Alleluia
Alme cunctis sator orbis
tota pio qui nomine
secula dignanter gubernas
accipe nunc preces petimus
tuorum supplicum singulas
et dicas

*

Alleluia.
Indulgent Creator of the whole world,
You who worthily command all eternity
by (Your) gracious name
hear now the individual prayers we,
your suppliants, offer
and say:

22. *Alleluia*
   ℣ Serve bone et fidelis

PROSULA: *Serve et amice bone*

SOURCE
Bu 2824 fols. 72v–73v (no rubric)

REFERENCE
  CT 2/1, 132.

TEXT AND TRANSLATION
Serve et amice **bone**
et fidelis qui supra pauca composita

militasti prudenter **Intra in gaudium**
quia talenta tradita
commutatare fatuisti
fruere supernis quapropter dapibus
pervigil merito preparatus **domini**
Domini tui recolentis quidem tempore prostratus laborum
accipe coronam stadii braviumque simul
euge per evum

*

"Oh good and faithful servant
and friend, you who prudently managed
a few things, enter into the joy:
for you have caused the talents handed
over (to you) to be increased.
Join in the perpetual celebrations
of heaven, prepared for the faithful of the Lord;
receive the prize garland and likewise the reward,
'Well done!' forever:
for indeed your Master recalls (your) prolonged struggle.
Always in the presence of God, Light of everlasting glory, let all the choruses
of angels and saints pray on our behalf for forgiveness forever."

23. *Alleluia* ℣ *Concussum est mare*

PROSULA: *Ante Deum semper gloriae*

SOURCES
Rn 1343 fols. 43r–v Concussum
Rc 1741 fols. 115r–v P<ro>sa de all<eluia> Concussu<m>.
Bu 2824 fol. 81r P<ro>s<a> de all<eluia>

REFERENCES
CT 2/1, 30–32; *GR*, 609–10.

TEXT AND TRANSLATION

Ante deum semper
gloriæ lux eternæ
omnes angelici et sanctorum chori implorent pro nobis
veniam concedentem in secula
Concussum

*

Always in the presence of God,
Light of everlasting glory,
let all the choruses of angels and saints pray
on our behalf for forgiveness forever.
Shaken.

MELODIC VARIANTS
Rc 1741 (ę)*ternae* c'G; *cho(ri)* a; *(con)ce(dentem)* ac. **Bu 2824** (æter)næ G; [2] *ar(va)* a(G); *(de)mer(sus)* d; *ex(pulit)* ac.

24. *Alleluia* ℣ *Concussum est mare*

PROSULA: *Concussum et percussum*

SOURCES
Rn 1343 fols. 43v (no rubric)
Rc 1741 fols. 115v–116r (no rubric)
Bu 2824 fols. 81r–v (no rubric)

REFERENCES
CT 2/1, 30–32; *GR*, 609–10.

TEXT AND TRANSLATION

Concussum
Concussum et per*cussum est*
mare fontes saxo et arva
et contremuit montes et expavit
draconem pestiferum serpens antiquus
qui eiectus est de cælo demersus sub *terra*
Ubi archan[gelus michael descendebat de **caelo]**
In monte garcanico
victoria christi expugnantes cum satan durius et expulit eum exinde
All<eluia>

*

Shaken.
Shaken and beaten were
the sea, the rivers, the rock, and the land,
and the mountain shook, and frightened
the pernicious dragon, the ageless serpent,
which was expelled from heaven (and) sunk beneath the earth,
where the archangel Michael descended from heaven.
On Mount Gargano,
the victory of Christ over harsh Satan was won
and he expelled him from that place.
Alleluia.

DISTINCTIVE VARIANTS
Rc 1741 *Concussum* lacking; *saxa* for *saxo*; *dracone* for *draconem*; *dimersus* for *demersus*; *Alleluia* lacking. **Bu 2824** *dimersus* for *demersus*; *victoriam . . . satam* for *victoria . . . satan*.

MELODIC VARIANTS
Rc 1741 *(sa)xa et ar(va)* cb'aG'aa~; *(de)mer(sus)* d; *ex(pulit)* ac; *(ex)in(de)* a. **Bu 2824** *ar(va)* a(G); *(de)mer(sus)* d; *ex(pulit)* ac.

25. Alleluia
℣ *Concussum est mare*

PROSULA: *Angele Michael atque Gabriel*

SOURCES
Rn 1343 fols. 43v (no rubric)
Rc 1741 fols. 116r (no rubric)
Bu 2824 fols. 81v–82r (no rubric)

REFERENCES
CT 2/1, 30–32; GR, 609–10.

TEXT AND TRANSLATION
All\<eluia\>
Angele michahel atque gabrihel simulque raphael
et omnes concives polorum sideris agmina
regnantem in secula

*

Alleluia.
The angels Michael and Gabriel, together with Raphael,
and all the fellow citizens of the skies, the armies of heaven,
prevailing forever.

DISTINCTIVE VARIANTS
Rc 1741 *raphahel* for *raphael*. **Bu 2824** *raphahel* for *raphael*.

MELODIC VARIANTS
Rc 1741 *(reg)nan(tem)* ac. **Bu 2824** *(reg)nan(tem)* ac.

26. Alleluia
℣ *O quam pulchra est*

PROSULA: *Psallat turba devota*

SOURCES
Rn 1343 fol. 47r P\<ro\>sa de all\<eluia\> O qua\<m\> pulchra
Rc 1741 fols. 122v–123v P\<ro\>sa de all\<eluia\> O quam
Bu 2824 fols. 89r–v P\<ro\>s\<a\> de v\<er\>so O qua\<m\> pulchra es

REFERENCES
CT 2/1, 113; GT, 501–2.

TEXT AND TRANSLATION
[1] Psallat turba devota christo
   melos atque canat dulce
   virginis sacratæ cælebrans officium
   natalis summi quo processit
   simul dicat corde fideli
   O qua\<m\> [pulchra est]

[2] Quæ suis sequacibus salutem competenter
   in excelsis condonat æternam
   angelorumque dignos facit consorcio
   ubi plaudat atque resultat
   Casta gen\<eratio\>

[3] Virginum corruscat chorus ante deum
   semper vocibus decoris
   nosque rogemus incessanter
   ut pro nostris intercedat sedule delictis
   Cum clari[tate]

*

[1] Let the devoted multitude chant a Psalm to Christ, and sing a sweet melody,
   celebrating the Office of the Blessed Virgin,
   who gave birth to the Most High;
   likewise, let it say with faithful heart:
   Oh how beautiful

[2] Who becomingly grants to her followers eternal well-being in heaven,
   and makes them worthy (of heaven),
   where the consort of angels applauds and dances.

[3] A chorus of virgins always warbles before God with beautiful voices;
   and let us beg incessantly
   that it diligently intercede for our sins.

DISTINCTIVE VARIANT
Bu 2824 [2] *exelsis . . . æterna* for *excelsis . . . æternam*.

MELODIC VARIANTS
Rc 1741 [1] *dul(ce)* D; *sum(mi)* G; *(fi)de(li)* GFE; [2] *(sa)lu(tem)* G; *(compe)ten(ter)* aG; *(ex)cel(sis)* D; *(ę)ter(nam)* ED(C); *fa(cit)* G; *plau(dat)* D; [3] *corus(cat)* F'G; *an(te)* aG; *sem(per)* D; *(inces)san(ter)* G; *(inter)ce(dat)* D; *(de)lic(tis)* GF. **Bu 2824** [1] *chris(to)* GG~; *di(cat)* DD~; [3] *(de)lic(tis)* GG~FE.

27. Alleluia
℣ *Dilexit Andream*

PROSULA: *In dulcedine amoris*

SOURCES
Rn 1343 fol. 47v P\<ro\>sa. [de] v\<ersu\> Dilexit [Andream]
Rc 1741 fol. 124r P\<ro\>sa de all\<eluia\> dilex\<it\> [Andream]
Bu 2824 fol. 90r P\<ro\>s[a] Dilex\<it\> andrea\<m\>

REFERENCES
CT 2/1, 41; GT, 625–26.

TEXT AND TRANSLATION
In dulcedine amoris redemptoris
vocantis duos fratres de navi

quorum unus fuit petrus qui fuit piscator bonus
atque frater andreas
hos dominus vocaverat
qui fuerant secuti *odorem*
In odo[rem]

*

In the sweetness of the Redeemer's love,
He called two brothers from the sea,
of whom one was Peter, who was a good fisherman,
and (his) brother, Andrew;
the Lord called these men
who had followed an odor.

DISTINCTIVE VARIANTS
   Rc 1741 and **Bu 2824** cue **In odo[rem]** lacking.

MELODIC VARIANTS
   Rc 1741 *dul(cedine)* CE; *(amo)ris* E; *(vo)can(tis)* G; *na(vi)* F; *pe(trus)* a; *(an)dre(as)* F. **Bu 2824** *dul(cedine)* CE; *(amo)ris* E; *na(vi)* F.

28. Alleluia
℣ *Verba mea*

PROSULA: *Alme domine noli claudere*

SOURCES
Rn 1343 fol. 48v P<ro>sa de all<eluia>
Rc 1741 fols. 129r–v P<ro>sa de all<eluia> Verba mea.
Bu 2824 fols. 93v–94r P<ro>s[a] de v<er>so Verba mea

REFERENCES
   CT 2/1, 148 (nos. 4b, 1b, 5b); *GT*, 280.

TEXT AND TRANSLATION
[1] Alme domine noli claudere aurem tuam
       sed exaudi
   Verba [mea]
[2] Arva cuncta et satu tu gubernas
   o domine redemptor populorum alme
[3] Corda nostra divini roris illustra
   tu deus confirma

*

[1] Kind Lord, do not close your ears, but hear my words.
[2] You rule over all the fields and crops,
   Oh Lord, gracious Redeemer of the people.
[3] Light up our hearts with divine dew:
   God, give us strength.

MELODIC VARIANTS
   Rc 1741 [1] *clau(dere)* F; [2] *(gu)ber(nas)* G; *al(me)* CDEFE(D); [3] *inlustra* G′D′EF; *confir(ma)* EF′E(D). **Bu 2824** [1] *clau(dere)* F; [3] *(illus)tra* EF.

29. Alleluia
℣ *Deus iudex iustus*

PROSULA: *Arbiter singulorum facta*

SOURCES
Rn 1343 fols. 48v–49r P<ro>sa de all<eluia>.
Rc 1741 fols. 129v–130r P<ro>sa de all<eluia> D<eu>s iudex

REFERENCES
   CT 2/1, 35; *GT*, 286.

TEXT AND TRANSLATION
Alleluia
Arbiter singulorum facta
qui prope pensat
in examinis tuis libra
neque scruteris servorum acta
sed ne in finem iratus reservet merita iniqua
sed pius misericorditer solvet commissa
℣ **Deus iudex**

*

Alleluia!
Judge of individuals,
who in Your close examination weighs (read *tui*) deeds on the scale (of justice):
neither examine too thoroughly the deeds of (Your) servants,
nor be angry forever, nor be mindful of our evil deserts,
but, O benevolent One, mercifully forgive (our) transgressions.
℣ God, the Judge.

DISTINCTIVE VARIANTS
   Rc 1741 Alleluia lacking; *reserves* for *reservet*; *solve* for *solvet*.

MELODIC VARIANTS
   Rc 1741 *fac(ta)* a; *pen(sat)* E; *(exa)mi(nis)* G; *li(bra)* a; *ac(ta)* a; *(re)ser(ves)* d; *(i)ni(qua)* G; *(mise)ricorditer* b′G′G′c; *(com)mis(sa)* a.

30. Alleluia
℣ *Ad te domine levavi*

PROSULA: *Alma voce canamus*

SOURCES
Rn 1343 fol. 49r (no rubric)
Rc 1741 fol. 130r P<ro>sa de all<eluia> Ad te d<omine>
Bu 2824 fol. 100v P<ro>s<a> da all<elluia> Ad te d<omine> levavi

REFERENCE
   CT 2/1, 19.

lxix

TEXT AND TRANSLATION
Alleluia
Alma voce canamus
supplices regi polorum
et arva sataque cuncta
ut sit scutum inexpugnabile
suo precio redemptis
Ad te d<omine>

*

Alleluia.
In one melodious voice
we suppliants sing to the King of the heavens
and all the fields and crops,
that there be an impenetrable shield
as Your reward for the redeemed.

DISTINCTIVE VARIANTS
  Rc 1741 and Bu 2824 **Alleluia** lacking; cue **Ad te domine** lacking.

MELODIC VARIANTS
  Rc 1741 and Bu 2824 *(ca)na(mus)* G; *(po)lo(rum)* G; *cunc(ta)* a; *(pre)ci(o)* G; *(redemp)tis* aG.

31. *Alleluia*
℣ *Eripe me*

PROSULA: *Laudes debitas vocibus*

SOURCES
Rn 1343 fol. 49r Alleluia P<ro>sa
Rc 1741 fol. 130r P<ro>sa de all<eluia> Eripe
Bu 2824 fol. 94r P<ro>s[a] de Eripe me

REFERENCES
  CT 2/1, 58; *GT*, 308–9.

TEXT AND TRANSLATION
Laudes debitas vocibus dulcisonis
omnes pariter nunc modulemur
omnipotenti atque precemur davitico spiritu dicentes
Eripe me

*

Let us all together sing due praises with sweet-
  sounding voices,
and let us also beg
the Almighty in the spirit of David, saying:
Deliver me

DISTINCTIVE VARIANTS
  Bu 2824 *dulcis sonis . . . modulemus* for *dulcisonis . . . modulemur.*

MELODIC VARIANTS
  Rc 1741 *Lau(des)* CD(E); *(modu)le(mur)* E; *(omnipo)ten(ti)* D; *(pre)ce(mur)* E; *(di)cen(tes)* F.

32. *Alleluia*
℣ *Eripe me*

PROSULA: *Et ab insurgentibus Deus*

SOURCES
Rn 1343 fols. 49r (no rubric)
Rc 1741 fols. 130r–v (no rubric)
Bu 2824 fols. 94r–v (no rubric)

REFERENCES
  CT 2/1, 58; *GT*, 308–9.

TEXT AND TRANSLATION
Eripe me
Et ab insurgentibus deus fortis rex
esto nobis turris fortitudinis
et clipeus inexpugnabilis
christe tuos eripe servos
Et ab insur[gentibus]
Redime nos pie christe
qui redemisti david prophetam
de gladio pessimo saulis
All<eluia>

*

And from those rising up (against us), O mighty God,
  King,
be for us a tower of strength
and an impregnable shield:
Oh Christ, deliver your servants
from the enemies.
Spare us, Oh good Christ,
You who rescued the prophet David
from Saul's injurious sword,
Alleluia.

DISTINCTIVE VARIANTS
  Rc 1741 cue **Et ab insurgentibus** lacking; **Alleluia** lacking. **Bu 2824** cue **Et ab insurgentibus** lacking; *propheta* for *prophetam.*

MELODIC VARIANTS
  Rc 1741 *for(tis)* F; *no(bis)* D; *(inex)pug(nabilis)* F; *(eri)pe* D; *chris(te)* E; *(rede)mis(ti)* D; *(pro)phe(tam)* E; *sau(lis)* D. **Bu 2824** *(eri)pe* D; *sau(lis)* D'F.

33. *Alleluia*
℣ *Eripe me*

PROSULA: *Lingua cor simul clamitet*

SOURCES
Rn 1343 fols. 49r–v (no rubric)
Rc 1741 fol. 130v (no rubric)
Bu 2824 fols. 94r–v

REFERENCES
CT 2/1, 58; *GT*, 308–9.

TEXT AND TRANSLATION
All\<eluia\>
*L*ingua cor simul clamitet ad te pie christe
precibus ut nos defendas
semper ubique ab omnibus malis
et corpore menteque tuere

*

Alleluia.
Let tongue and heart together cry out to You,
  Oh good Christ, (read *clamitent*)
with prayers that You defend us
always from every evil everywhere,
and watch over us, mind and body.

DISTINCTIVE VARIANT
  Rc 1741 cue **Libera** for *Lingua*.

MELODIC VARIANTS
  Rc 1741 *Lin(gua)* CE(E); *(de)fen(das)* E; *ma(lis)* E; *(men)te(que)* F; *(tu)e(re)* F. **Bu 2824** [3] *Lin(gua)* CD(E).

34. *Alleluia*
℣ *Benedictus es domine*

PROSULA: *Semper sonet nostra lingua*

SOURCE
Bu 2824 fol. 100r P\<ro\>s\<a\>

REFERENCES
  CT 2/1, 27; *GT*, 375.

TEXT AND TRANSLATION
Semper sonet nostra lingua
que puro corde tibi laudat
quod voces nostras melliflua
cuncta resonet
℣ Tibi laudes cunctaque voce persolvat
te que conlaudat *in* sempiterna *secula* amen

*

Let our tongue, which praises You
with a pure heart, always sound;
let every one of our voices, flowing with honey, resound.
℣ And let every voice that extols You render praises to You forever and ever. Amen.

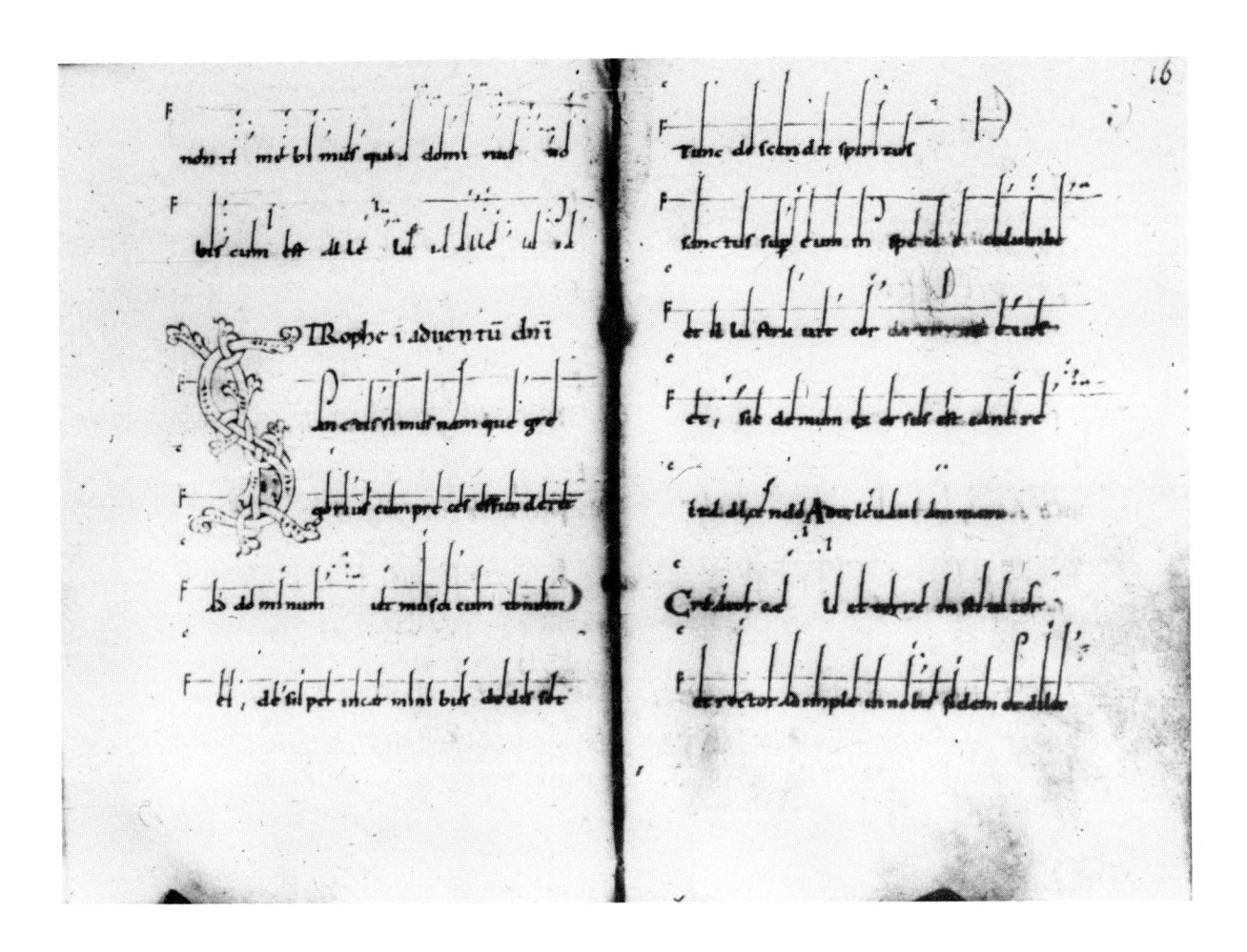

Plate 1. Bologna, Biblioteca Universitaria, MS 2824, fols. 15v–16r, including the introductory Introit trope (no. 1), *Sanctissimus namque Gregorius*

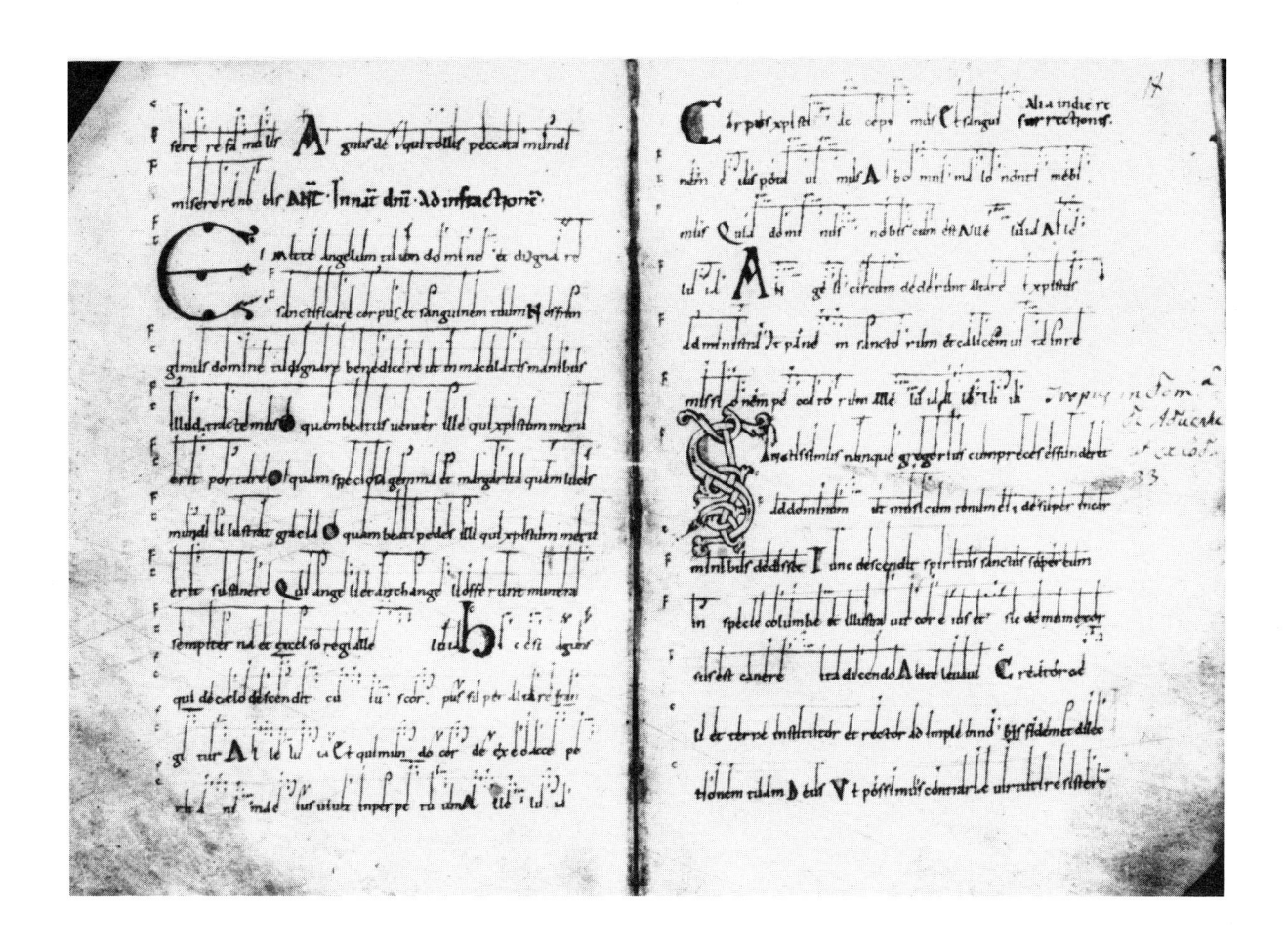

Plate 2. Rome, Biblioteca Universitaria, MS 1343 (*olim* Sessoriano 62), fols. 17v–18r, including the introductory Introit trope (no. 1), *Sanctissimus namque Gregorius*

1. Introit: Ad te levavi
Sanctissimus namque Gregorius

Rn 1343

[1] Sanc- tis- si- mus nam- que gre- go- ri- us cum pre- ces ef- fun- de- ret

ad do- mi- num ut mu- si- cum to-num e- i de- su- per in car- mi- ni- bus de- dis- set

Tunc de- scen- dit spi- ri- tus sanc-tus su- per e- um in spe- ci- e co- lum- bæ

et il- lus- tra- vit cor e- ius et sic de-mum ex-or-sus est ca- ne- re i- ta di- cen-do

Ad te le- va- vi [a- ni- mam me- am] [2] Cre- a- tor cæ- li

et ter-ræ in- sti- tu- tor et rec- tor ad-im-ple in no- bis fi- dem et di- lec- ti- o- nem tu- am

De- us [me- us in te con- fi- do non e- ru- bes- cam]

[3] Ut pos- si- mus con- tra- ri- æ vir- tu- ti re- si- ste- re ac ti- bi

fi- de- li- ter ser- vi- re ne- que [ir- re- ant me in- i- mi- ci me- i et- e- nim u- ni- ver- si qui te ex- spec- tant non con- fun- den- tur]

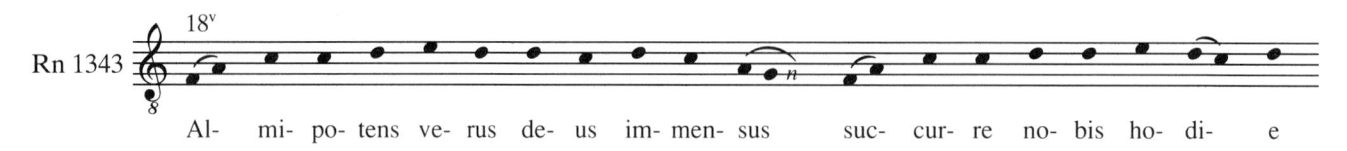

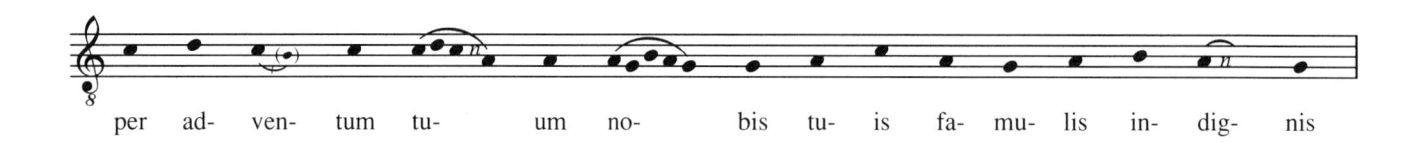

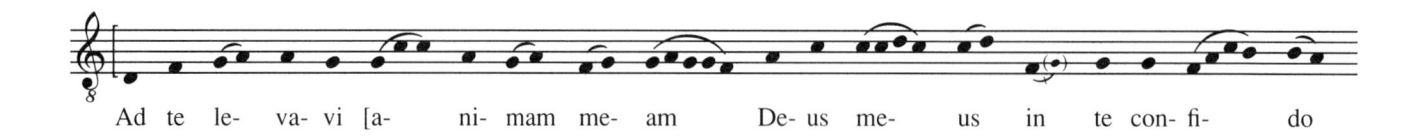

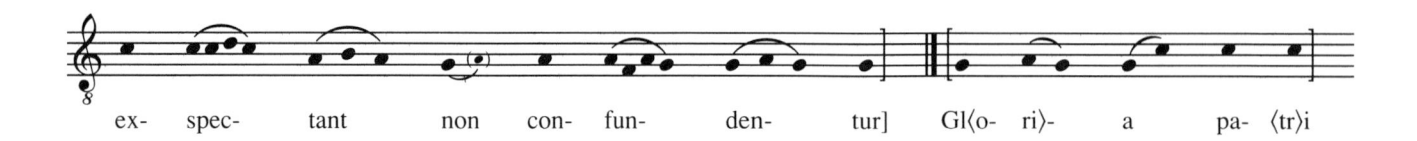

[Ps.] Vi- as tu- as do- mi- ne

2. Introit: Ad te levavi
Almipotens verus Deus

Rn 1343

Al- mi- po- tens ve- rus de- us im- men- sus suc- cur- re no- bis ho- di- e

per ad- ven- tum tu- um no- bis tu- is fa- mu- lis in- dig- nis

Ad te le- va- vi [a- ni- mam me- am De- us me- us in te con- fi- do

non e- ru- bes- cam ne- que ir- ri- de- ant me in- i-

-mi- ci me- i et- e- nim u- ni- ver- si qui te

ex- spec- tant non con- fun- den- tur] Gl⟨o- ri⟩- a pa- ⟨tr⟩i

3. Introit: Ad te levavi
Ecce iam Christus

[1] Ec- ce iam chris-tus quem sanc- ti pa- tres pro- phe- ta- runt ad- ve- nit no- bis

Ad te [le- va- vi an- i- mam me- am]

[2] Su- am nos sal- vet per na- ti- vi- ta- tem glo- ri- o- sam

De- us [me- us in te con- fi- do non e- ru- bes- cam]

[3] Cu- i om- nes oc- cur- ren- tes cla- me- mus sal- va nos de- us rex is- ra- hel

Ne- que [ir- ri- de- ant me in- i- mi- ci me- i]

[4] Rex chris-te de- us ab- ra- ham de- us i- sa- ac de- us ia- cob mi- se- re- re no- bis

Qui- a tu es sal- va- tor et mi- se- ri- cors ve- rax pi- us et sanc- tis- si- mus a- men

Et e- nim [u- ni- ver- si qui te ex- spec- tant non con- fun- den- tur]

4. Introit: Dominus dixit
Verbo altissimi patris

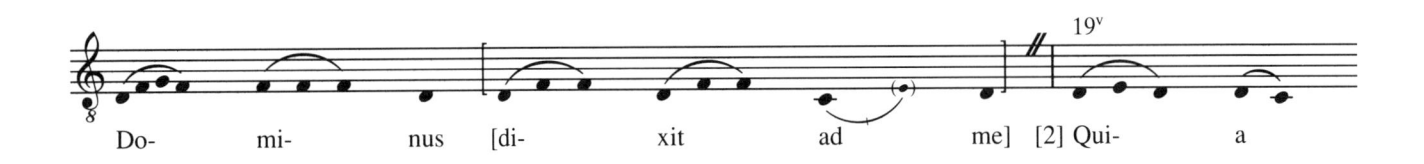

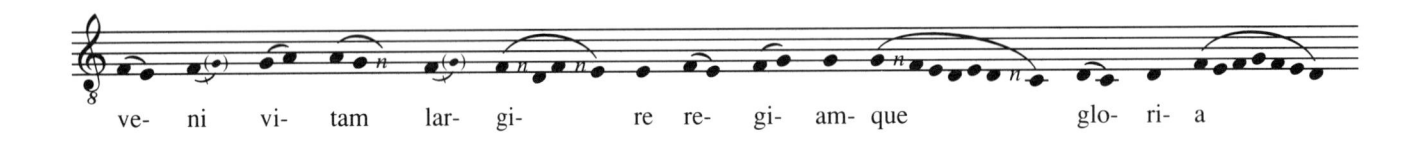

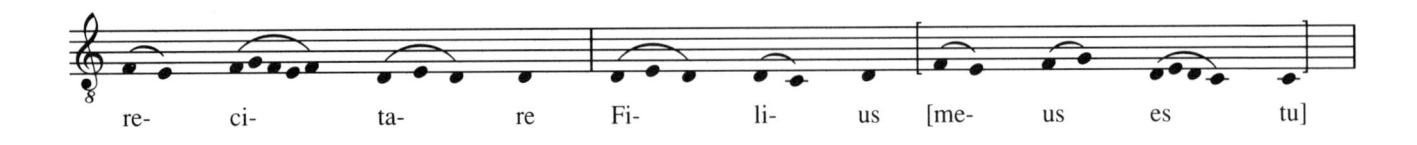

[1] Ver- bum al- tis- si- mi pa- tris ge- ni- to- que re- gis pro- phe- ti- ca lau- de psal- len- do Do- mi- nus [di- xit ad me] [2] Qui- a ve- ni vi- tam lar- gi- re re- gi- am- que glo- ri- a re- ci- ta- re Fi- li- us [me- us es tu] [3] Ve- ne- ran- te fi- li- um va- ti- ci- nan- do pro- phe- tan- do at- que di- cen- do E- go ho- [di- e ge- nu- i te]

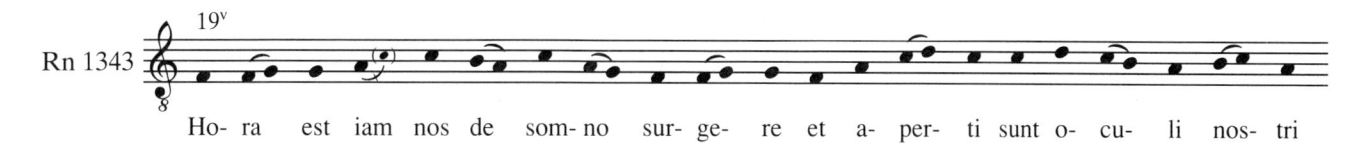

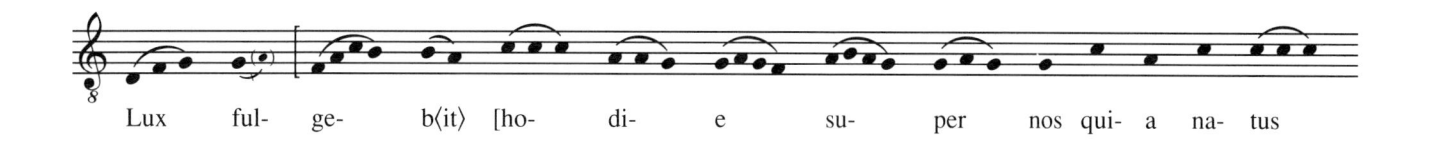

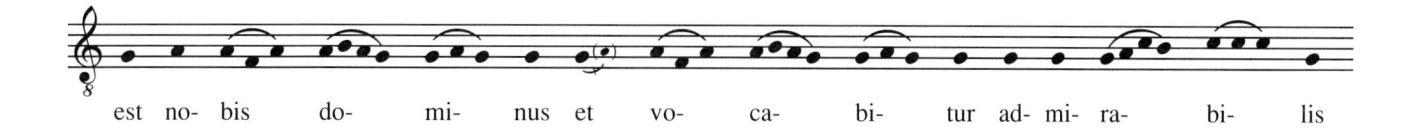

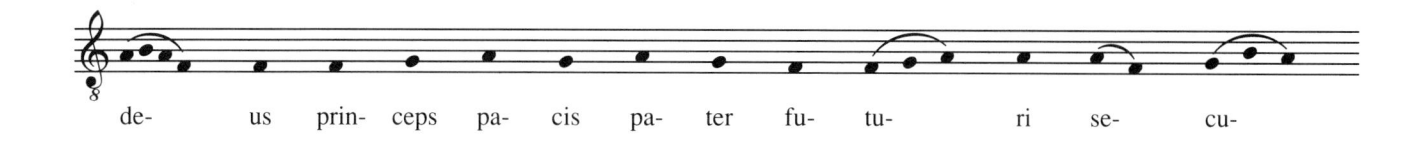

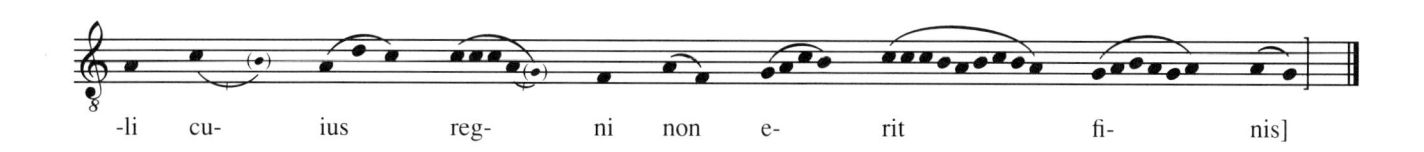

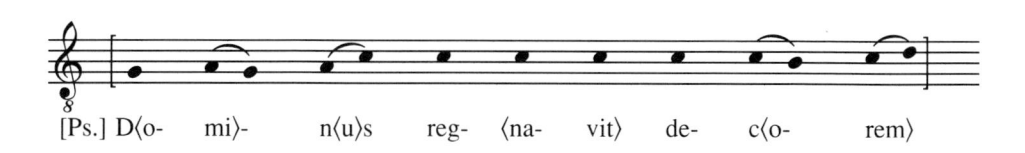

5. Introit: Lux fulgebit

Hora est iam nos

Rn 1343

Ho- ra est iam nos de som- no sur- ge- re et a- per- ti sunt o- cu- li nos- tri

sur- ge- re ad lu- cem qui- a lux ve- ra ful- get in cæ- lo

Lux ful- ge- b⟨it⟩ [ho- di- e su- per nos qui- a na- tus

est no- bis do- mi- nus et vo- ca- bi- tur ad- mi- ra- bi- lis

de- us prin- ceps pa- cis pa- ter fu- tu- ri se- cu-

-li cu- ius reg- ni non e- rit fi- nis]

[Ps.] D⟨o- mi⟩- n⟨u⟩s reg- ⟨na- vit⟩ de- c⟨o- rem⟩

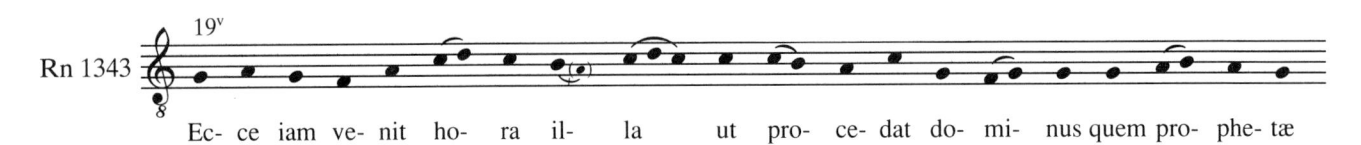

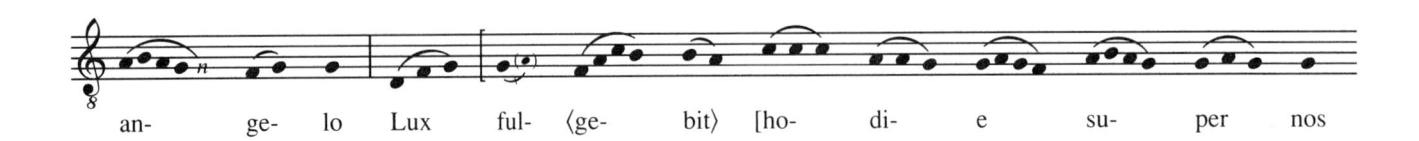

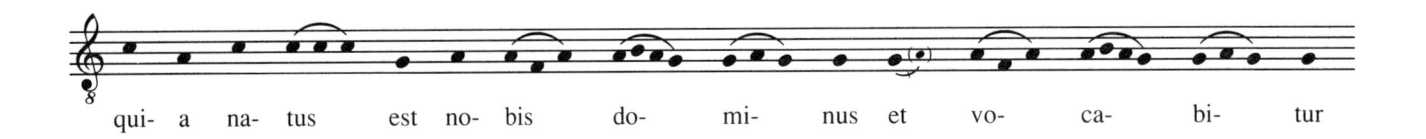

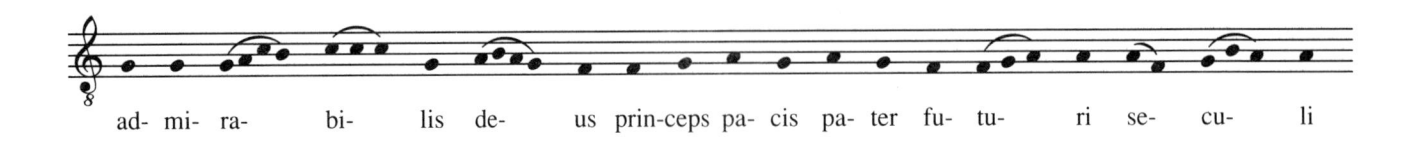

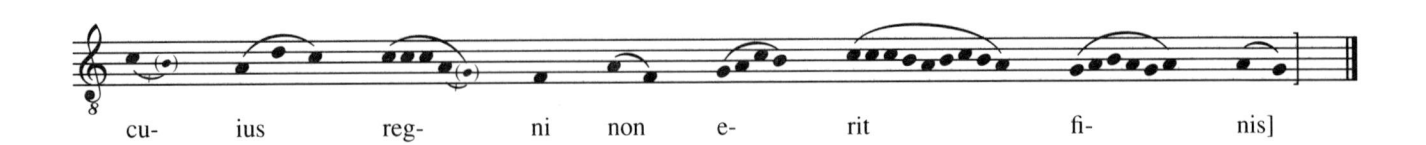

6. Introit: Lux fulgebit
Ecce iam venit hora

Rn 1343

Ec- ce iam ve- nit ho- ra il- la ut pro- ce- dat do- mi- nus quem pro- phe- tæ

pre- di- xe- runt im- ple- ta sunt om- ni- a per ma- ri- am vir- gi- nem ad- nun- ci- an- te

an- ge- lo Lux ful- ⟨ge- bit⟩ [ho- di- e su- per nos

qui- a na- tus est no- bis do- mi- nus et vo- ca- bi- tur

ad- mi- ra- bi- lis de- us prin- ceps pa- cis pa- ter fu- tu- ri se- cu- li

cu- ius reg- ni non e- rit fi- nis]

Gl⟨o-ri⟩- a pa- tri

7. Introit: Lux fulgebit
Iam surgens aurora

Rn 1343

Iam sur- gens au- ro- ra iam ve- ni- et di- es

iam ve- nit do- mi- nus il- lu- mi- na- re no- bis lu- men vi- tæ

Lux ful- g⟨e- bit⟩ [ho- di- e su- per nos qui- a na- tus

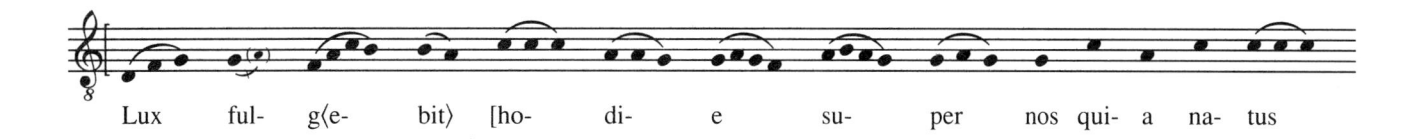

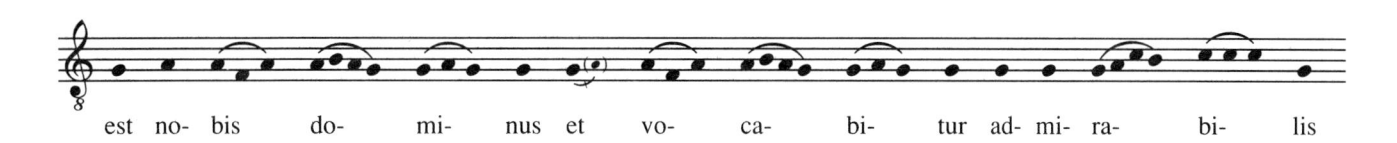

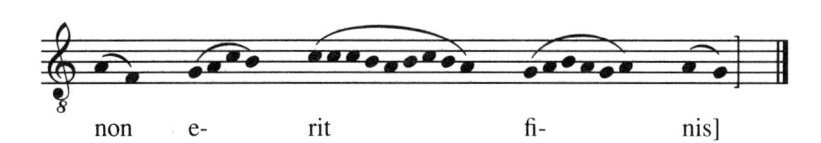

est no- bis do- mi- nus et vo- ca- bi- tur ad- mi- ra- bi- lis

de- us prin- ceps pa- cis pa- ter fu- tu- ri se- cu- li cu- ius reg- ni

non e- rit fi- nis]

8. Introit: Puer natus est nobis
Hodie salvator mundi per virginem

Bu 2824

[1] Ho- di- e sal- va- tor mun- di per vir- gi- nem nas- ci dig- na- tus

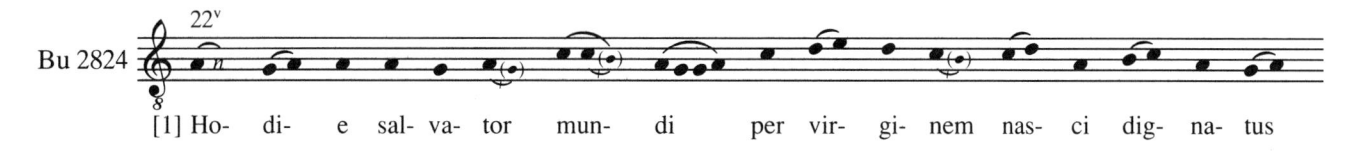

est gau- de- a- mus om- nes de chri- sto do- mi- no qui na- tus est no- bis e- ia et e- ia

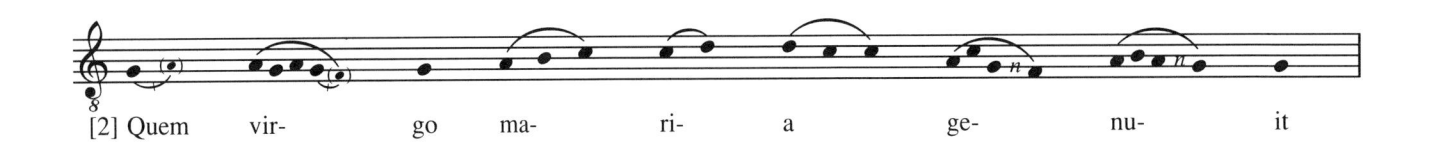

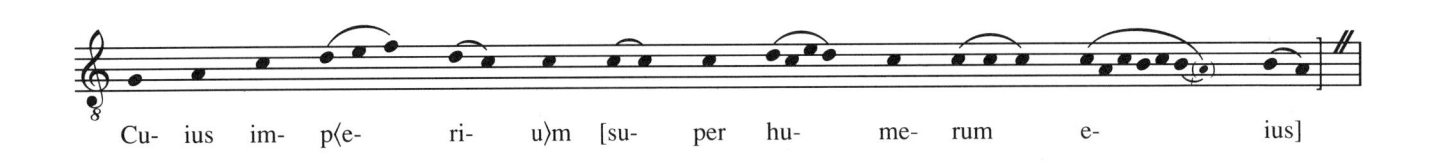

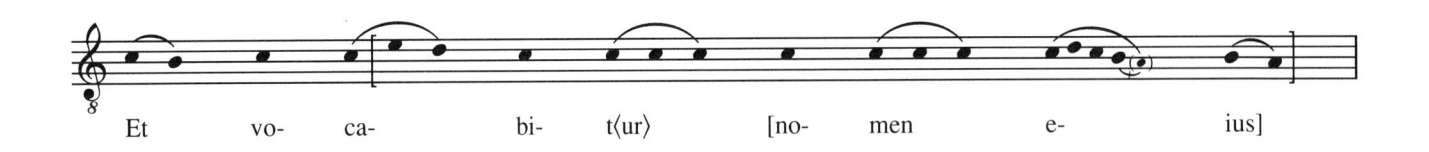

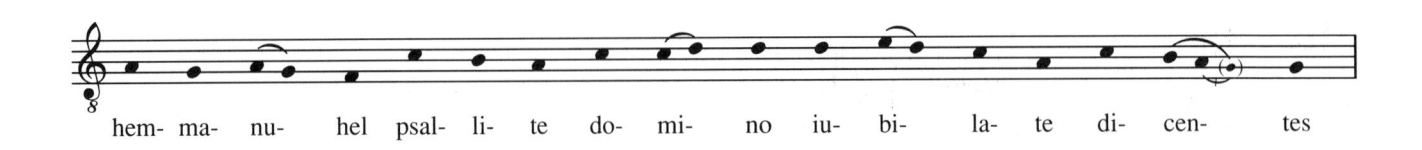

Pu- er na- tus [est no- bis et fi- li- us da- tus est no- bis]

[2] Quem vir- go ma- ri- a ge- nu- it

Cu- ius im- p⟨e- ri- u⟩m [su- per hu- me- rum e- ius]

[3] No- men e- ius hem- ma- nu- hel vo- ca- bi- tur

Et vo- ca- bi- t⟨ur⟩ [no- men e- ius]

[4] Mag- ni con- sci- li- i an- ge- lus e- ia is- te vo- ca- bi- tur no- men

hem- ma- nu- hel psal- li- te do- mi- no iu- bi- la- te di- cen- tes

Mag- ni [con- si- li- i an- ge- lus]

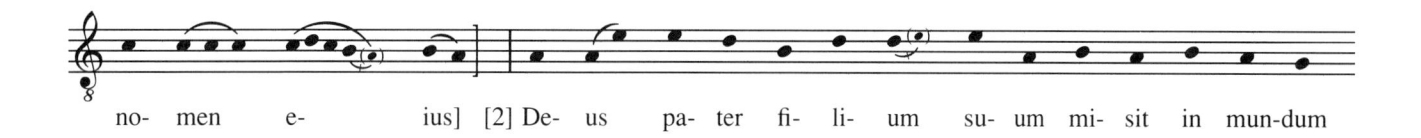

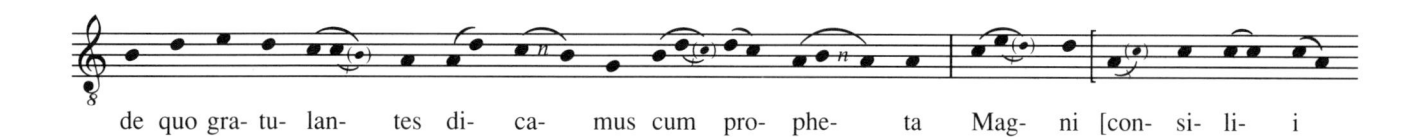

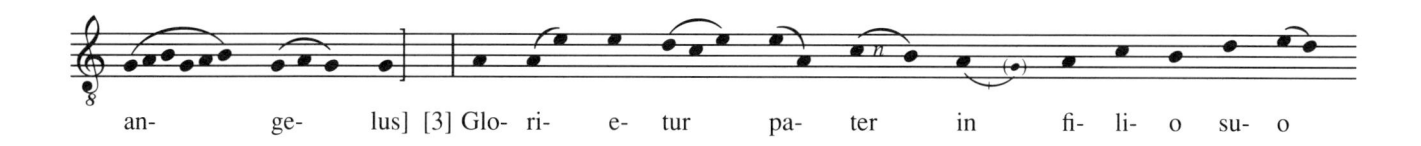

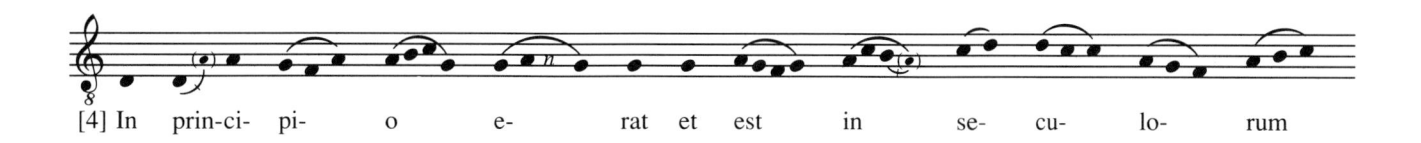

9. Introit: Puer natus est nobis
Hodie exultent iusti natus est

Rn 1343

[1] Ho- di- e ex- ul- tent iu- sti na- tus est fi- li- us de- i de- o gra- ci- as di- ci- te e- ia Pu- er [na- tus est no- bis et fi- li- us da- tus est no- bis cu- ius im- pe- ri- um su- per hu- me- rum e- ius et vo- ca- bi- tur no- men e- ius] [2] De- us pa- ter fi- li- um su- um mi- sit in mun- dum de quo gra- tu- lan- tes di- ca- mus cum pro- phe- ta Mag- ni [con- si- li- i an- ge- lus] [3] Glo- ri- e- tur pa- ter in fi- li- o su- o u- ni- ge- ni- to Gl⟨o- ri⟩- a pa- tri [et fi- li- o et spi- ri- tu- i sanc- to] [4] In prin- ci- pi- o e- rat et est in se- cu- lo- rum

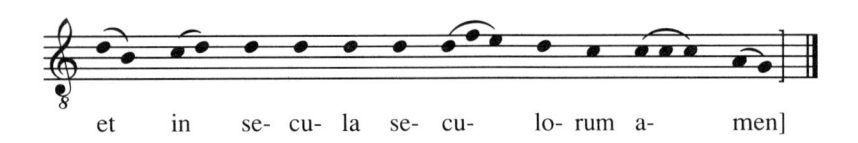

se- cu- la Sic- ut e- rat [in prin- ci- pi- o et nunc et sem- per

et in se- cu- la se- cu- lo- rum a- men]

10. Introit: Puer natus est nobis
Hic enim est de quo prophetae

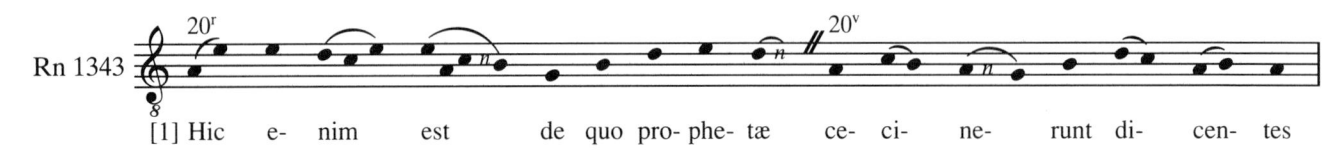

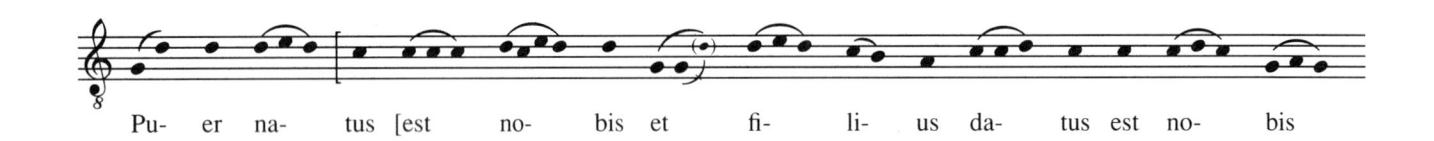

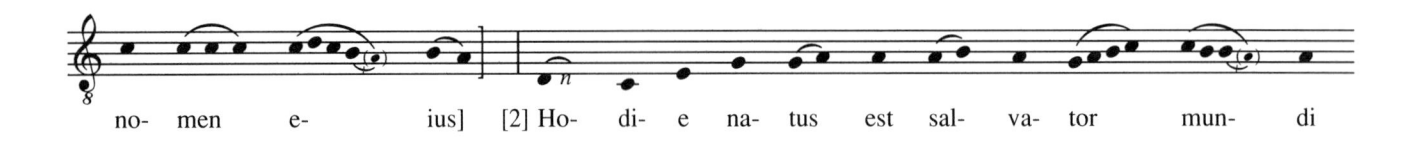

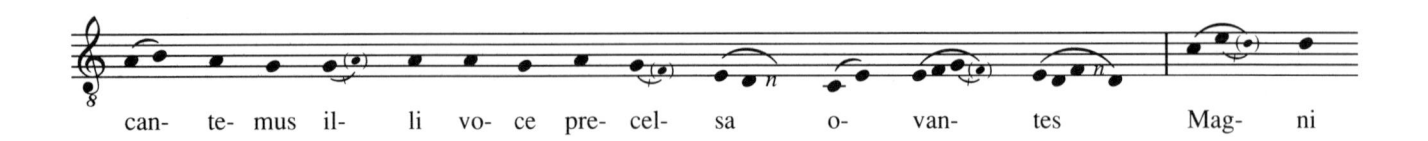

Rn 1343

[1] Hic e- nim est de quo pro- phe- tæ ce- ci- ne- runt di- cen- tes

Pu- er na- tus [est no- bis et fi- li- us da- tus est no- bis

cu- ius im- pe- ri- um super hu- me- rum e- ius et vo- ca- bi- tur

no- men e- ius] [2] Ho- di- e na- tus est sal- va- tor mun- di

can- te- mus il- li vo- ce pre- cel- sa o- van- tes Mag- ni

[con- si- li- i an- ge- lus]

11. Introit: Etenim sederunt principes
Hodie inclitus martyr Stephanus

Rn 1343

[1] Ho- di- e in- cly- tus mar- tyr ste- pha- nus pa- ra- di- sum lau- re- a- tus as- cen- dit Et- e- nim [se- de- runt prin- ci- pes et ad- ver- sum me lo- que- ban- tur]

[2] In- sur- re- xe- runt con- tra me iu- de- o- rum po- pu- li in- i- qui Et in- i- q⟨ui⟩ [per- se- cu- ti sunt me]

[3] In- vi- di- o- sæ la- pi- di- bus op- pres- se- runt me Ad- iu- va [me do- mi- ne de- us me- us]

[4] Su- sci- pe me- um in pa- ce spi- ri- tum Qui- a ser- vus [tu- us ex- er- ce- ba- tur in tu- is ius- ti- fi- ca- ti- o- ni- bus] [Ps.] Be- a- ti [immaculati]

12. Introit: Etenim sederunt principes
Grandine lapidum

Rn 1343

Gran- di- ne la- pi- dum mox mo- ri- tu- rus sanc- tus ste- pha- nus spe vi- tæ ma- nen- tis læ- ta- bun- dus i- ta di- ce- bat Ad- iu- va me [do- mi- ne de- us qui- a ser- vus tu- us ex- er- ce- ba- tur in tu- is ius- ti- fi- ca- ti- o- ni- bus] Glo- ri- a patri

13. Introit: Etenim sederunt principes
Qui primus meruit

Bu 2824

[1] Qui pri- mus me- ru- it post cris- tum o- cur- re- re mar- tir iu- re su- o ta- li tes- ta- tur vo- ce la- bo- re

Et- e- nim [se- de- runt prin- ci- pes et ad- ver- sum me lo- que- ban- tur]

[2] Non nul- lum no- cu- i nec le- gum iu- ra re- sol- vi

Et in- i- q⟨ui⟩ [per- se- cu- ti sunt me]

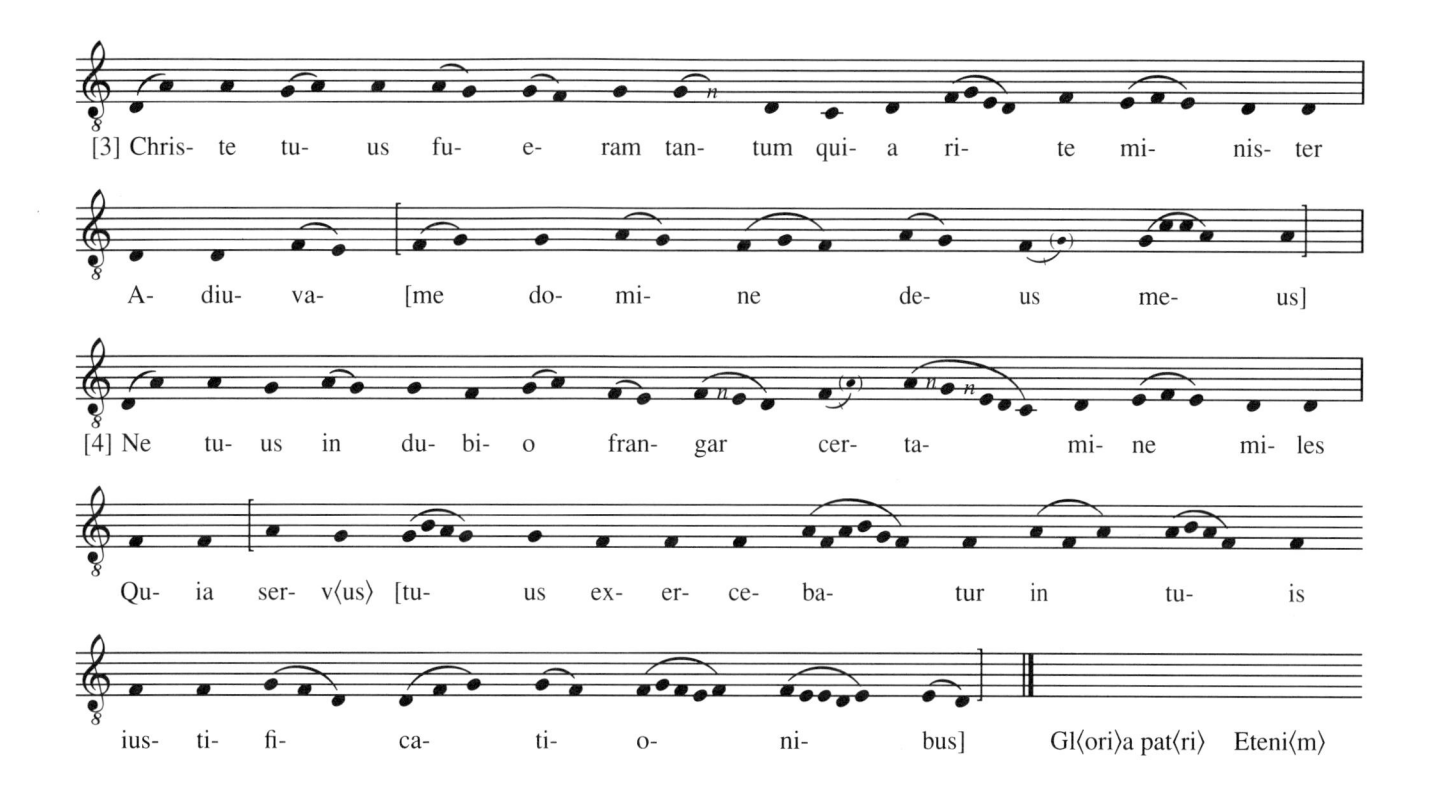

[3] Chris- te tu- us fu- e- ram tan- tum qui a ri- te mi- nis- ter

A- diu- va- [me do- mi- ne de- us me- us]

[4] Ne tu- us in du- bi- o fran- gar cer- ta- mi- ne mi- les

Qui- ia ser-⟨us⟩ [tu- us ex- er- ce- ba- tur in tu- is

ius- ti- fi- ca- ti- o- ni- bus] Gl⟨ori⟩a pat⟨ri⟩ Eteni⟨m⟩

14. Communion: Video caelos apertos
Magnus et felix

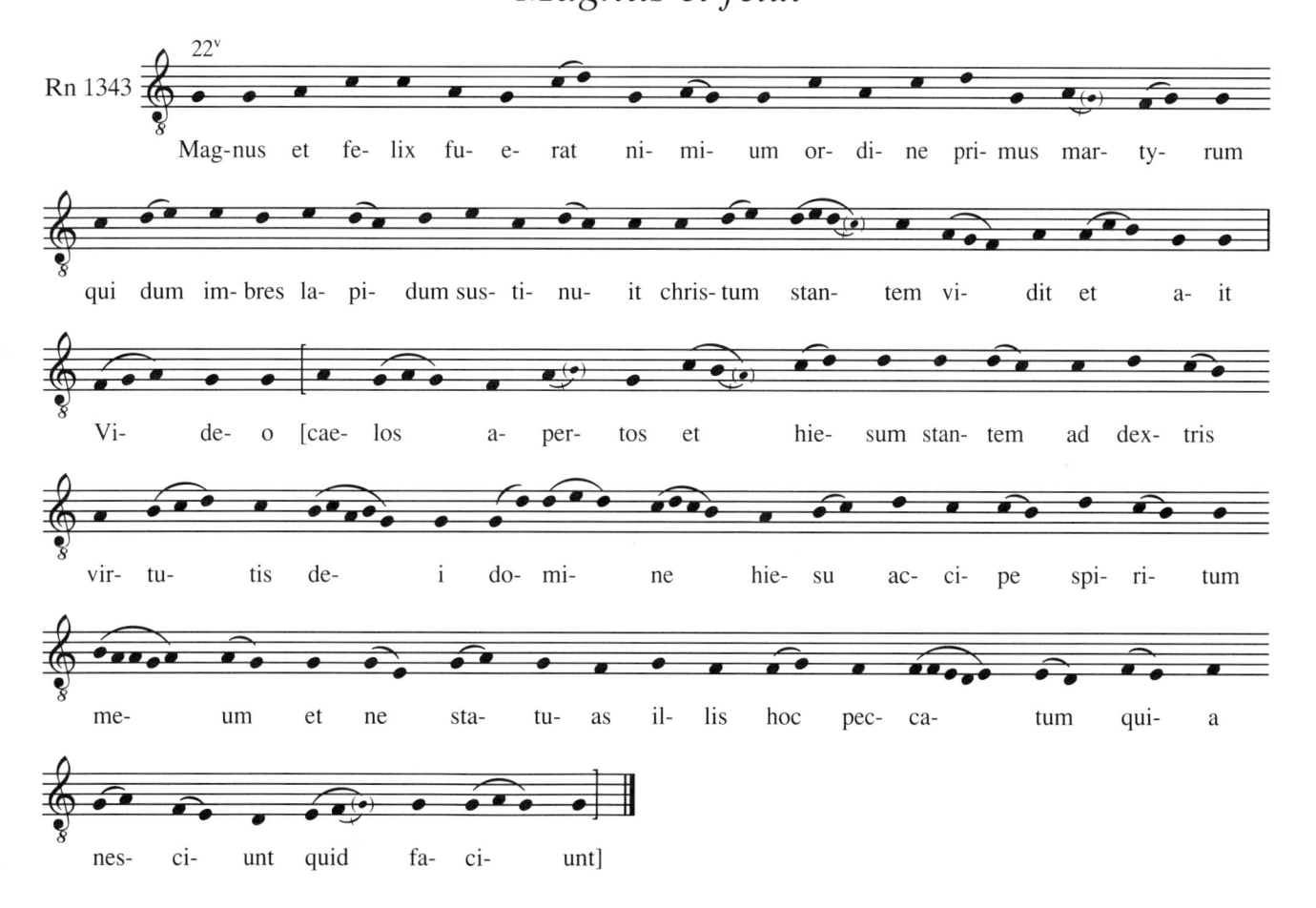

Rn 1343

Mag- nus et fe- lix fu- e- rat ni- mi- um or- di- ne pri- mus mar- ty- rum

qui dum im- bres la- pi- dum sus- ti- nu- it chris- tum stan- tem vi- dit et a- it

Vi- de- o [cae- los a- per- tos et hie- sum stan- tem ad dex- tris

vir- tu- tis de- i do- mi- ne hie- su ac- ci- pe spi- ri- tum

me- um et ne sta- tu- as il- lis hoc pec- ca- tum qui- a

nes- ci- unt quid fa- ci- unt]

15. Introit: In medio ecclesiae
Aeterno genitus genitore

Rn 1343

[1] E- ter- no ge- ni- tus ge- ni- to- re ex tem- po- re chris- tus

In me- di- o [ec- cle- si- ae a- pe- ru- it os e- ius]

[2] Pec- to- ris at- que sa- cri pan- dit mys- te- ri- a sanc- ta

Et im- [ple- vit e- um do- mi- nus spi- ri- tu sa- pi- en- ti- ae

et in- tel- lec- tus] [3] Men- ti- bus er- go pi- is

can- te- mus que- so de- o qui Sto- lam

[glo- ri- ae in- du- it e- um] [4] Om- nes vo- ce

de- o can- ta- te et psal- li- te cor- de

[Ps.] Bo- num est [confiteri domino et psallere nomini tuo altissime]

16. Introit: In medio ecclesiae
Ille qui dixit

[1] Il- le qui di- xit a- pe- ri os tu- um

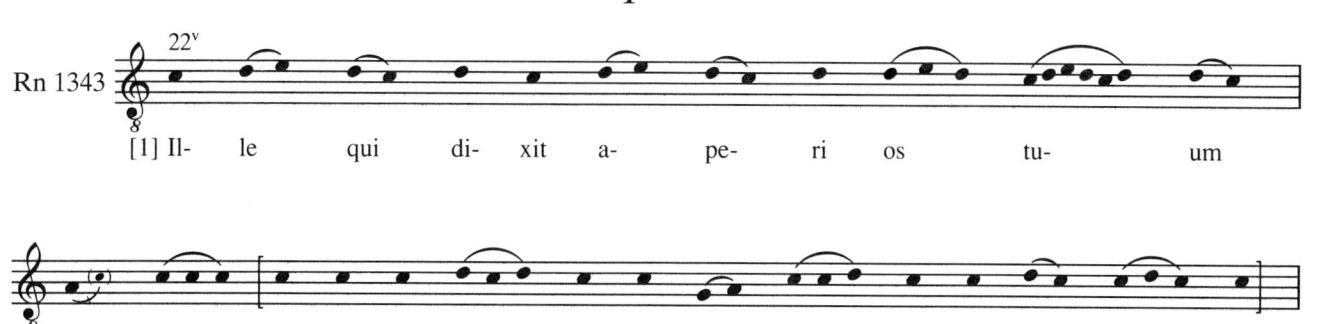

In me- [di- o ec- cle- si- ae a- pe- ru- it os e- ius]

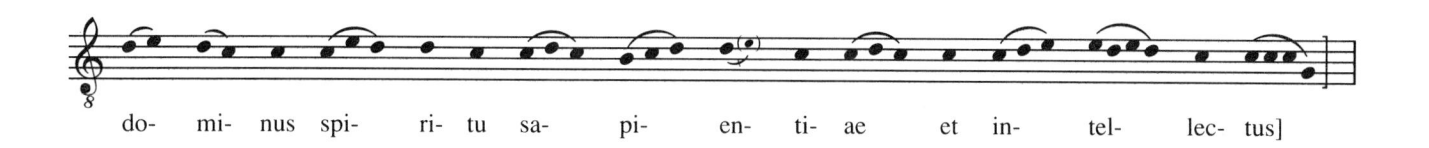

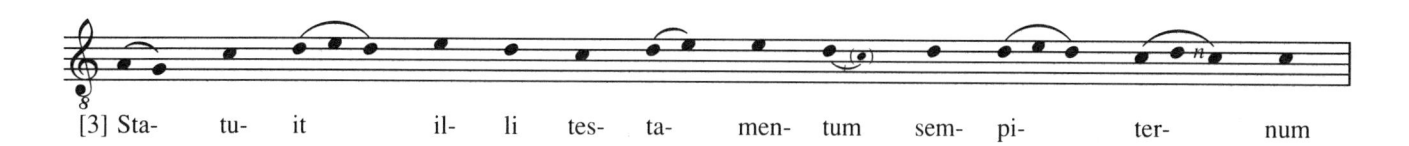

[2] Ci- ba- vit il- lum pa- nem vi- tæ Et im- ple- [vit e- um

do- mi- nus spi- ri- tu sa- pi- en- ti- ae et in- tel- lec- tus]

[3] Sta- tu- it il- li tes- ta- men- tum sem- pi- ter- num

Sto- lam [glo- ri- ae in- du- it e- um] Glo- ri- a patri

17. Introit: In medio ecclesiae
Amor angelorum et gaudium

[1] A- mor an- ge- lo- rum et gau- di- um

chris- tus io- han- nem di- li- gens

In me- [di- o ec- cle- si- ae a- pe- ru- it os e- ius]

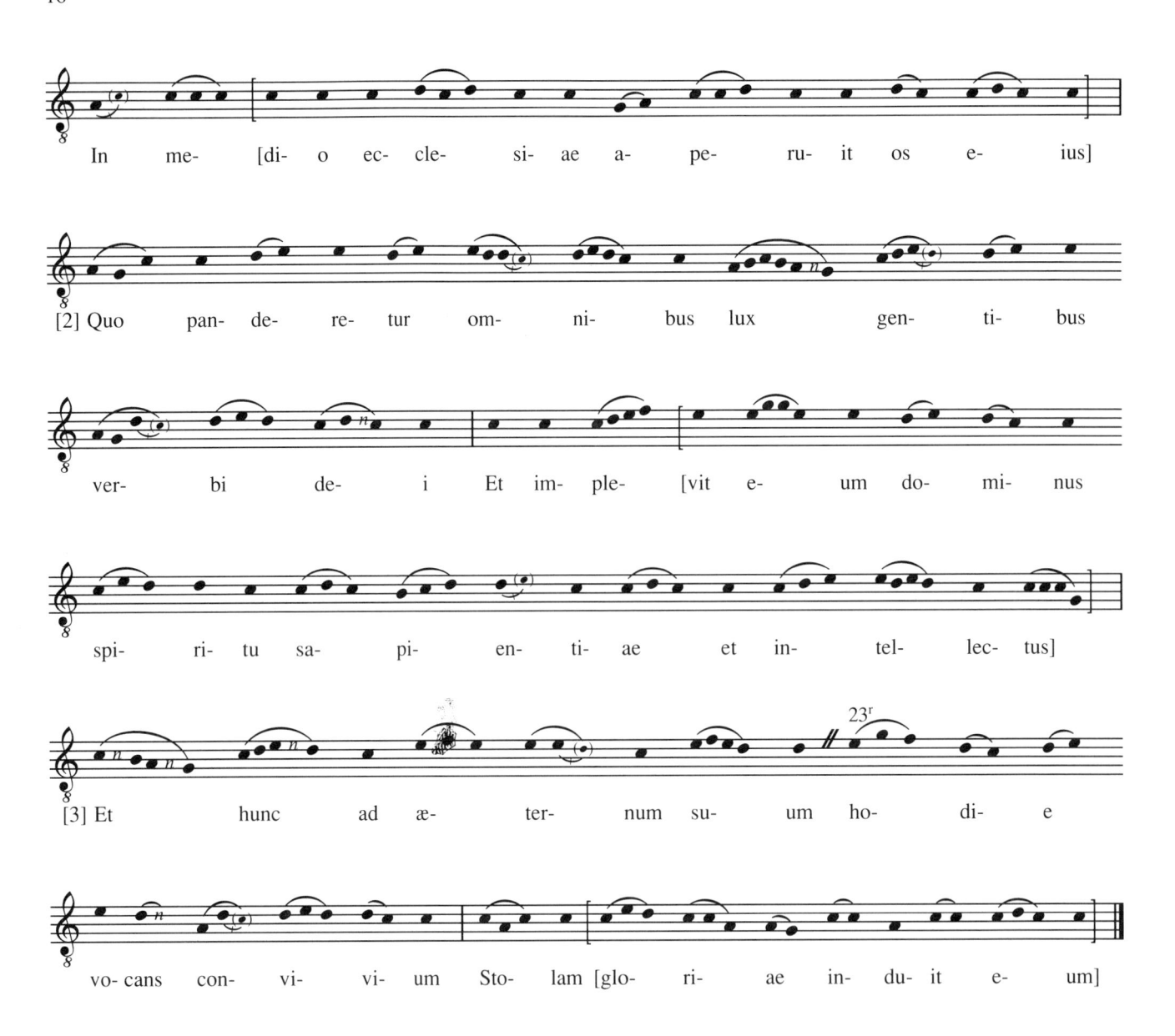

[2] Quo pan- de- re- tur om- ni- bus lux gen- ti- bus

ver- bi de- i Et im- ple- [vit e- um do- mi- nus

spi- ri- tu sa- pi- en- ti- ae et in- tel- lec- tus]

[3] Et hunc ad æ- ter- num su- um ho- di- e

vo- cans con- vi- vi- um Sto- lam [glo- ri- ae in- du- it e- um]

18. Introit: In medio ecclesiae
Dilectus iste domini

Bu 2824

[1] Di- lec- tus is- te do- mi- nus io- han- nes est a- pos- to- lus

scrip- tis e- ius et mo- ni- tis pol- let de- cus ec- cle- si- e

Glo- ri- a pa[tri] [2] Os tu- um in- qui- ens a- pe- ri me- que il- lud ip- sum pro cer- to s[c]i- as im- ple- re Et im- ple- [vit e- um do- mi- nus

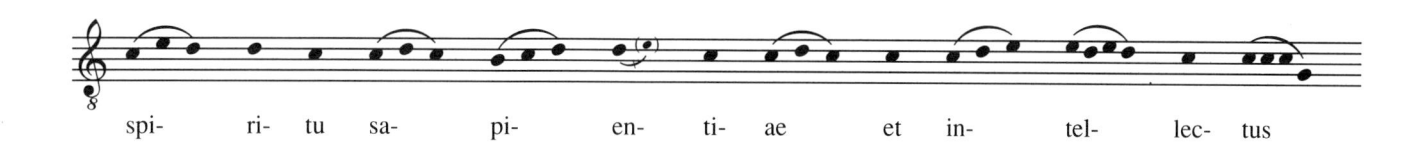

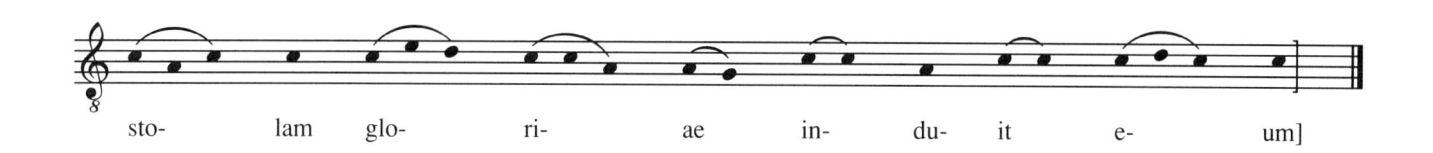

spi- ri- tu sa- pi- en- ti- ae et in- tel- lec- tus

sto- lam glo- ri- ae in- du- it e- um]

19. Offertory: Iustus ut palma
Florebit iustus ut palma

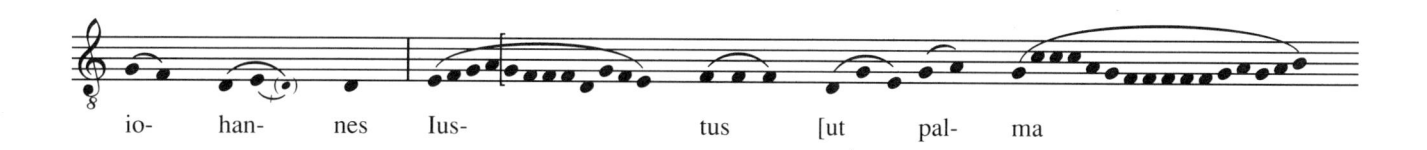

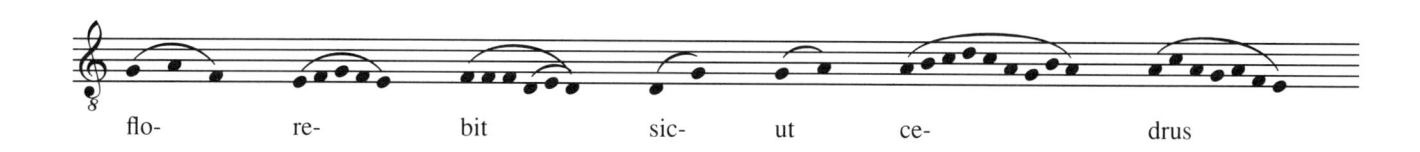

Rn 1343

Flo- re- bit ius- tus ut pal- ma mul- ti- pli- ca- bi- tur ut ce- drus

io- han- nes Ius- tus [ut pal- ma

flo- re- bit sic- ut ce- drus

quae in li- ba- no est

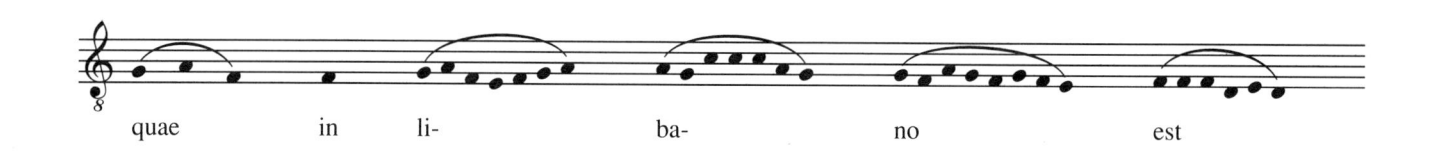

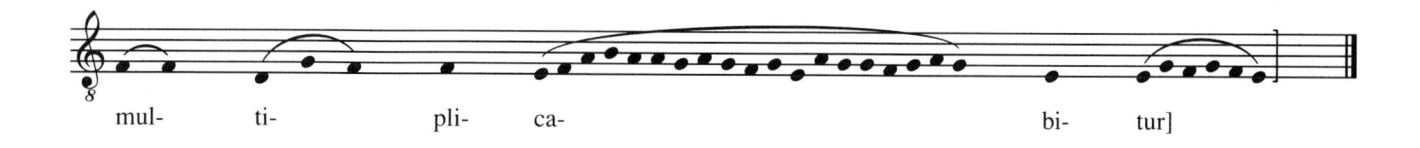

mul- ti- pli- ca- bi- tur]

20. Introit: Ex ore infantium
Hodie te domine suggentes

Bu 2824

[1] Ho- di- e te do- mi- ne sug- gen- tes u- be- ra ma- tri- bus cla- mant nos- que lau- di- bus e- ia Ex o- re [in- fan- ti- um de- us] [2] Te- ne- ri ex- er- ci- tus pre- co- ni- a spar- si- sti or- bis cir- cu- la mi- ran- da Et lac- ten- [ti- um per- fe- cis- ti lau- dem] [3] Ut tu- a glo- ri- a in mi- ni- mis ful- ge- ret al- ta Prop- ter [in- i- mi- cos tu- os]

21. Introit: Statuit ei dominus
Venite populi ad conlaudandum

Rn 1343

[1] Ve- ni- te po- pu- li ad col- lau- dan- dum re- gem re- gum do- mi- num qui tri- um- phat in con- fes- so- re su- o Sil- ves- tro a- gi- te Sta- tu- it [e- i do- mi- nus

tes- ta- men- tum pa- cis] [2] Cel- sa nunc ru- ti- la[n]t fes- ta
be- a- ti sil- ves- tri di- ca- mus om- nes vo- ce pre- cel- sa
o- van- tes Et prin- [ci- pem fe- cit e- um]
[3] Quo u- ni- ti su- mus fi- de Ut sit [il- li sa- cer- do- ti- i
dig- ni- tas] [4] Ma- net in- de- fi- ci- ens
In æ- t[er- num] [Ps.] Mi- ⟨se- ricordi⟩as tuas

22. Introit: Statuit ei dominus
Hic est Silvester

Rn 1343

[1] Hic est sil- ves- ter pa- pa de quo pro- phe- ta ce- ci- nit di- cens

Sta- tu- it [e- i do- mi- nus tes- ta- men- tum pa- cis]

[2] Quem au- gus- tus con- stan- ti- nus sta- tu- it sum- mum es- se sa- cer- do- tem

de- i se- cun- dum or- di- nem mel- chi- se- dech

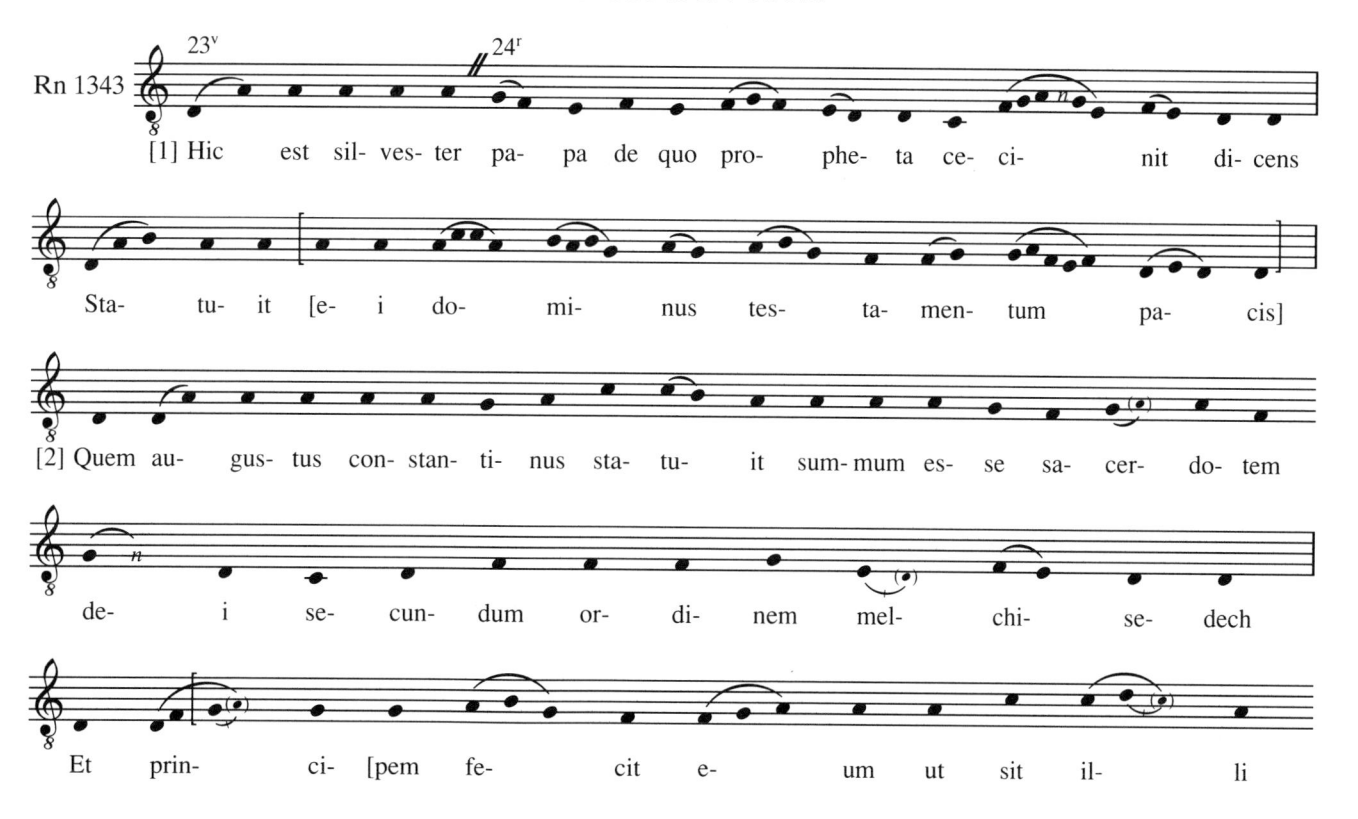

Et prin- ci- [pem fe- cit e- um ut sit il- li

sa- cer- do- ti dig- ni- tas] [3] Per ip- sum il- lu- mi- na- ta est om- nis æc- cle- si- a sanc- ta de- i In ae- ter- [num] Gloria patri

23. Offertory: Veritas mea
Usque in saeculum saeculi

Rn 1343

[1] Us- que in se- cu- lum se- cu- li con- ser- va- bo sanc- tum me- um Ve- ri- tas [me- a] [2] Non de- re- lin- quam e- um sed in per- pe- tu- um cum e- o per- ma- ne- bo Et mi- ⟨se- ri- cor- di⟩- a [me- a cum ip- so] [3] Sta- tu- am tes- ta- men- tum cum e- o et sta- bi- li- am us- que in æ- ter- num thro- num e- ius Et in no- mi- [ne me- o ex- al- ta- bi- tur cor- nu e- ius]

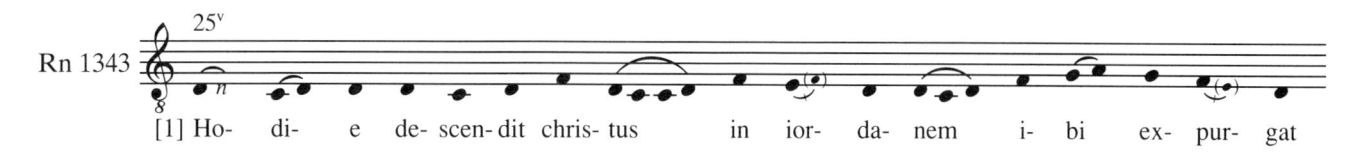

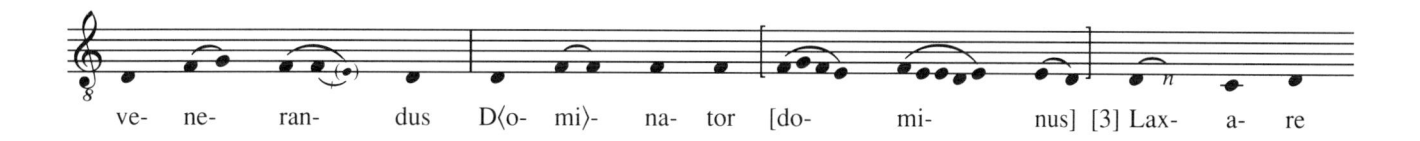

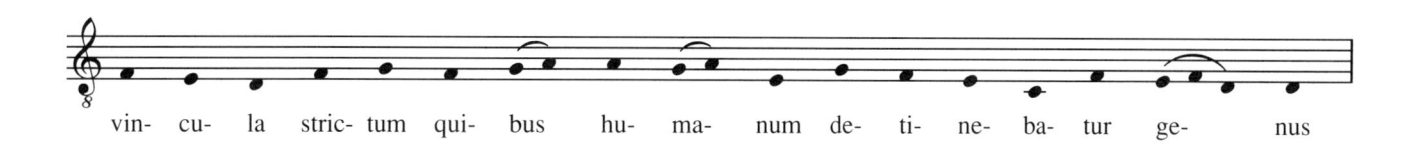

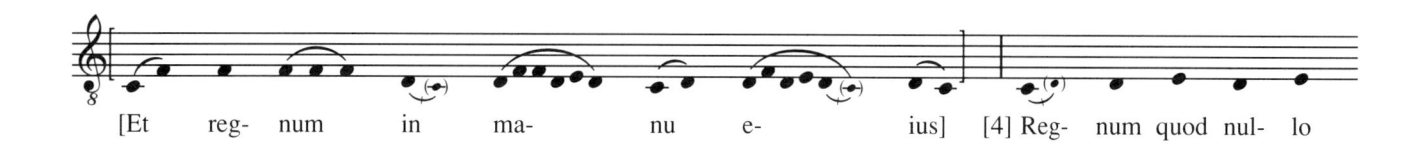

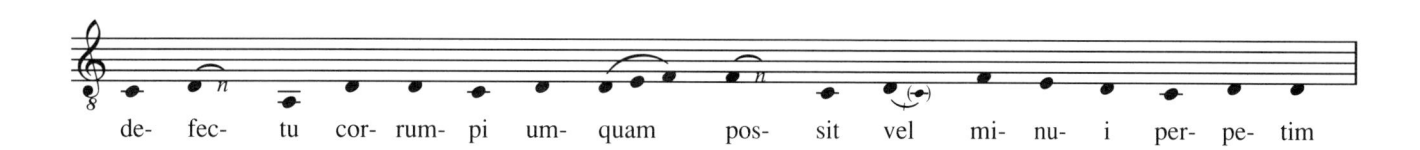

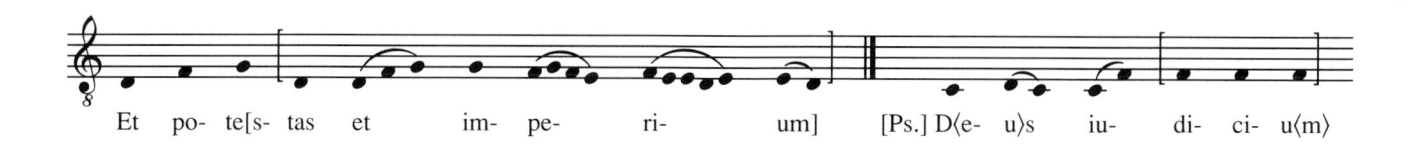

24. Introit: Ecce advenit
Hodie descendit Christus

Rn 1343

[1] Ho- di- e de- scen- dit chris- tus in ior- da- nem i- bi ex- pur- gat nos- tra fa- ci- no- ra de- o gra- ci- as di- ci- te Ec- ce ad- [ve- nit] [2] O- lim pro- mis- sus a[c] cu- pi- dis pa- tri- bus ve- ne- ran- dus D⟨o- mi⟩- na- tor [do- mi- nus] [3] Lax- a- re vin- cu- la stric- tum qui- bus hu- ma- num de- ti- ne- ba- tur ge- nus [Et reg- num in ma- nu e- ius] [4] Reg- num quod nul- lo de- fec- tu cor- rum- pi um- quam pos- sit vel mi- nu- i per- pe- tim Et po- te[s- tas et im- pe- ri- um] [Ps.] D⟨e- u⟩s iu- di- ci- u⟨m⟩

25. Introit: Ecce advenit
Forma speciosissimus

Rn 1343

For- ma spe- ci- o- sis- si- mus ma- nu- que po- ten- tis- si- mus ex da- vid o- ri- gi- ne na- tus ma- ri- æ vir- gi- nis Gl⟨o- ri⟩- a patri

26. Introit: Ecce advenit
Haec est praeclara dies

Rn 1343

[1] Hæc est pre- cla- ra di- es tri- bus sa- cra- ta mi- ra- cu- lis in qua cum pro- phe- ta ca- na- mus di- cen- tes Ec- ce [ad- ve- nit] [2] Quem ma- gi ho- di- e mu- ne- ri- bus ho- no- rant et ut re- gem su- per- num a- do- rant qui est D⟨o- mi⟩- na- tor [do- mi- nus] [3] In ior- da- ne a io- han- ne bap- ti- za- tus pa- ter- na vo- ce fi- li- us pa- tris

est ho- di- e ad- cla- ma- tus Et reg-⟨num⟩ [in ma- nu

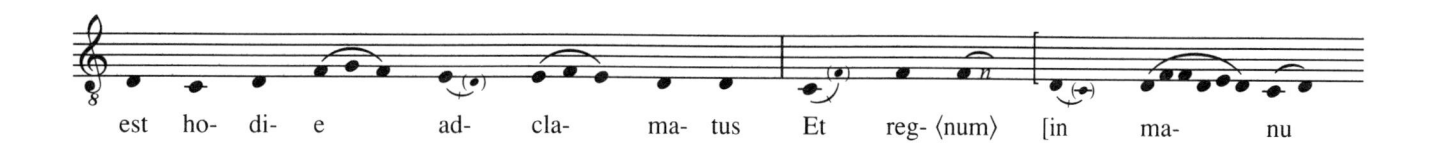

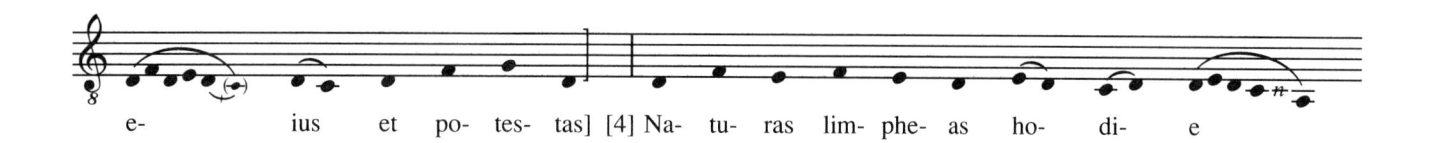

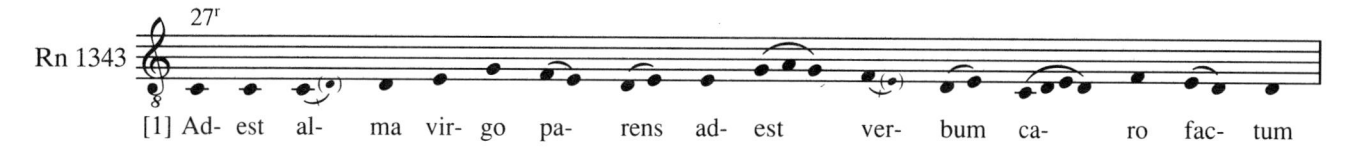

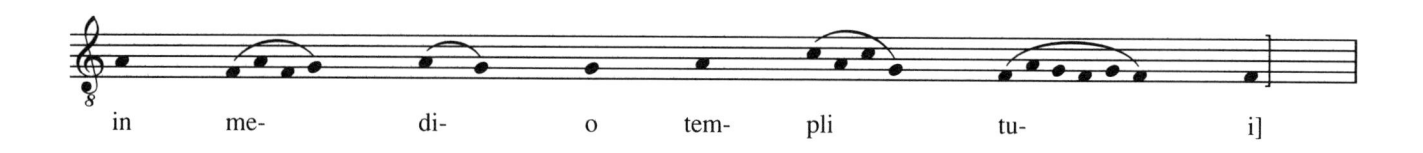

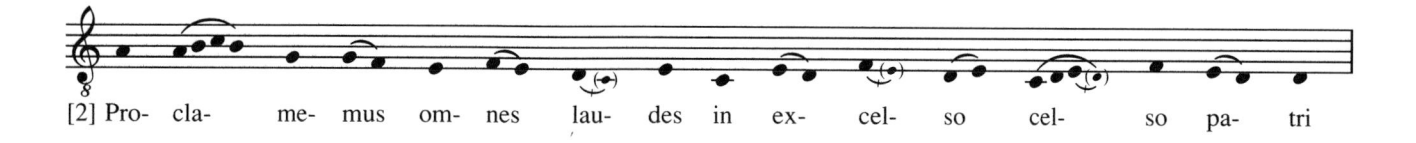

e- ius et po- tes- tas] [4] Na- tu- ras lim- phe- as ho- di- e

mu- ta- vit in sa- po- ri- fe- ros aus- tus per

po- tes- ta- tem Et im- pe- [ri- um]

27. Introit: Suscepimus
Adest alma virgo

Rn 1343

[1] Ad- est al- ma vir- go pa- rens ad- est ver- bum ca- ro fac- tum

Su- sce- pi- m⟨us⟩ [de- us mi- se- ri- cor- di- am tu- am

in me- di- o tem- pli tu- i]

[2] Pro- cla- me- mus om- nes lau- des in ex- cel- so cel- so pa- tri

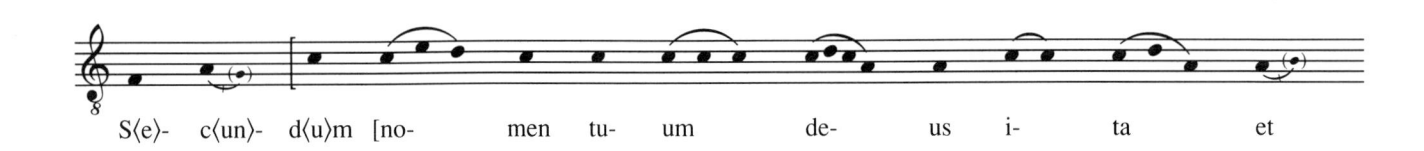

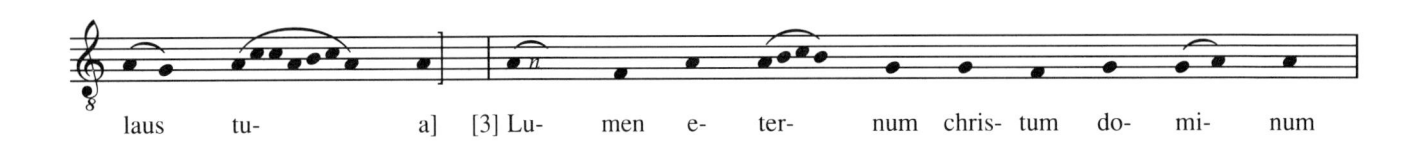

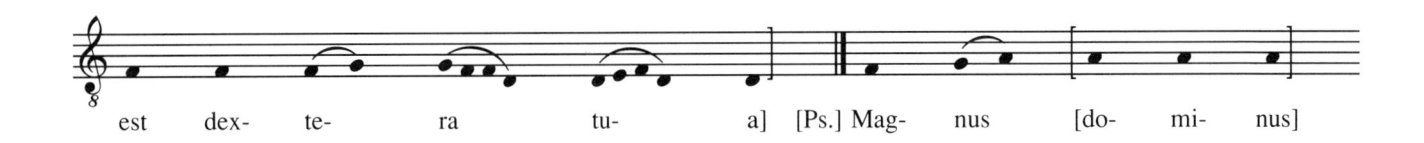

S⟨e⟩- c⟨un⟩- d⟨u⟩m [no- men tu- um de- us i- ta et laus tu- a] [3] Lu- men e- ter- num chris- tum do- mi- num In fi- ne[s ter- rae] [4] In bra- chiis sanc- ti sy- me- o- nis Ius- ti- ci- a [ple- na est dex- te- ra tu- a] [Ps.] Mag- nus [do- mi- nus]

28. Introit: Suscepimus
Psallentes legimus

Rn 1343

[1] Psal- len- tes le- gi- mus da- vid ce- ci- nis- se pro- phe- ta Su- sce- [pi- mus de- us mi- se- ri- cor- di- am tu- -am in me- di- o tem- pli tu- i se- cun- dum no- men

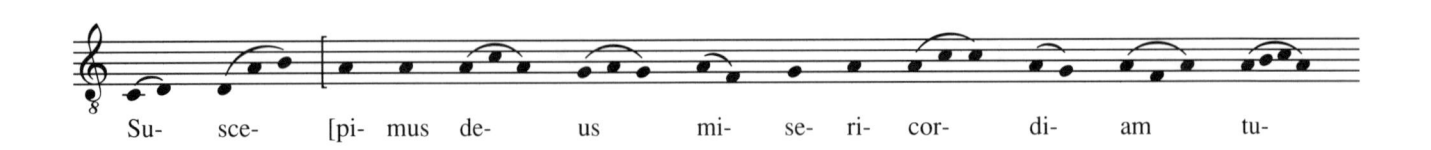

tu- um de- us i- ta et laus tu- a]

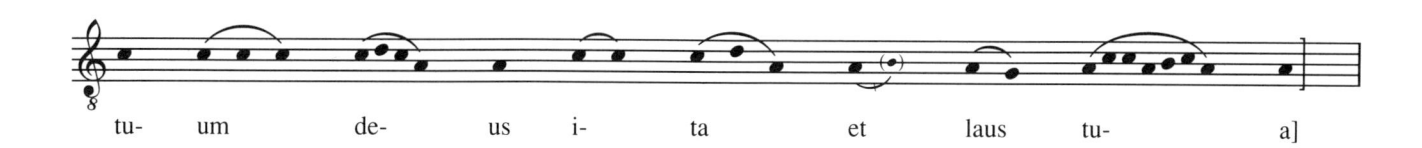

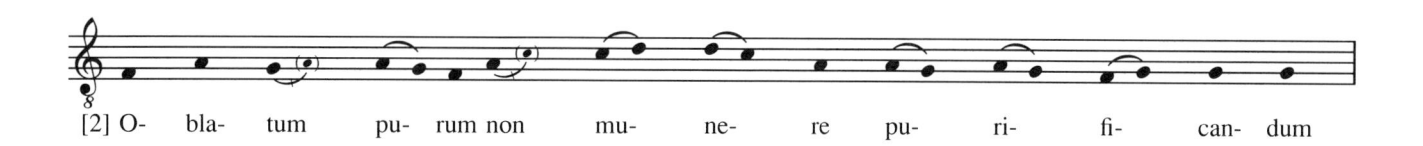

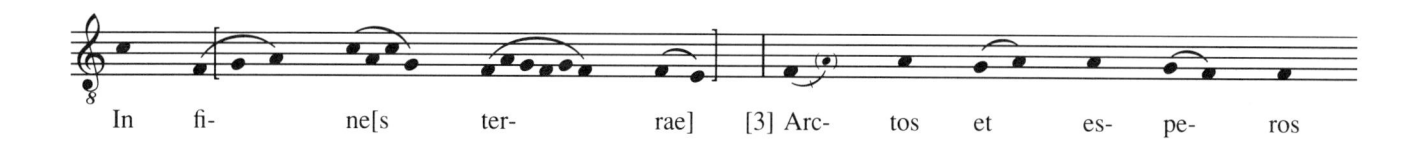

[2] O- bla- tum pu- rum non mu- ne- re pu- ri- fi- can- dum

In fi- ne[s ter- rae] [3] Arc- tos et es- pe- ros

au- ster et e- o- us Ius- ti- [ti- a ple- na est dex- te- ra tu- a]

29. Introit: Domine ne longe facias
Ingresso Iesu

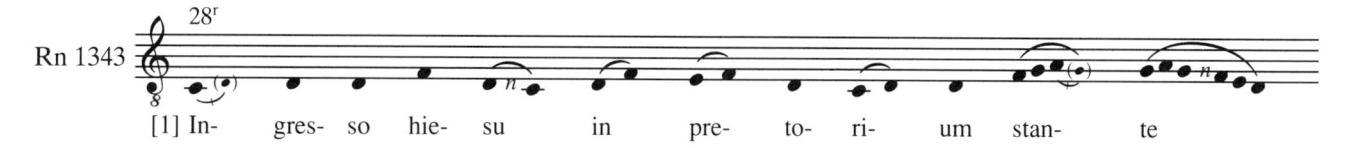

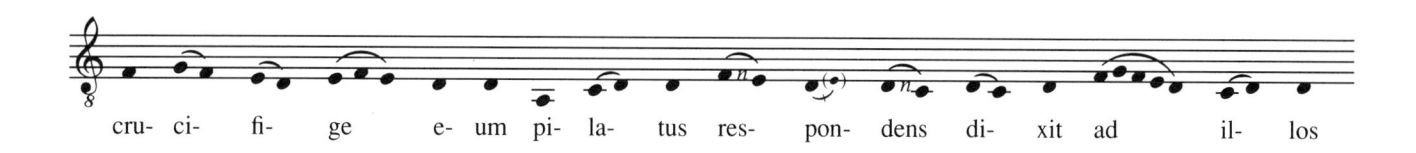

Rn 1343

[1] In- gres- so hie- su in pre- to- ri- um stan- te

an- te pi- la- tum iu- de- i cla- ma- bant cru- ci- fi- ge

cru- ci- fi- ge e- um pi- la- tus res- pon- dens di- xit ad il- los

re- gem ves- trum ve- rum non cru- ci- fi- gam e- go de

quo da- vid pro- phe- ta ce- ci- nit di- cens Do- mi- ne

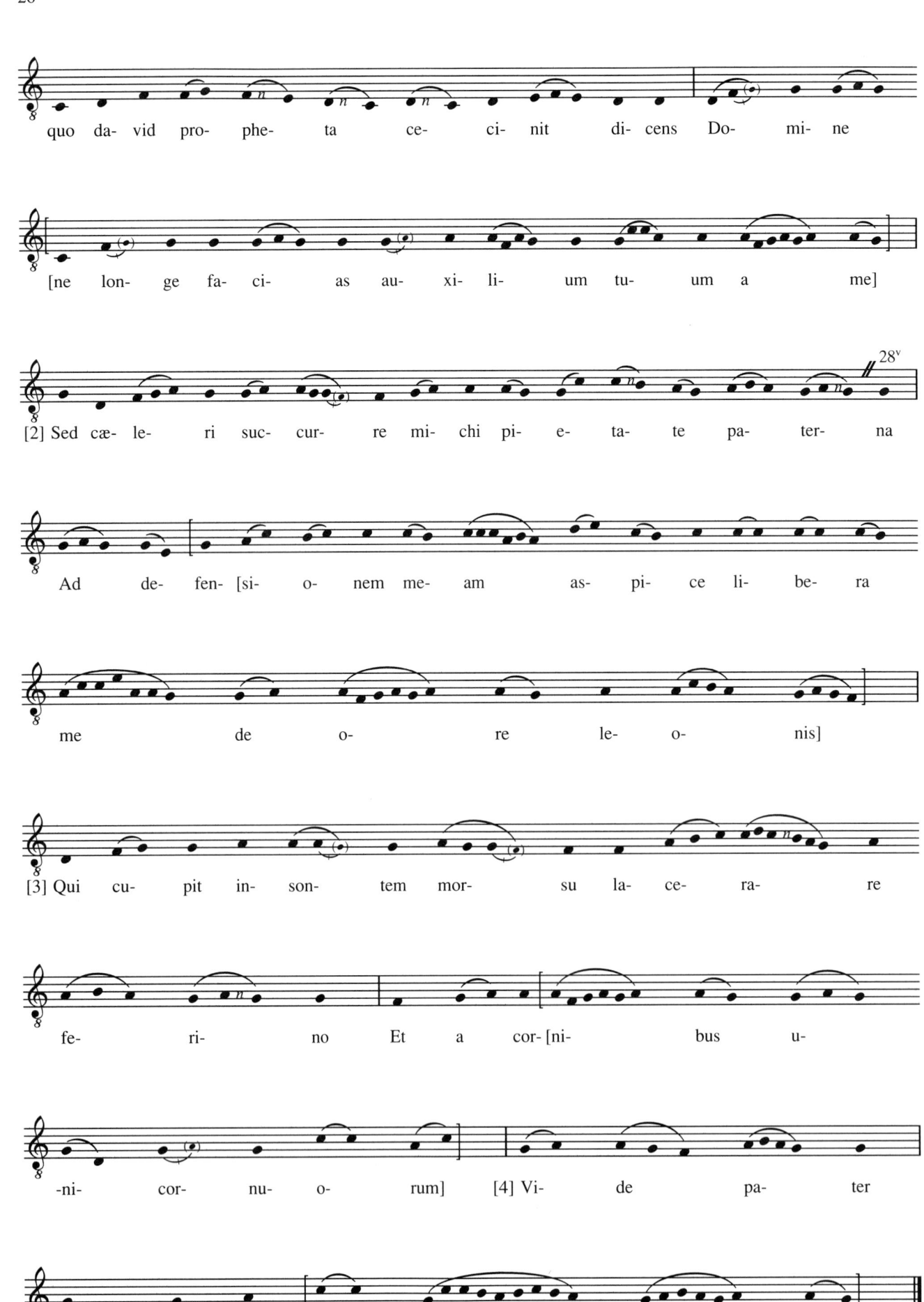

[ne lon- ge fa- ci- as au- xi- li- um tu- um a me]

[2] Sed cæ- le- ri suc- cur- re mi- chi pi- e- ta- te pa- ter- na

Ad de- fen- [si- o- nem me- am as- pi- ce li- be- ra

me de o- re le- o- nis]

[3] Qui cu- pit in- son- tem mor- su la- ce- ra- re

fe- ri- no Et a cor- [ni- bus u-

-ni- cor- nu- o- rum] [4] Vi- de pa- ter

Hu- mi- li- ta- [tem me- am]

30. Introit: Domine ne longe facias
Suspensus ligno patri

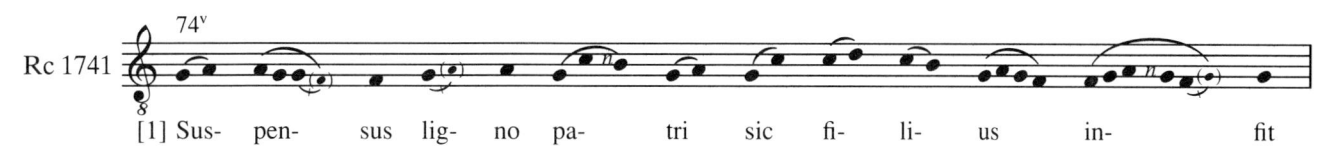

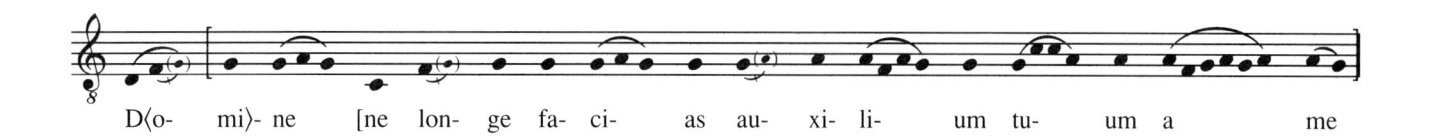

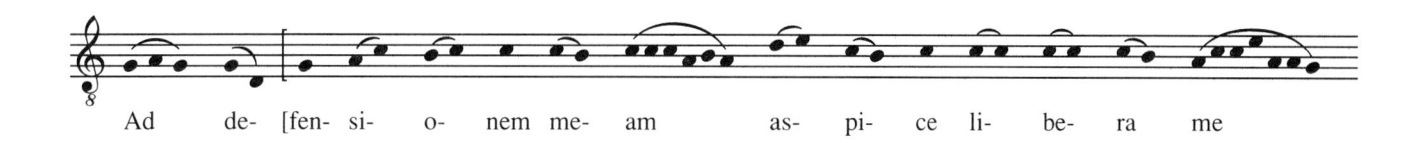

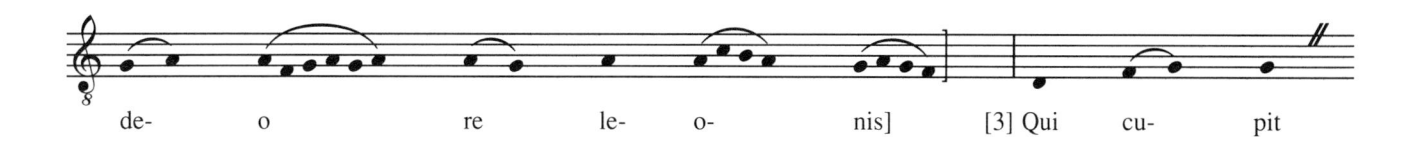

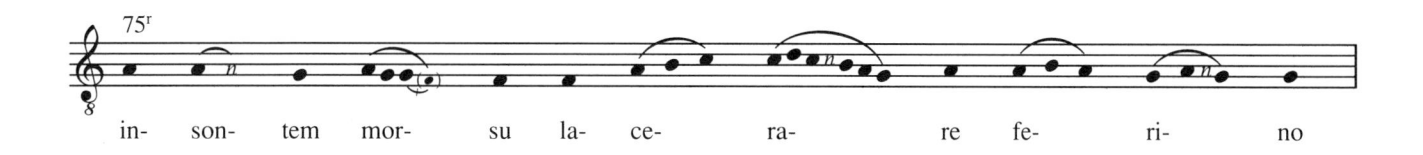

Rc 1741

[1] Sus- pen- sus lig- no pa- tri sic fi- li- us in- fit

D⟨o- mi⟩- ne [ne lon- ge fa- ci- as au- xi- li- um tu- um a me

[2] Sed ce- le- ri suc- cur- re mi- chi pi- e- ta- te pa- ter- na

Ad de- [fen- si- o- nem me- am as- pi- ce li- be- ra me

de- o re le- o- nis] [3] Qui cu- pit

in- son- tem mor- su la- ce- ra- re fe- ri- no

Et a cor- [ni- bus u- ni- cor- nu- o- rum]

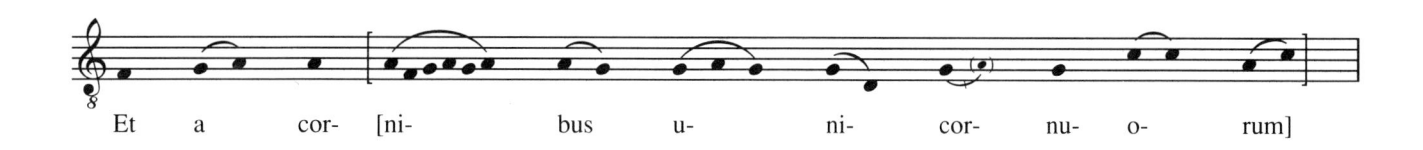

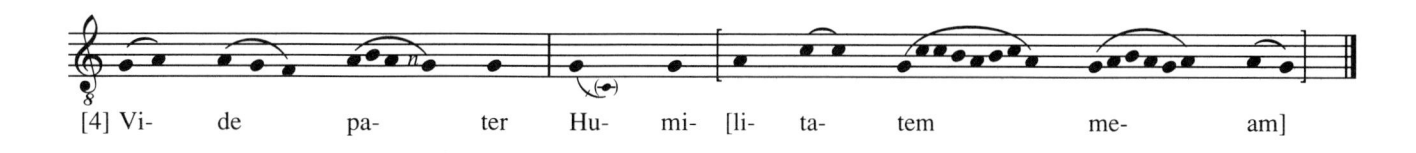

[4] Vi- de pa- ter Hu- mi- [li- ta- tem me- am]

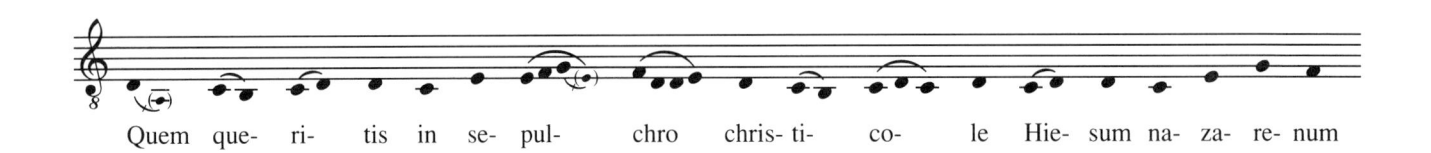

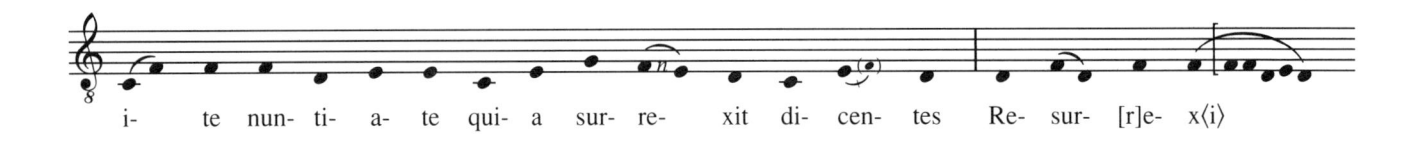

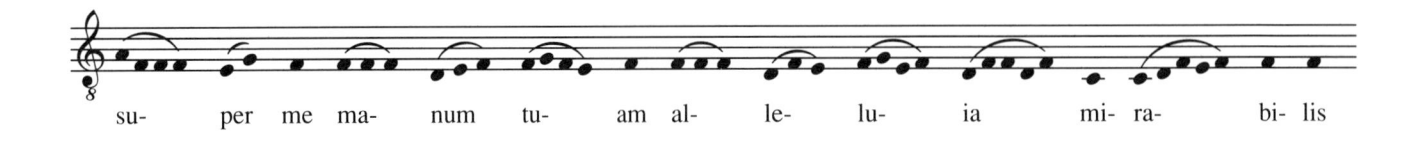

31. Introit: Resurrexi
Hora est surgite / Quem quaeritis

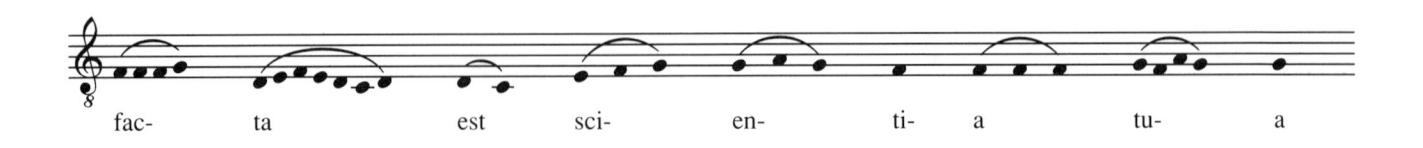

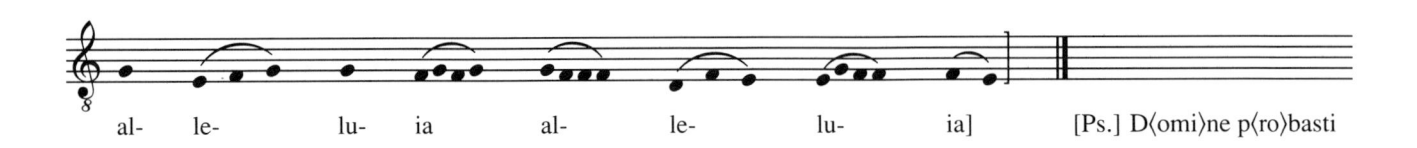

Rn 1343

Ho-ra est sur-gi- te iu- bet dom-nus ca- ne- re e- ia di- ci- te

Quem que- ri- tis in se- pul- chro chris-ti- co- le Hie-sum na- za- re- num

cru- ci- fi- xum o ce- li- co- le Non est hic sur- re- xit sic- ut pre- di- xe- rat

i- te nun- ti- a- te qui- a sur- re- xit di- cen- tes Re- sur- [r]e- x⟨i⟩

[et ad- huc te- cum sum al- le- lu- ia po- su- is- ti

su- per me ma- num tu- am al- le- lu- ia mi- ra- bi- lis

fac- ta est sci- en- ti- a tu- a

al- le- lu- ia al- le- lu- ia] [Ps.] D⟨omi⟩ne p⟨ro⟩basti

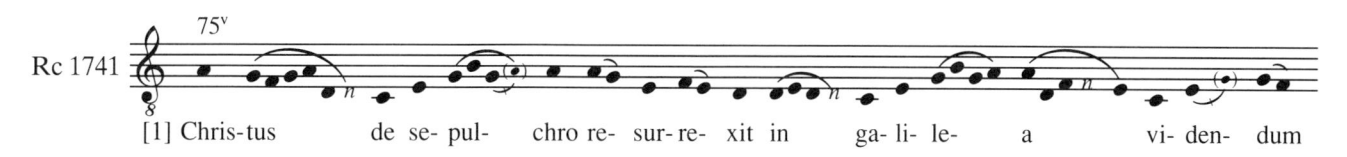

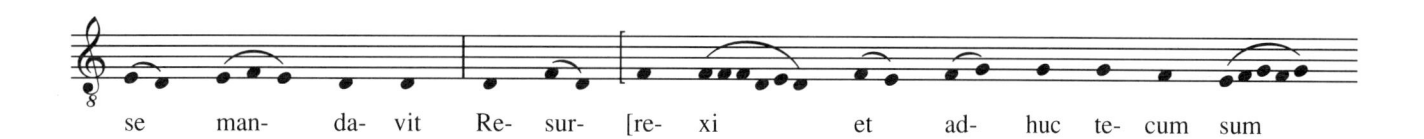

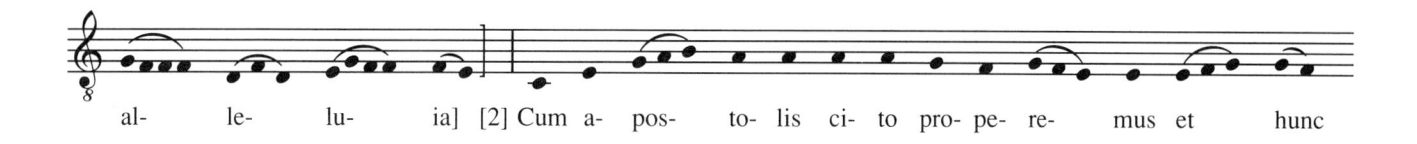

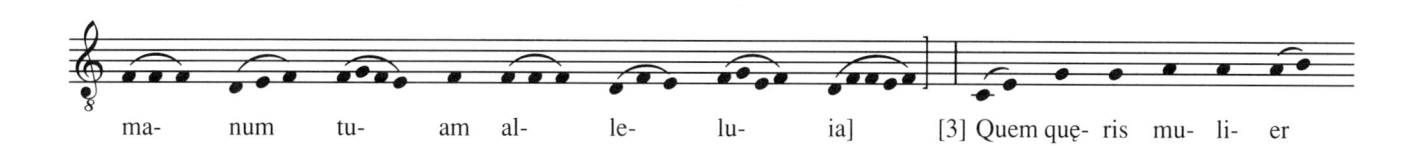

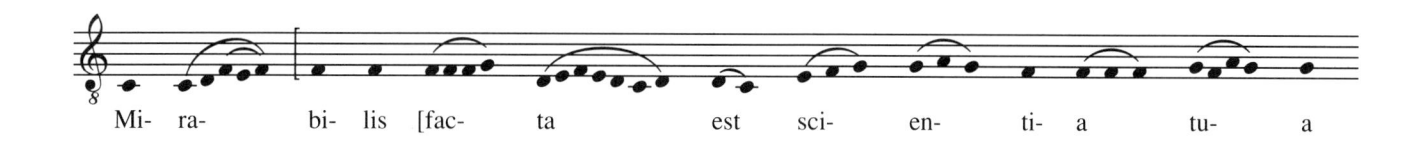

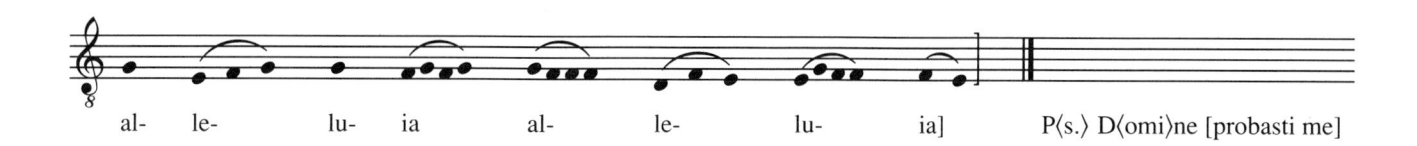

32. Introit: Resurrexi

Christus de sepulchro resurrexit

Rc 1741

[1] Christus de sepulchro resurrexit in galilea videndum se mandavit Resur[rexi et adhuc tecum sum alleluia] [2] Cum apostolis cito properemus et hunc resurgentem cum eis adoremus Posuisti [super me manum tuam alleluia] [3] Quem quęris mulier in monumento resumpto corpore iam vivit et est in galilea Mirabilis [facta est scientia tua alleluia alleluia] P⟨s.⟩ D⟨omi⟩ne [probasti me]

33. Introit: Resurrexi
Hodie resurrexit leo fortis

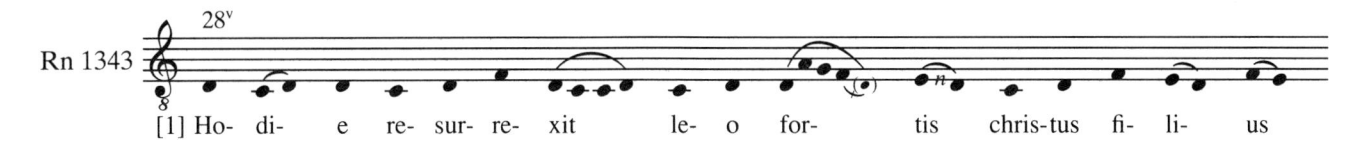

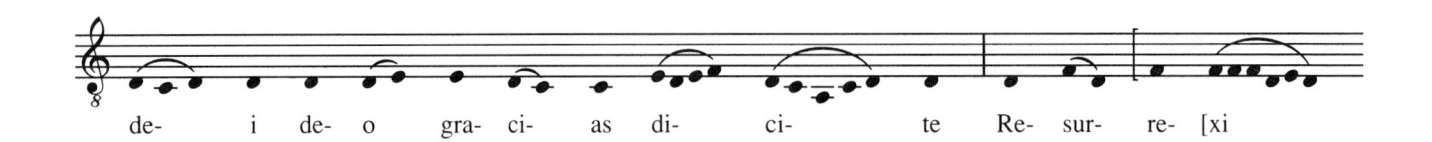

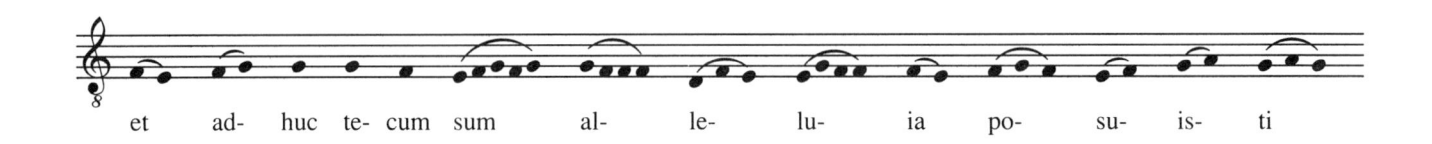

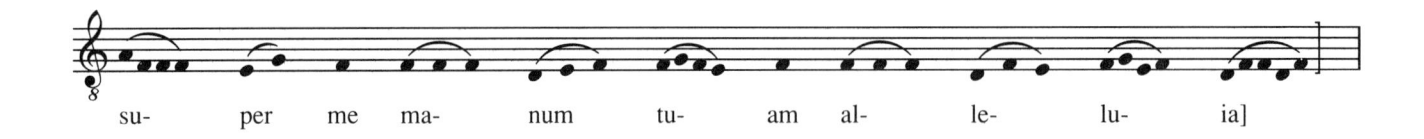

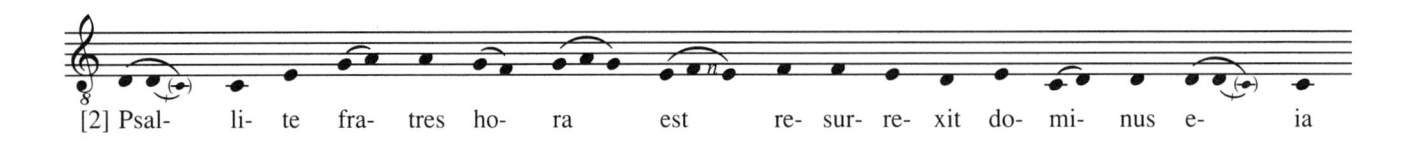

Rn 1343

[1] Ho- di- e re- sur- re- xit le- o for- tis chris-tus fi- li- us de- i de- o gra- ci- as di- ci- te Re- sur- re- [xi et ad- huc te- cum sum al- le- lu- ia po- su- is- ti su- per me ma- num tu- am al- le- lu- ia]

[2] Psal- li- te fra- tres ho- ra est re- sur- re- xit do- mi- nus e- ia et e- ia Mi- ra- bi- lis [fac- ta est sci- en- ti- a tu- a al- le- lu- ia al- le- lu- ia]

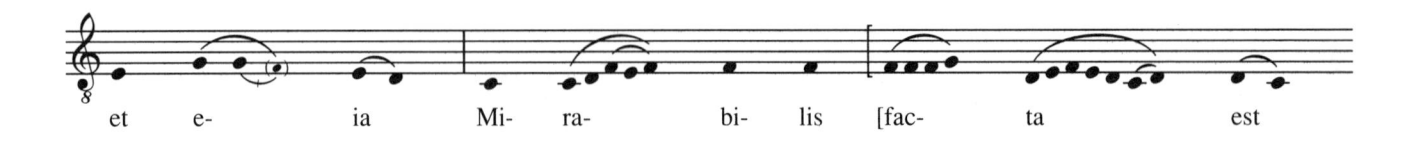

34. Offertory: Terra tremuit
Ab increpatione et ira

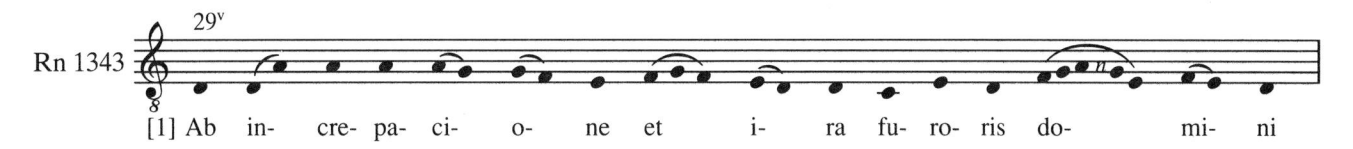

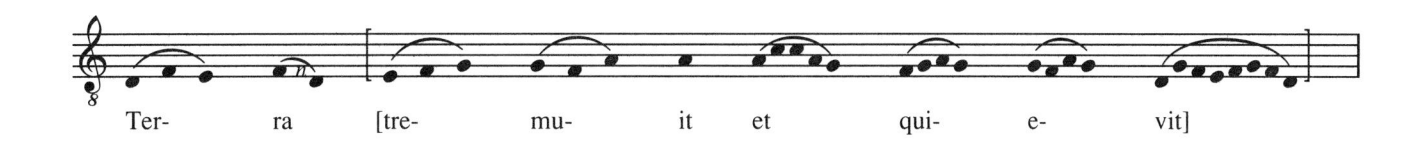

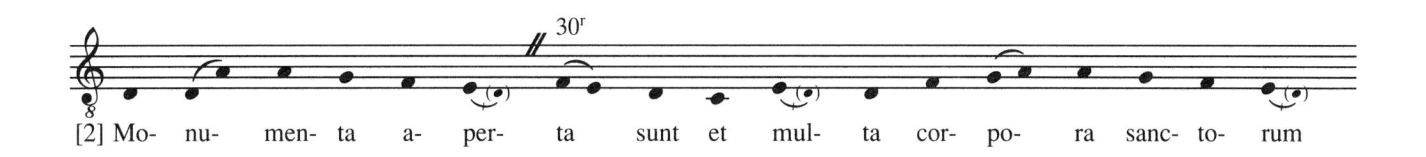

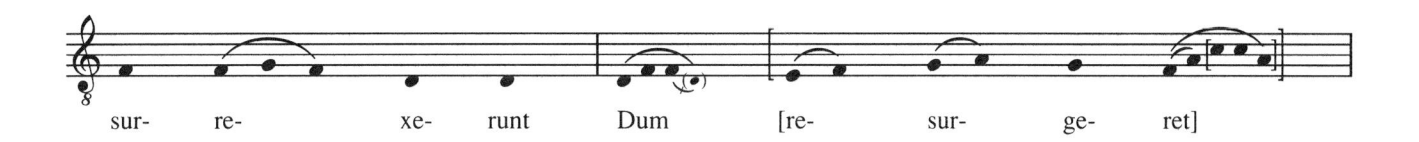

Rn 1343

[1] Ab in- cre- pa- ci- o- ne et i- ra fu- ro- ris do- mi- ni

Ter- ra [tre- mu- it et qui- e- vit]

[2] Mo- nu- men- ta a- per- ta sunt et mul- ta cor- po- ra sanc- to- rum

sur- re- xe- runt Dum [re- sur- ge- ret]

[3] Chris- tus iu- di- ca- tu- rus est vi- vos et mor- tu- os quan- do ve- ne- rit

In iu- di- c⟨i- o⟩ [de- us] [4] Chris- tus sur- re- xit a

mor- tu- is ve- ni- te a- do- re- mus e- um om- nes u- na vo- ce pro- cla- man- tes

Al- le- lu- [ia]

35. Communion: Pascha nostrum
Laus honor virtus

Rn 1343

[1] Laus ho- nor vir- tus de- o nos- tro de- cus et im- pe- ri- um

re- gi nos- tro qui pre- ci- o re- demp- ti- o- nis nos- træ

Pas- cha [nos- trum im- mo- la- tus est]

[2] Pec- ca- ta nos- tra ip- se por- ta- vit et prop- ter sce- le- ra

nos- tra ob- la- tus est Chris- tus [al- le- lu- ia]

[3] Le- o for- tis de tri- bu iu- da ho- di- e sur- re- xit a mor- tu- is

al- le- lu- ia I- ta- que [e- pu- le- mur

in a- zy- mis sin- ce- ri- ta- tis et ve- ri- ta- tis]

[4] In cu- ius lau- de cel- sa vo- ce per- to- na- te

Al- le- [lu- ia al- le- lu- ia al- le- lu- ia]

36. Introit: Gaudeamus . . . Senesii
Cuncti fideles Christi

[1] Cuncti fideles christi venite ad hanc sollem(m)pnitatem beatorum martyrum Senesii et theopontii de qua in cælis gaudent angeli et nos in terris Gaudea-[mus omnes in domino]

[2] Agentes gracias illi qui triumphat in sanctis suis atque Diem [festum celebrantes]

[3] Debitis laudibus venerantes Sub ho-[nore sanctorum Senesii et Theopontii]

[4] Quo ethereapecierunt regna De quorum [solemnitate gaudent angeli]

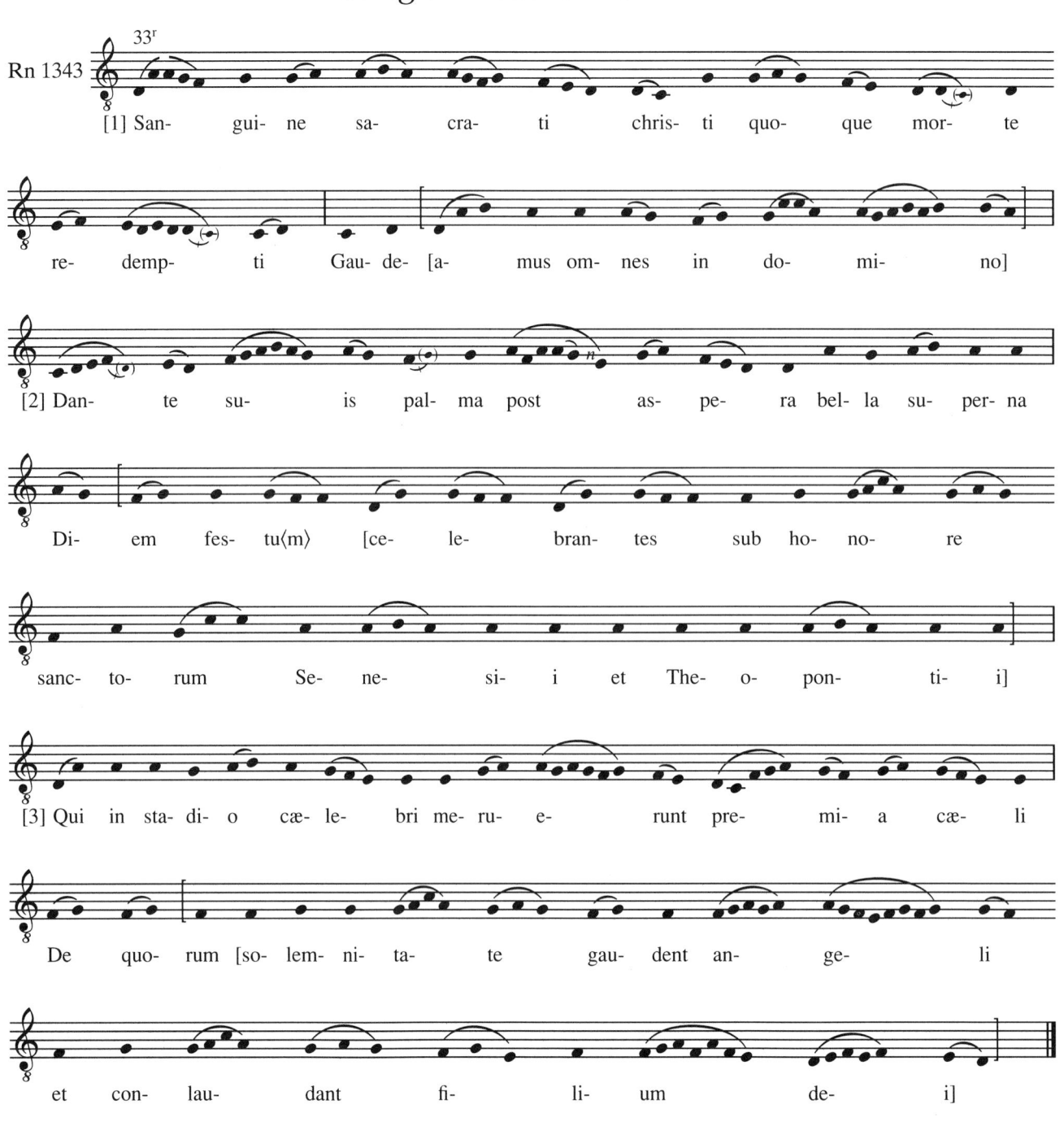

[5] Con- sor- tes su- o- rum ef- fec- tos at- que so- ci- os
Et con- lau- d[ant fi- li- um de- i] Gaudeamus

37a. Introit: Gaudeamus . . . Senesii
Sanguine sacrati Christi

Rn 1343

[1] San- gui- ne sa- cra- ti chris- ti quo- que mor- te re- demp- ti Gau- de- [a- mus om- nes in do- mi- no]

[2] Dan- te su- is pal- ma post as- pe- ra bel- la su- per- na Di- em fes- tu⟨m⟩ [ce- le- bran- tes sub ho- no- re sanc- to- rum Se- ne- si- i et The- o- pon- ti- i]

[3] Qui in sta- di- o cæ- le- bri me- ru- e- runt pre- mi- a cæ- li De quo- rum [so- lem- ni- ta- te gau- dent an- ge- li et con- lau- dant fi- li- um de- i]

37b. Introit: Gaudeamus . . . sanctorum omnium
Sanguine sacrati Christi

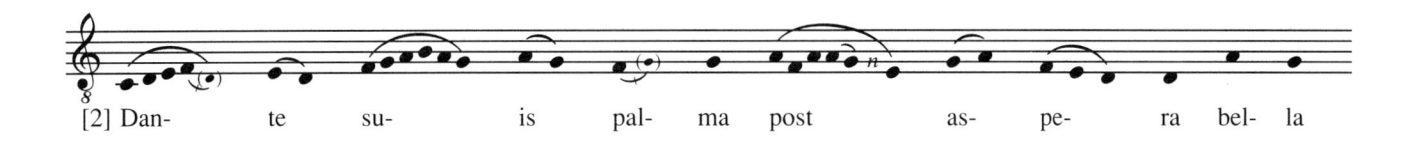

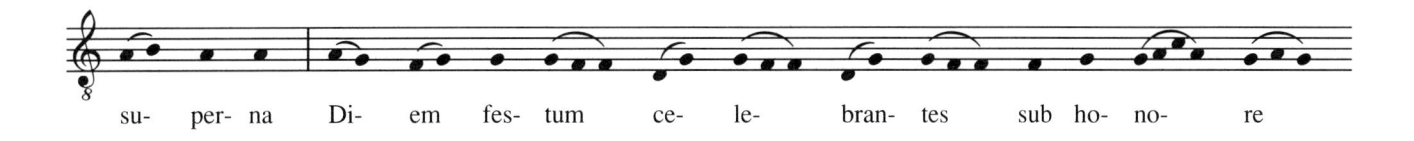

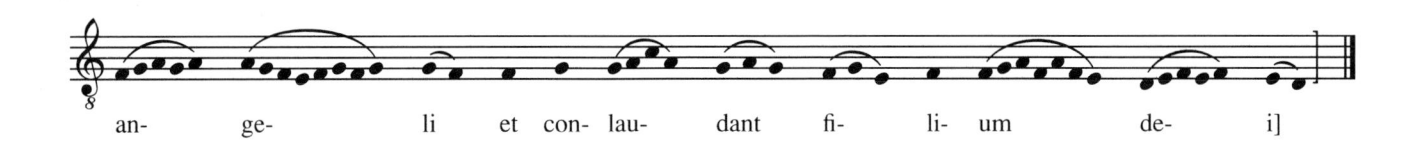

Rn 1343

[1] San- gui- ne sa- cra- ti [chris- ti quo- que mor- te re- demp- ti Gau- de- a- mus omnes in do- mi- no

[2] Dan- te su- is pal- ma post as- pe- ra bel- la su- per- na Di- em fes- tum ce- le- bran- tes sub ho- no- re sanc- to- rum om- ni- um [3] Qui in sta- di- o cae- le- bri me- ru- e- runt pre- mi- a cae- li De quo- rum so- lem- ni- ta- te gau- dent an- ge- li et con- lau- dant fi- li- um de- i]

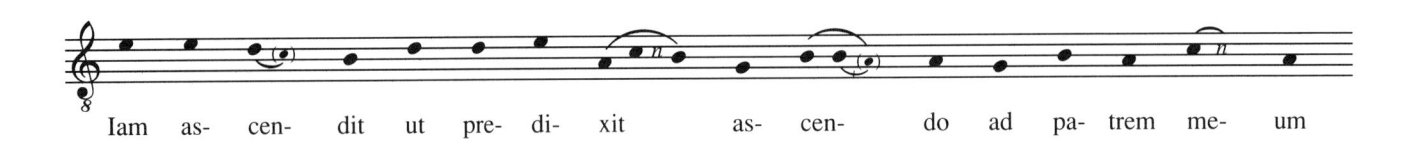

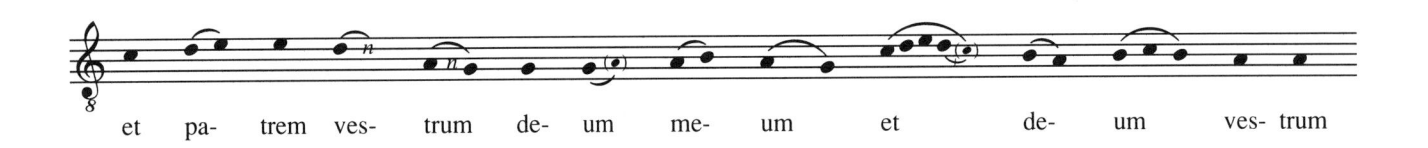

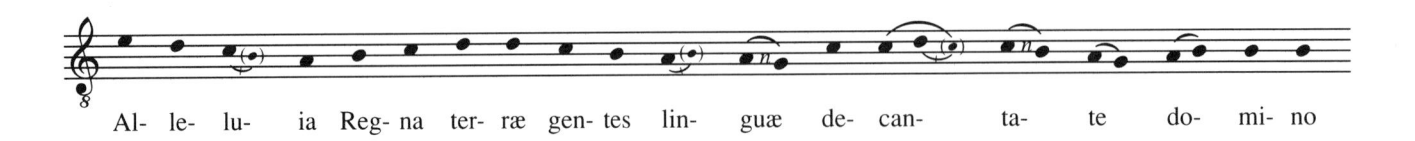

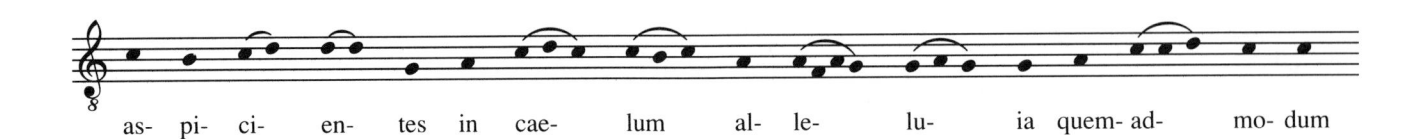

38. Introit: Viri Galilaei
Quem creditis super astra

Rn 1343

Quem cre- di- tis su- per as- tra as- cen- dis- se o de- i- co- le

Chris- tum qui sur- re- xit de se- pul- chro o cæ- li- co- le

Iam as- cen- dit ut pre- di- xit as- cen- do ad pa- trem me- um

et pa- trem ves- trum de- um me- um et de- um ves- trum

Al- le- lu- ia Reg- na ter- ræ gen- tes lin- guæ de- can- ta- te do- mi- no

quem a- do- rant cæ- li ci- ves in pa- ter- no so- li- o

Vi- ri ga- li- le- i [quid ad- mi- ra- mi- ni

as- pi- ci- en- tes in cae- lum al- le- lu- ia quem- ad- mo- dum vi- dis- tis e- um as- cen- den- tem in cae- lum i- ta ve- ni- et

al- le- lu- ia al- le- lu- ia al- le- lu- ia]

39. Introit: Viri Galilaei
Hodie redemptor mundi ascendit

Rn 1343

[1] Ho- di- e re-demp-tor mun- di as- cen- dit cæ- los mi- ran- tur a- pos- to- li

an- ge- li- que e- i lo- cu- ti sunt di- cen- tes Vi- ri ga- [li- lae- i quid

ad- mi- ra- mi- ni as- pi- ci- en- tes in cae- lum al- le- lu- ia]

[2] Quem e- un- tem an- ge- li- ci gra- tu- lan- tes or- di- nes in- tu- en- ti- bus

hinc cla- ma[n]t a- pos- to- li[s] Quem- ad- [mo- dum vi- dis- tis

e- um as- cen- den- tem in cae- lum i- ta ve- ni- et

al- le- lu- ia al- le- lu- ia al- le- lu- ia]

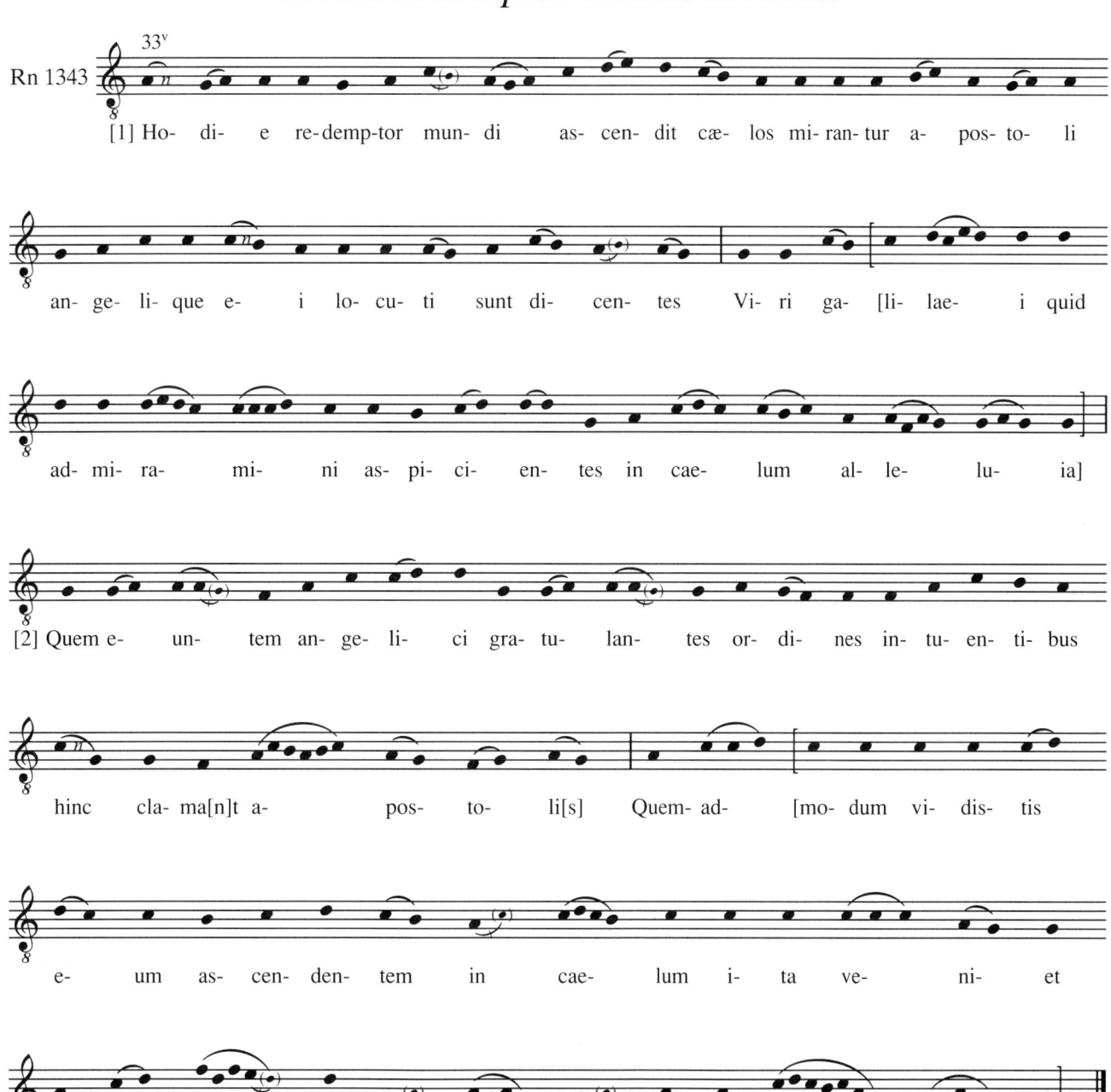

40. Introit: Viri Galilaei
Terrigenas summos affatur

Rc 1741

[1] Ter- ri- ge- nas sum- mos af- fa- tur ce- li- cus or- do

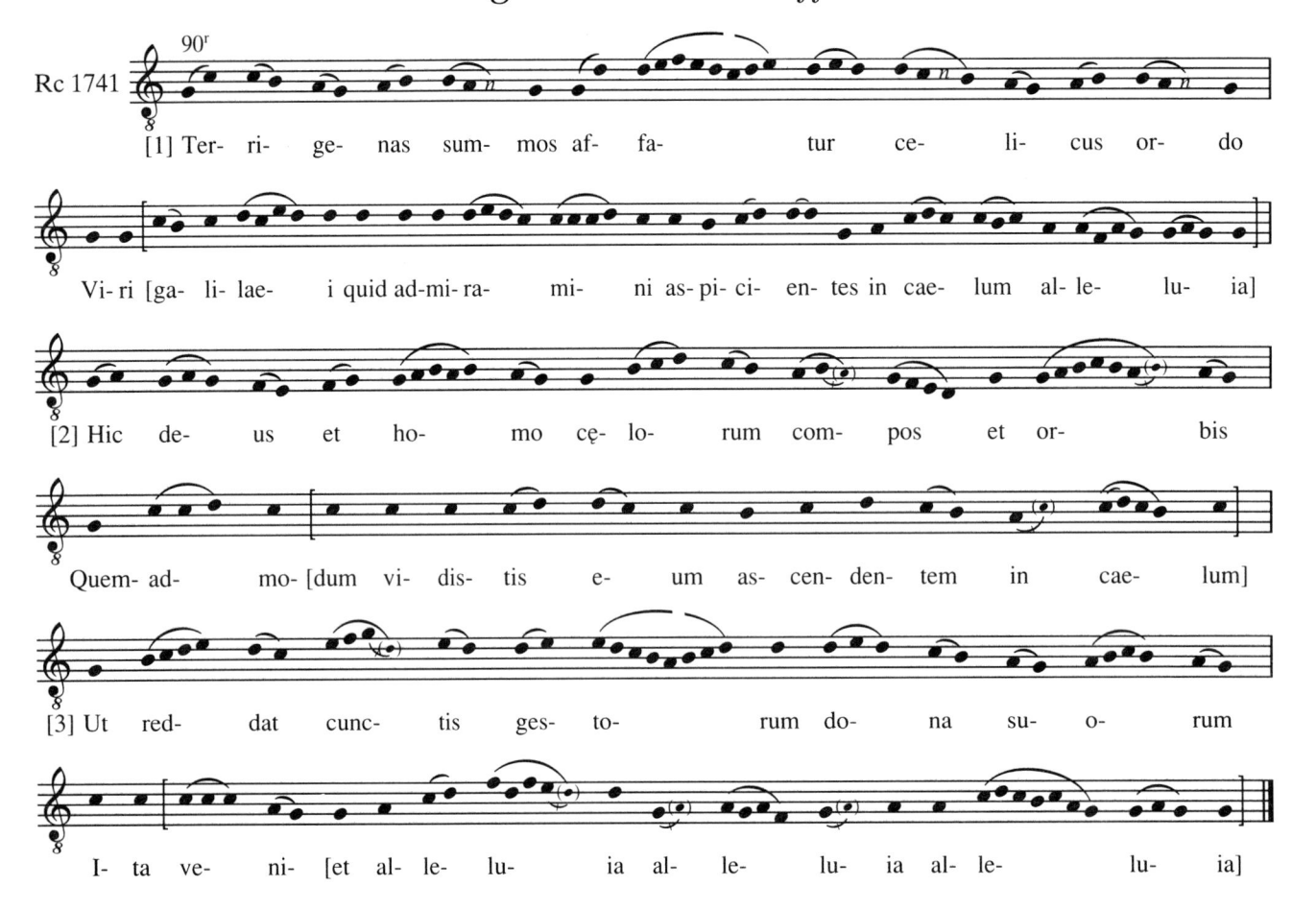

Vi- ri [ga- li- lae- i quid ad-mi-ra- mi- ni as- pi- ci- en- tes in cae- lum al- le- lu- ia]

[2] Hic de- us et ho- mo cę- lo- rum com- pos et or- bis

Quem- ad- mo- [dum vi- dis- tis e- um as- cen- den- tem in cae- lum]

[3] Ut red- dat cunc- tis ges- to- rum do- na su- o- rum

I- ta ve- ni- [et al- le- lu- ia al- le- lu- ia al- le- lu- ia]

41. Introit: Viri Galilaei
Hodie rex gloriae Christus

Bu 2824

[1] Ho- di- e rex glo- ri- e chris-tus cæ-lum pa-ten-ter scan-dens pa- te- fe- cit in- gres-sum

Vi- ri ga- [li- lae- i quid ad- mi- ra- mi- ni as- pi- ci- en- tes in cae- lum

al- le- lu- ia] [2] Quem e- un- tes an- ge- li- ci gra-tu- lan- tes

or- di- nes in- tu- en- ti- bus hinc cla- mant a- pos- to- li

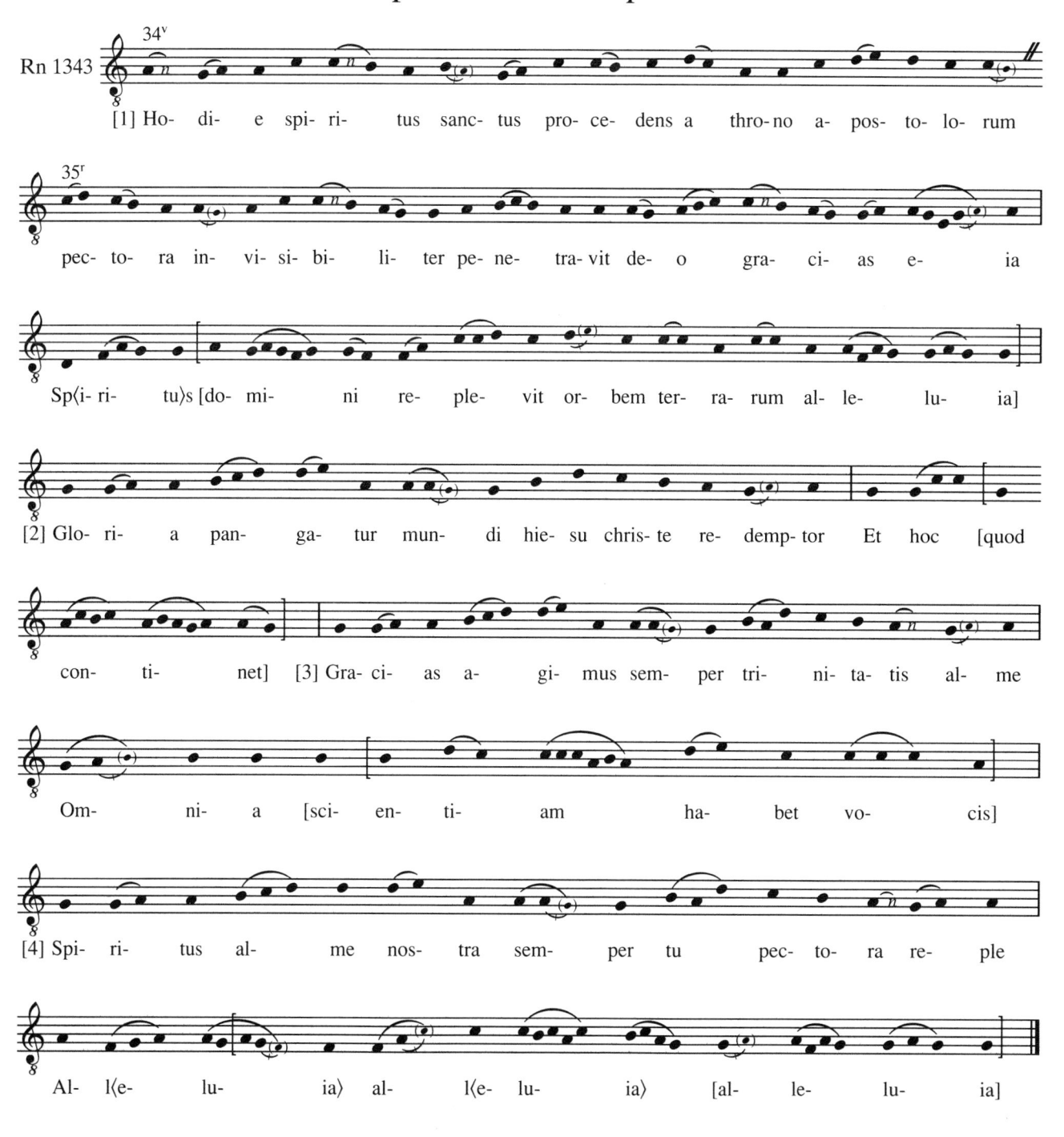

Quem-ad- [mo- dum vi- dis- tis e- um as- cen- den- tem in cae- lum i- ta ve- ni- et al- le- lu- ia al- le- lu- ia al- le- lu- ia]

42. Introit: Spiritus domini
Hodie spiritus sanctus procedens

Rn 1343

[1] Ho- di- e spi- ri- tus sanc- tus pro- ce- dens a thro- no a- pos- to- lo- rum pec- to- ra in- vi- si- bi- li- ter pe- ne- tra- vit de- o gra- ci- as e- ia Sp⟨i- ri- tu⟩s [do- mi- ni re- ple- vit or- bem ter- ra- rum al- le- lu- ia]

[2] Glo- ri- a pan- ga- tur mun- di hie- su chris- te re- demp- tor Et hoc [quod con- ti- net] [3] Gra- ci- as a- gi- mus sem- per tri- ni- ta- tis al- me Om- ni- a [sci- en- ti- am ha- bet vo- cis]

[4] Spi- ri- tus al- me nos- tra sem- per tu pec- to- ra re- ple Al- l⟨e- lu- ia⟩ al- l⟨e- lu- ia⟩ [al- le- lu- ia]

43. Introit: Spiritus domini
Hodie spiritus sanctus processit

Rn 1343

Ho- di- e spi- ri- tus sanc- tus pro- ces- sit a thro- no et
re- ple- vit to- tum mun- dum de- o gra- ci- as di- ci- te
pa- ri- ter Spi- ri- tus [do- mi- ni re- ple- vit or- bem ter- ra- rum
al- le- lu- ia et hoc quod con- ti- net om- ni- a
sci- en- ti- am ha- bet vo- cis al- le- lu- ia
al- le- lu- ia al- le- lu- ia]

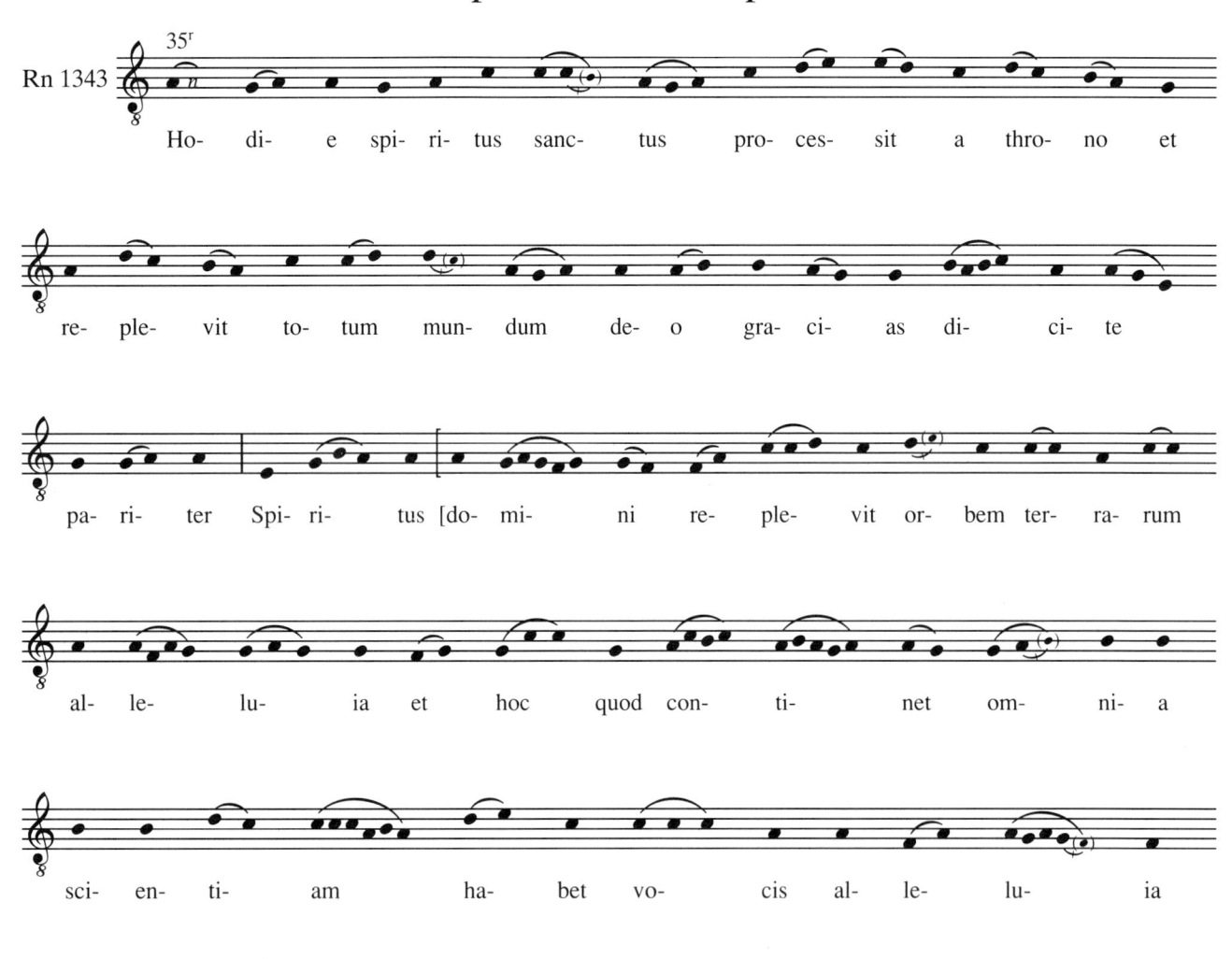

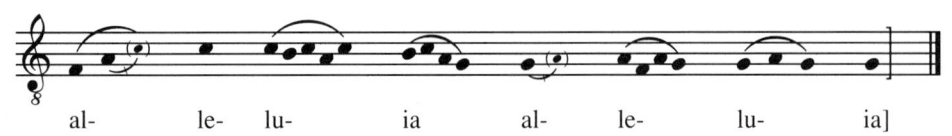

44. Introit: Spiritus domini
Cum essent apostoli

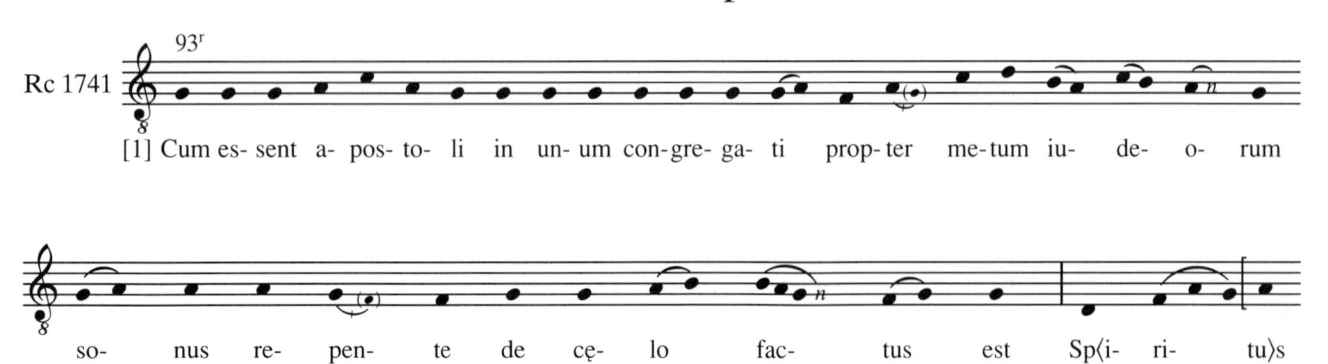

Rc 1741

[1] Cum es- sent a- pos- to- li in un- um con- gre- ga- ti prop- ter me- tum iu- de- o- rum
so- nus re- pen- te de cę- lo fac- tus est Sp⟨i- ri- tu⟩s

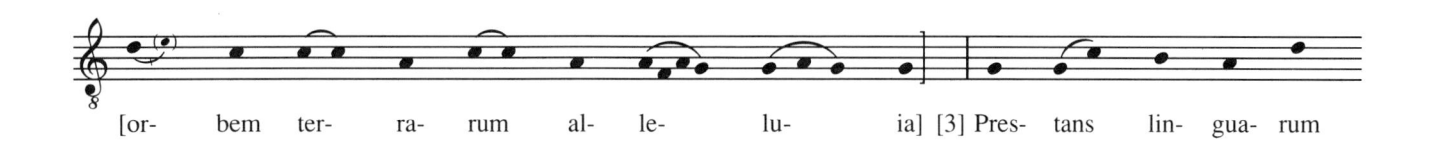

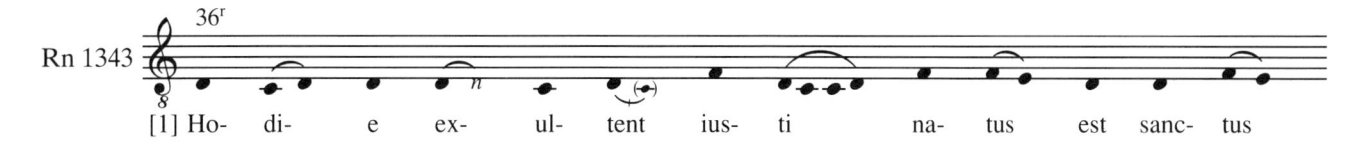

[do-mi-ni] [2] De-us im-men-sus et ex-cel-sus Re-ple-vit [or-bem ter-ra-rum al-le-lu-ia] [3] Pres-tans lin-gua-rum pe-ri-ti-am Et hoc [quod con-ti-net om-ni-a] [4] Ter-res-tri-a at-que su-per-na Sci-en-ti-a[m ha-bet vo-cis al-le-lu-ia al-le-lu-ia al-le-lu-ia]

45. Introit: De ventre matris meae
Hodie exultent iusti . . . Iohannes

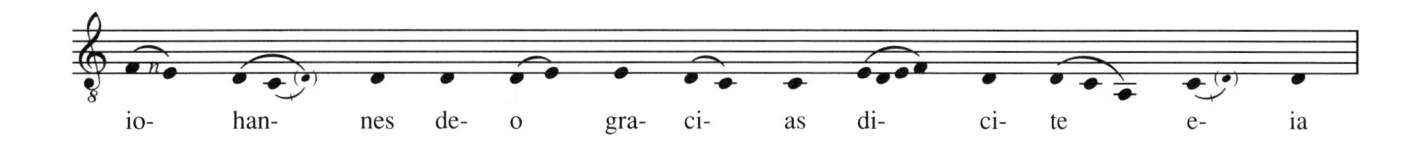

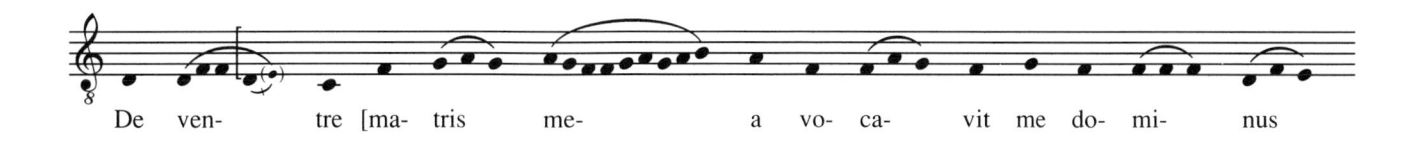

Rn 1343

[1] Ho-di-e ex-ul-tent ius-ti na-tus est sanc-tus io-han-nes de-o gra-ci-as di-ci-te e-ia De ven-tre [ma-tris me-a vo-ca-vit me do-mi-nus

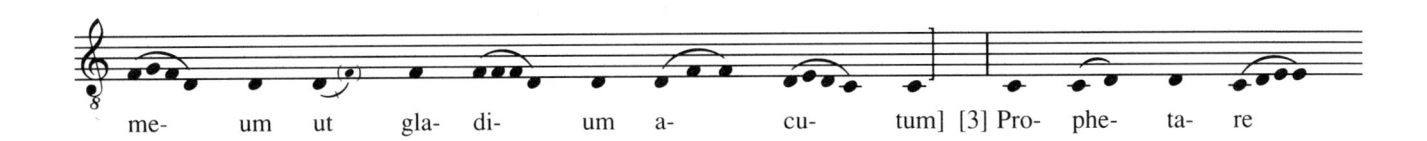

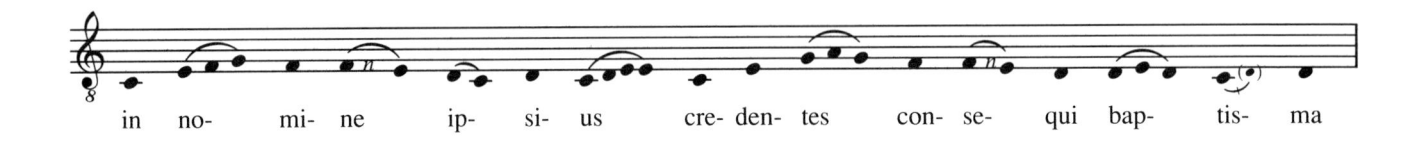

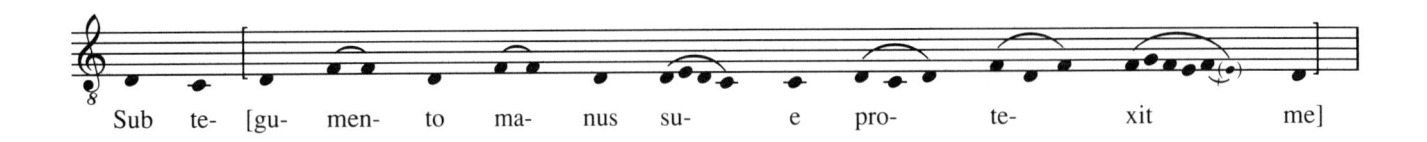

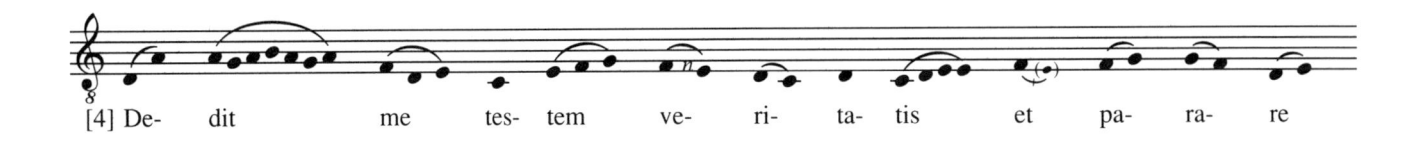

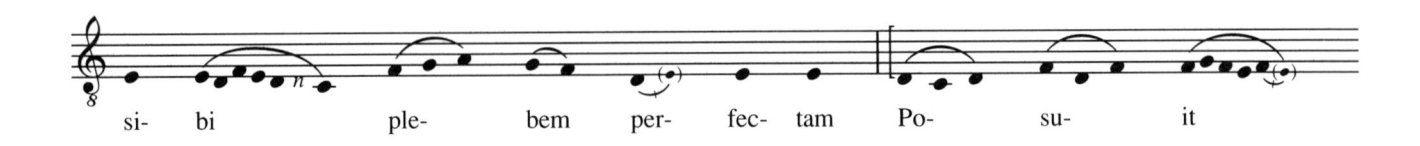

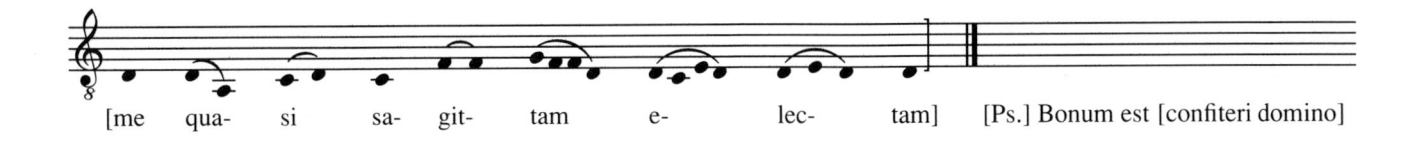

no- mi- ne me- o] [2] Ser- vum si- bi io- han- ne

me vo- cans za- cha- ri- e fi- li- um Et po- su- it [os

me- um ut gla- di- um a- cu- tum] [3] Pro- phe- ta- re

in no- mi- ne ip- si- us cre- den- tes con- se- qui bap- tis- ma

Sub te- [gu- men- to ma- nus su- e pro- te- xit me]

[4] De- dit me tes- tem ve- ri- ta- tis et pa- ra- re

si- bi ple- bem per- fec- tam Po- su- it

[me qua- si sa- git- tam e- lec- tam] [Ps.] Bonum est [confiteri domino]

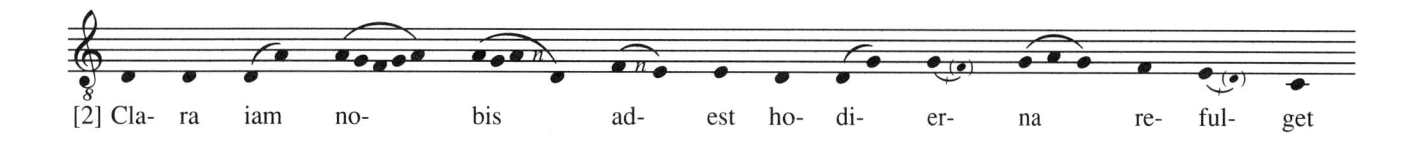

46. Introit: De ventre matris meae
Deus pater clamat Iohannem

Rn 1343

[1] Deus pater clamat iohannem in ventre matris de quo gratulantes dicamus cum propheta De ventre [matris mea vocavit me dominus nomine meo et posuit os meum ut gladium acutum]

[2] Clara iam nobis adest hodierna refulget iohannis nativitas dicentis Sub tegu-[mento manus sue protexit me posuit me quasi sagittam electam] Gl⟨ori⟩a patri

47. Introit: De ventre matris meae
Audite insulae

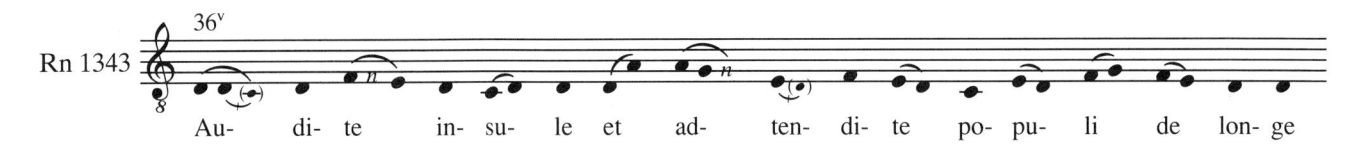

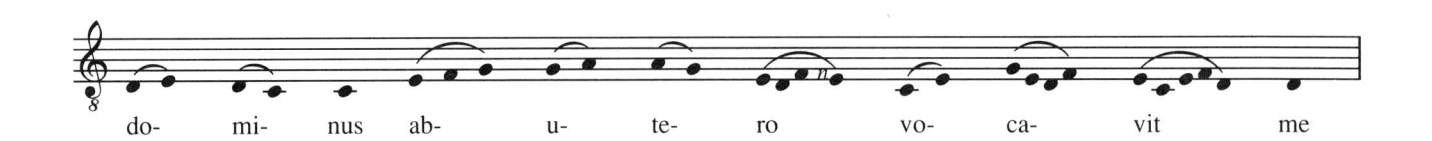

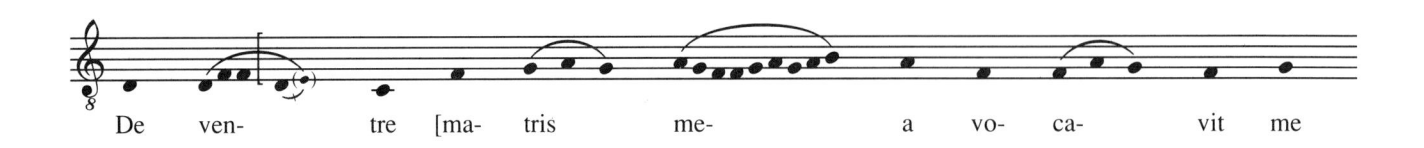

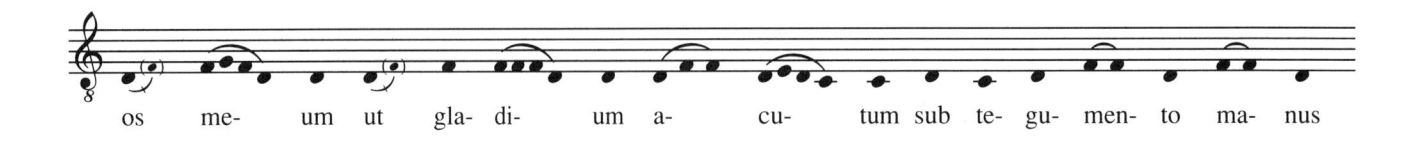

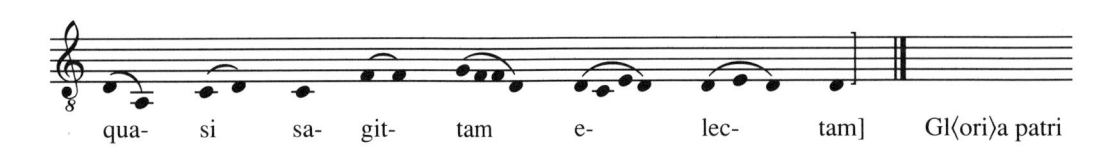

Rn 1343

Au- di- te in- su- le et at- ten- di- te po- pu- li de lon- ge

do- mi- nus ab u- te- ro vo- ca- vit me

De ven- tre [ma- tris me- a vo- ca- vit me

do- mi- nus no- mi- ne me- o et po- su- it

os me- um ut gla- di- um a- cu- tum sub te- gu- men- to ma- nus

su- e pro- te- xit me po- su- it me

qua- si sa- git- tam e- lec- tam] Gl⟨ori⟩a patri

48. Introit: Nunc scio vere
Beatissimus Petrus catenis

Rn 1343

[1] Be- a- tis- si- mus pe- trus ca- te- nis in car- ce- re

vinc- tus cum fu- is- set ab an- ge- lo po- ten- ter so- lu- tus

et de ma- nu he- ro- dis li- be- ra- tus a- it

Nunc sci- o [ve- re qui- a mi- sit do- mi- nus an- ge- lum su- um]

[2] De- us ex- er- ci- tu- um et mi- li- ci- a- rum rex

Et e- ri- pu- [it me de ma- nu he- ro- dis]

[3] O ad- mi- ra- bi- les cle- men- ci- æ ple- ne sunt in pe- tro

de quo gra- tu- lan- tes di- ca- mus cum il- lo Et de om- ⟨n⟩i

[ex- spec- ta- ti- o- ne ple- bis iu- de- o- rum]

49. Introit: Nunc scio vere
Hodie sanctissimi patroni nostri Petri

Rn 1343

Ho- di- e sanc- tis- si- mi pa- tro- ni nos- tri pe- tri a- ni- ma

cho- ris su- per- nis iunc- ta iu- bi- lat qua- prop- ter et nos

ex- ul- te- mus ca- nen- tes Nunc sci- o [ve- re qui- a

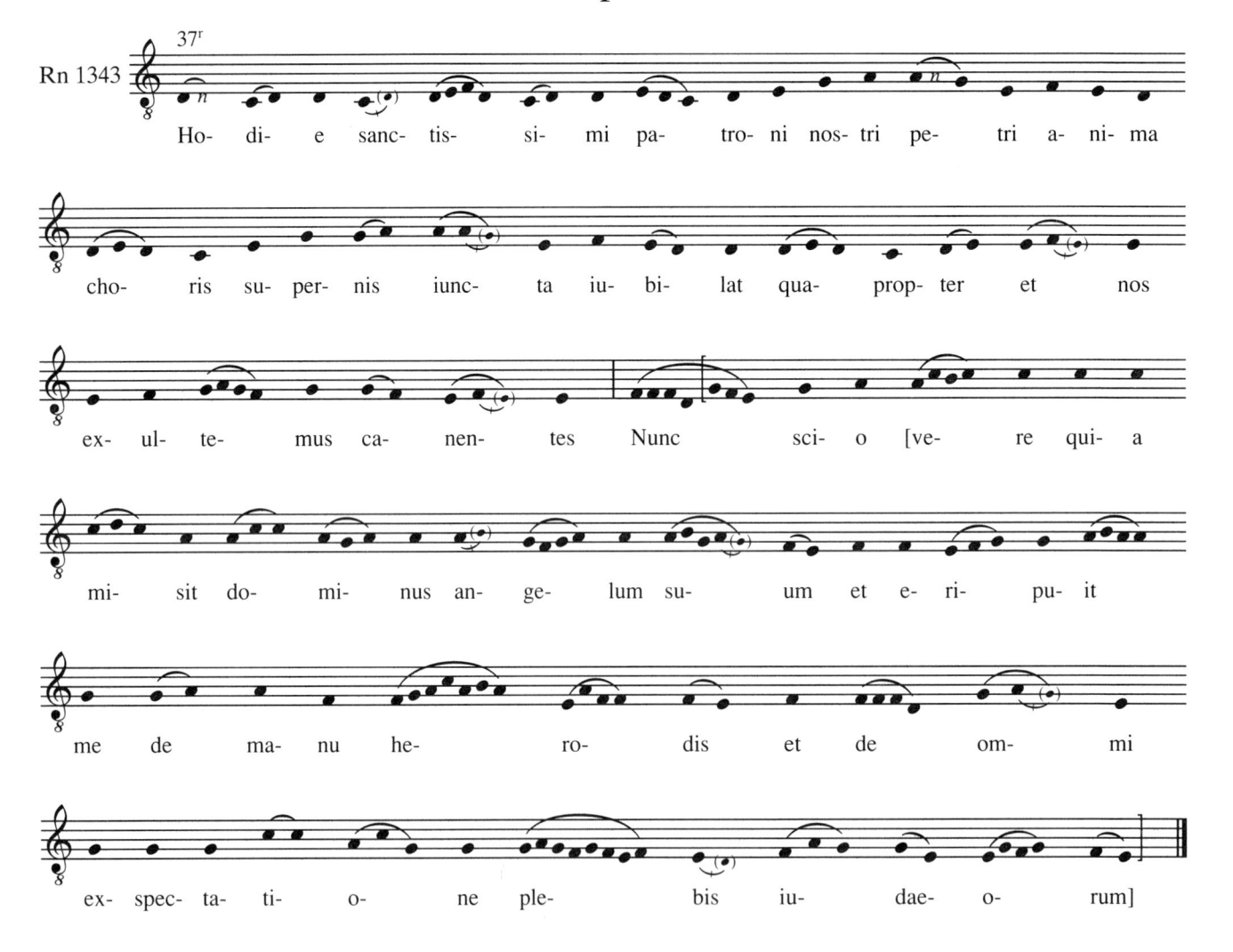

mi- sit do- mi- nus an- ge- lum su- um et e- ri- pu- it

me de ma- nu he- ro- dis et de om- mi

ex- spec- ta- ti- o- ne ple- bis iu- dae- o- rum]

50. Introit: Nunc scio vere
Divina beatus Petrus

Rn 1343

[1] Di- vi- na be- a- tus pe- trus e- rec- tus cle- men- ci- a in se

re- di- ens dic- it Nunc sci- o [ve- re qui- a mi- sit

do- mi- nus an- ge- lum su- um] [2] Lux ius- ti- ci- æ in te- ne- bris me il- lu- mi- na- vit et de car- ce- re e- du- xit Et e- ri- pu- it [me de

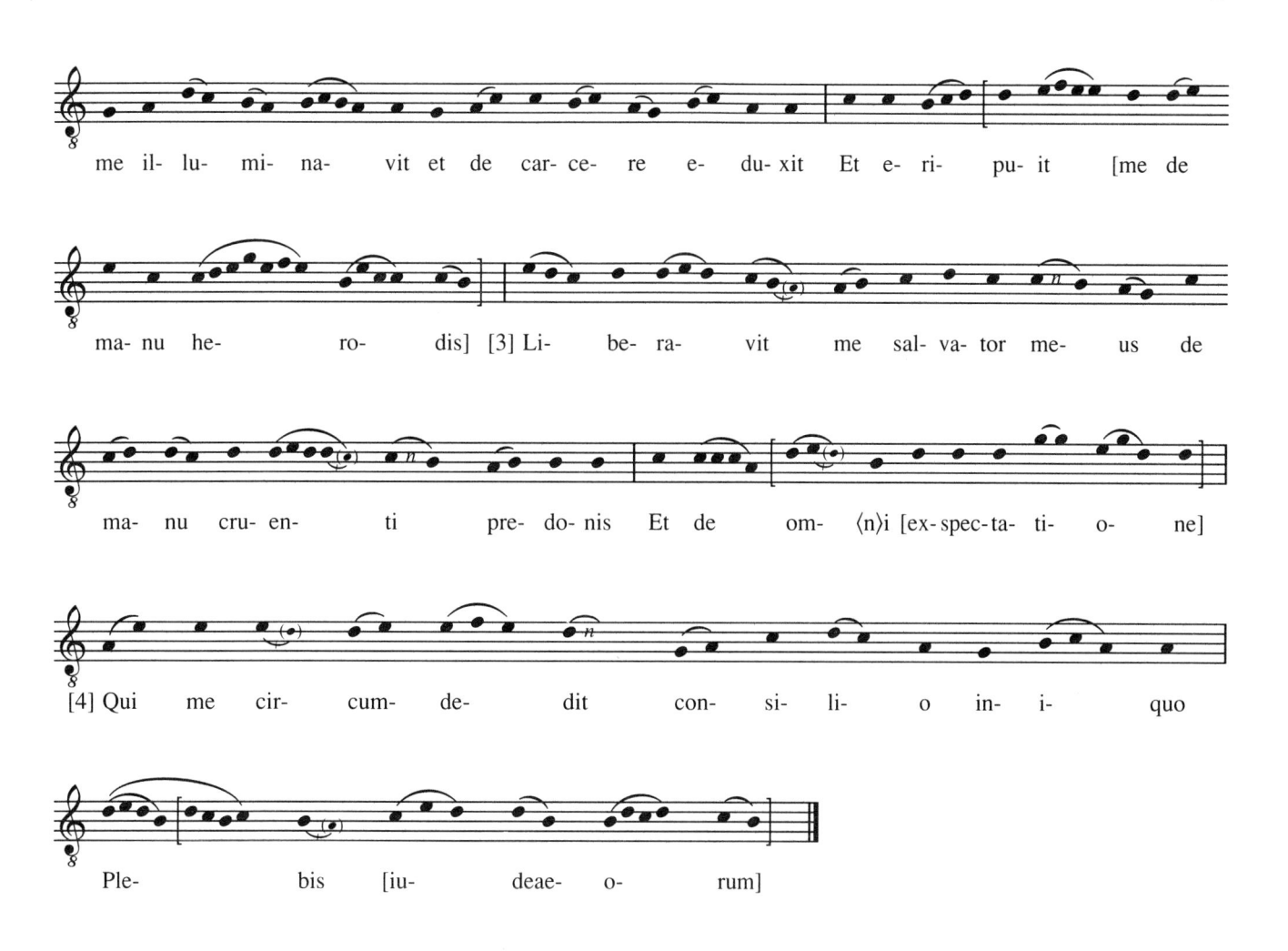

ma- nu he- ro- dis] [3] Li- be- ra- vit me sal- va- tor me- us de

ma- nu cru- en- ti pre- do- nis Et de om- ⟨n⟩i [ex- spec- ta- ti- o- ne]

[4] Qui me cir- cum- de- dit con- si- li- o in- i- quo

Ple- bis [iu- deae- o- rum]

51. Introit: Os iusti
A domino impletum

Rn 1343

[1] A do- mi- no im- ple- tum sa- cro quo- que dog- ma- te ple- no

Os ius- ti [me- di- ta- bi- tur sa- pi- en- ti- am]

[2] Per- so- nas om- nes e- quo dis- cri- mi- ne pen- dens

Et lin- gua [e- ius lo- que- tur iu- di- ci- um]

[3] Ut iugiter tra[c]tet quæ sunt moderamina vitæ

Lex d⟨e⟩i [eius in corde ipsius] [4] Unde et psalmis-

-te versus sapienter adimplens obsequitur regi

tali nos voce monendo [Ps.] Noli emu[lari in malignantibus]

52. Introit: Os iusti
In iubilo vocis

Rc 1741 103ʳ

[1] In iubilo vocis benedicto psallite patri

Os iusti [meditabitur sapientiam]

[2] Namque sophia struit sedem sibi pectore iusti

Et lingua [eius loquetur iudicium]

[3] Neumate docti logo cordis rigante secreta

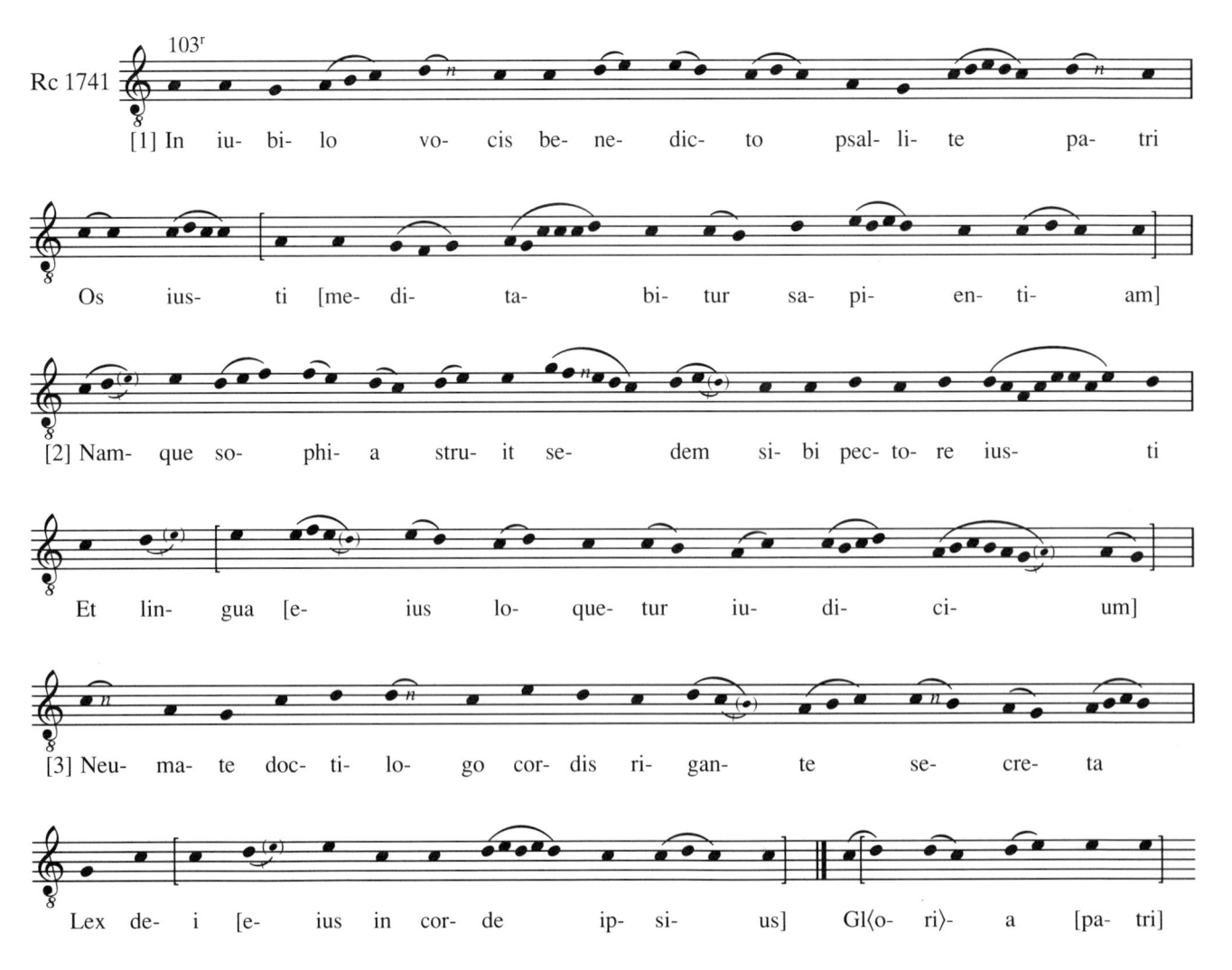

Lex dei [eius in corde ipsius] Gl⟨ori⟩a [patri]

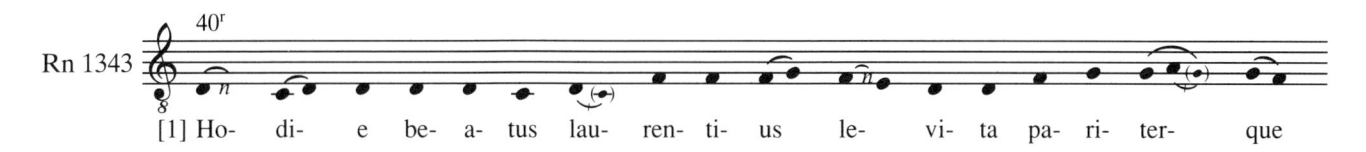

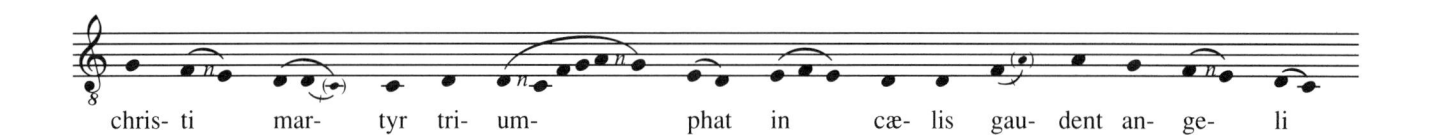

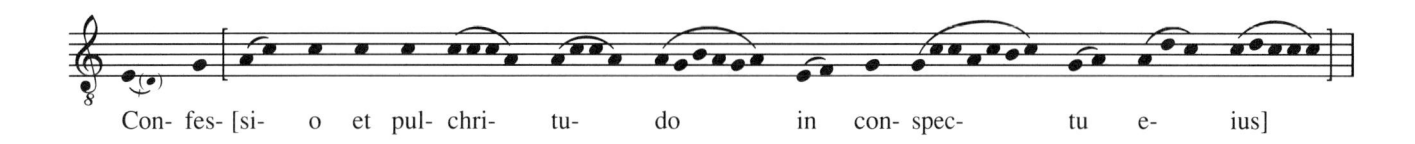

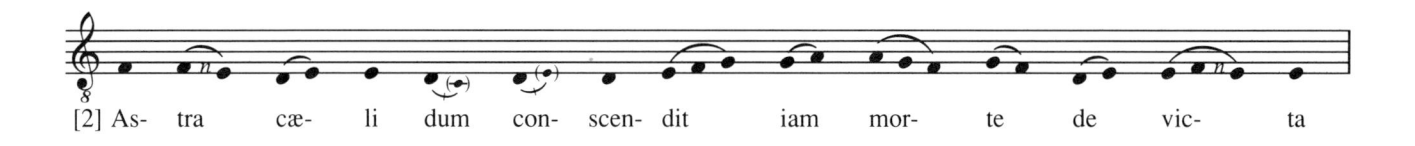

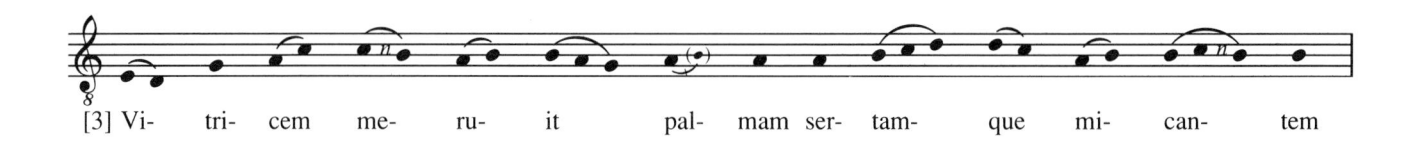

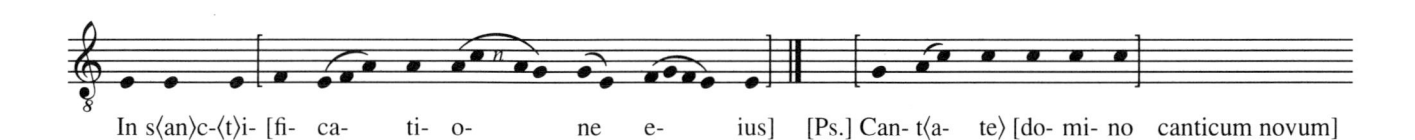

53. Introit: Confessio
Hodie beatus Laurentius levita

[1] Ho- di- e be- a- tus lau- ren- ti- us le- vi- ta pa- ri- ter- que chris- ti mar- tyr tri- um- phat in cæ- lis gau- dent an- ge- li et arch- an- ge- li et nos in ter- ris lau- des de- o ca- na- mus e- ia Con- fes- [si- o et pul- chri- tu- do in con- spec- tu e- ius]

[2] As- tra cæ- li dum con- scen- dit iam mor- te de vic- ta Sanc- ti- [tas et mag- ni- fi- cen- ti- a]

[3] Vi- tri- cem me- ru- it pal- mam ser- tam- que mi- can- tem In s⟨an⟩c-⟨t⟩i- [fi- ca- ti- o- ne e- ius] [Ps.] Can- t⟨a- te⟩ [do- mi- no canticum novum]

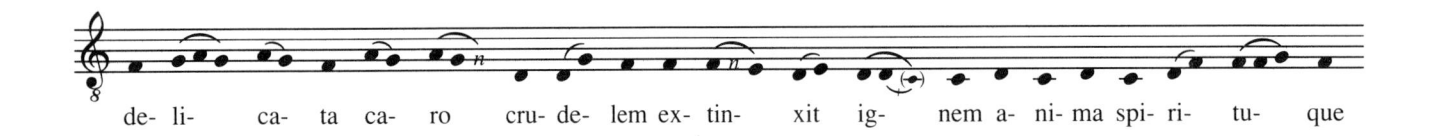

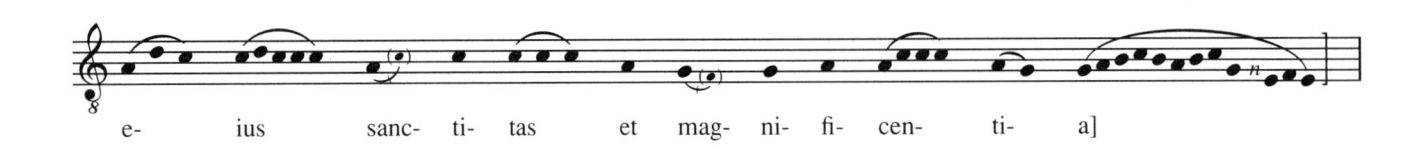

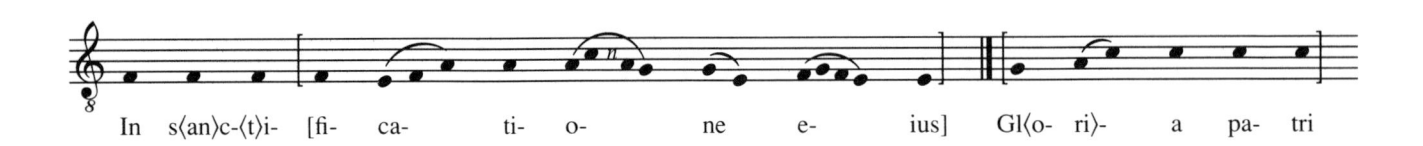

54. Introit: Confessio
Prunas extensa

Rn 1343

[1] Pru- nas ex- ten- sa su- per cra- ti- cu- lam men- bra vi- ven- ci- a de- li- ca- ta ca- ro cru- de- lem ex- tin- xit ig- nem a- ni- ma spi- ri- tu- que cum an- ge- lis cæ- li ia- nu- as in- gre- di- tur u- bi ful- get si- ne fi- ne Con- fes- [si- o et pul- chri- tu- do in con- spec- tu e- ius sanc- ti- tas et mag- ni- fi- cen- ti- a]

[2] Lau- ren- ti post men- bra so- lu- ta ca- lo- re pru- na- rum In s⟨an⟩c-⟨t⟩i- [fi- ca- ti- o- ne e- ius] Gl⟨o- ri⟩- a pa- tri

55. Introit: Confessio
Qui tibi dedit Laurenti

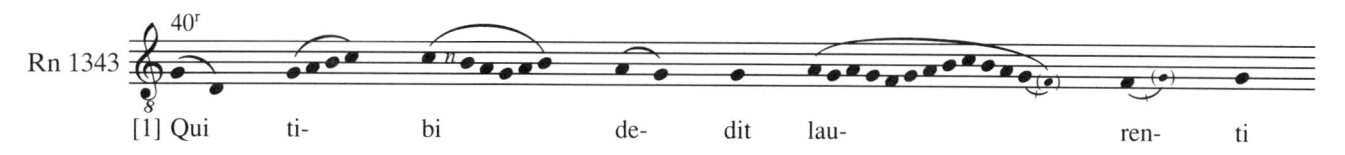

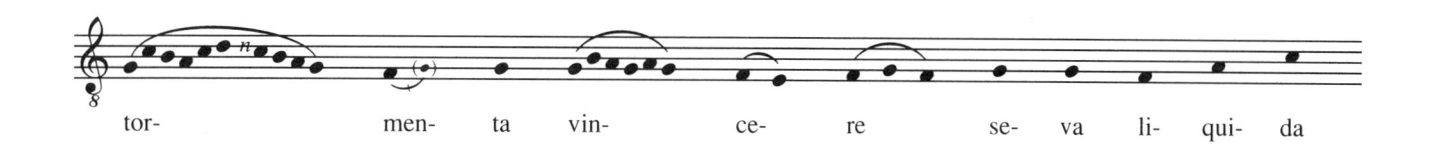

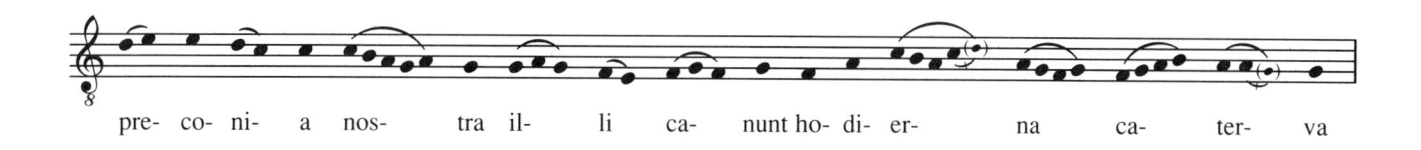

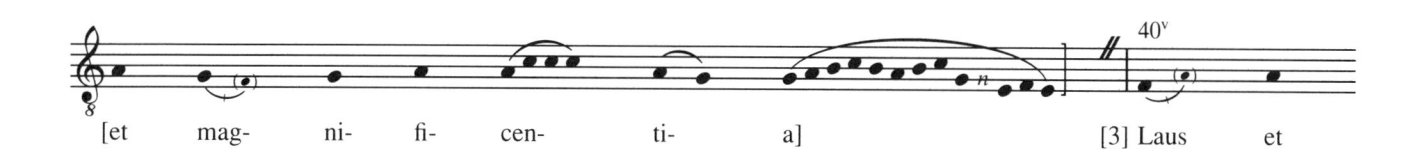

Rn 1343

[1] Qui tibi dedit laurenti tormenta vincere seva liquida preconia nostra illi canunt hodierna caterva Confessio [et pulchritudo in conspectu eius]

[2] Simulque consonn[i]s addatur hymnis S⟨an⟩c-⟨t⟩itas [et magnificentia] [3] Laus et iubilacio per cuncta tempora ac secla In s⟨an⟩c-⟨t⟩i-[ficatione eius]

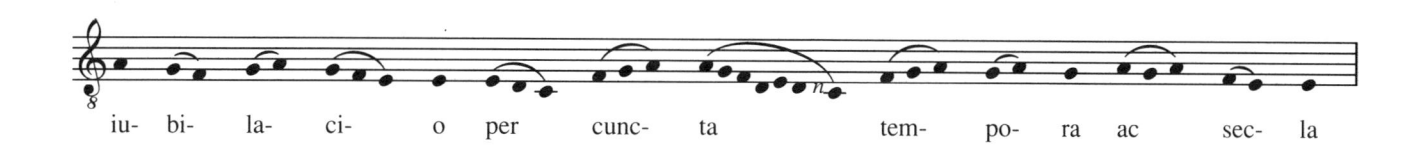

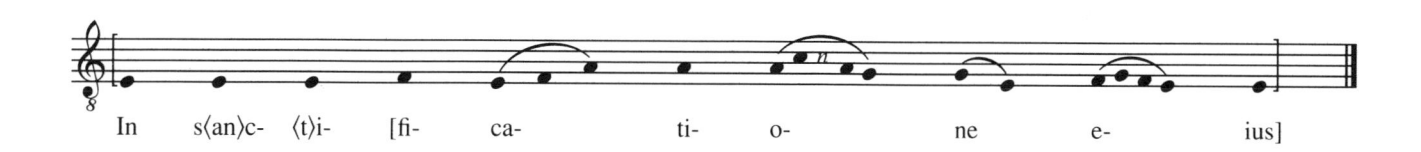

56. Introit: Gaudeamus ... Mariae ... assumptione
Exaudi virgo virginum

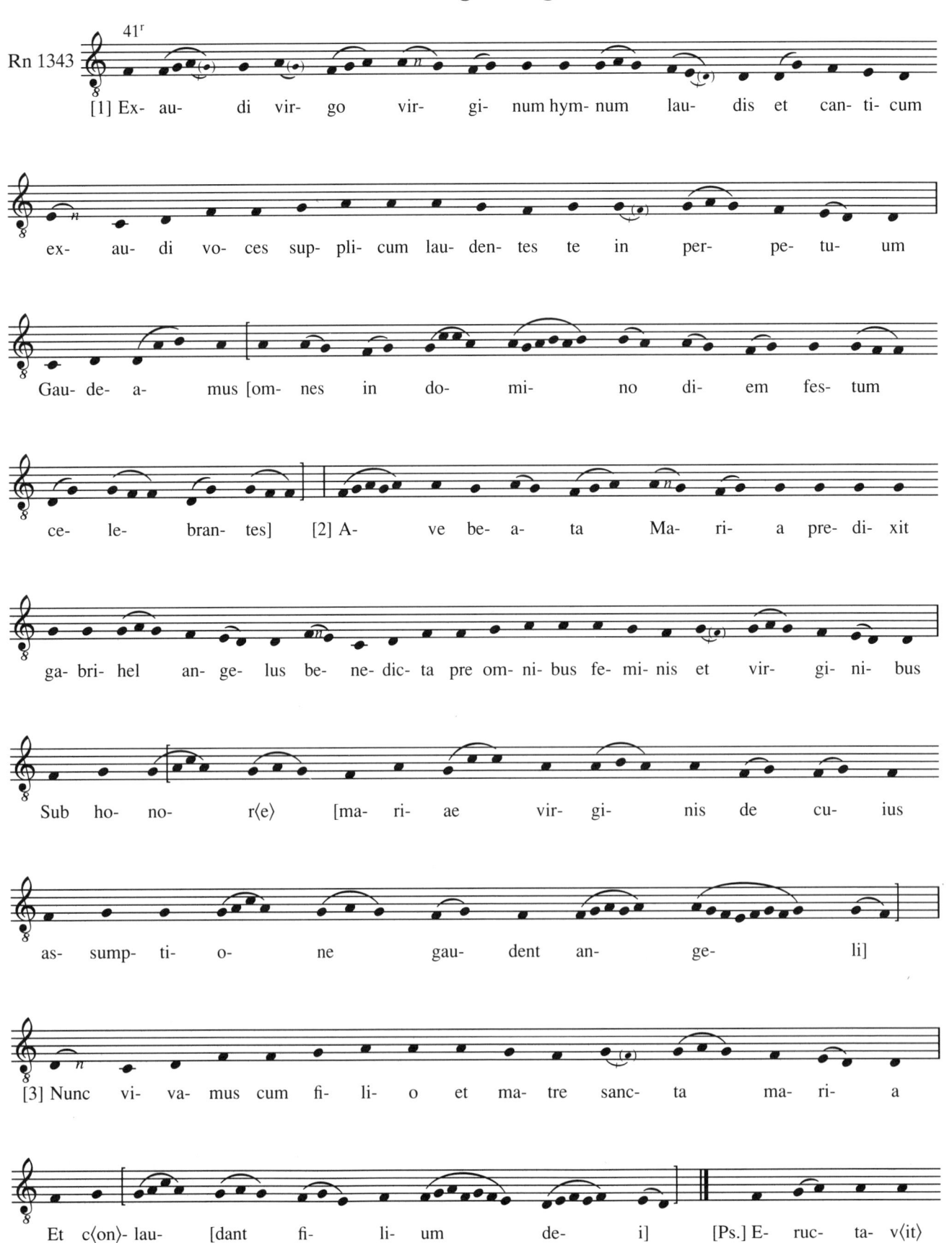

Rn 1343

[1] Ex- au- di vir- go vir- gi- num hym- num lau- dis et can- ti- cum

ex- au- di vo- ces sup- pli- cum lau- den- tes te in per- pe- tu- um

Gau- de- a- mus [om- nes in do- mi- no di- em fes- tum

ce- le- bran- tes] [2] A- ve be- a- ta Ma- ri- a pre- di- xit

ga- bri- hel an- ge- lus be- ne- dic- ta pre om- ni- bus fe- mi- nis et vir- gi- ni- bus

Sub ho- no- r⟨e⟩ [ma- ri- ae vir- gi- nis de cu- ius

as- sump- ti- o- ne gau- dent an- ge- li]

[3] Nunc vi- va- mus cum fi- li- o et ma- tre sanc- ta ma- ri- a

Et c⟨on⟩- lau- [dant fi- li- um de- i] [Ps.] E- ruc- ta- v⟨it⟩

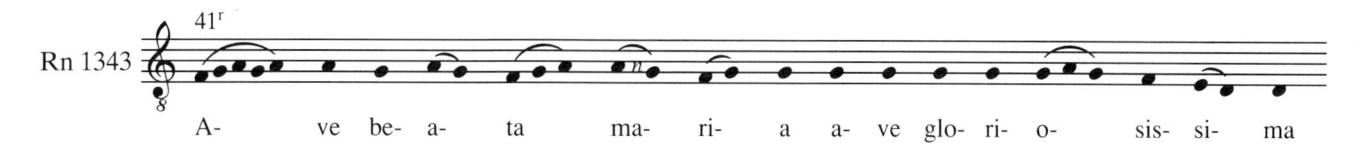

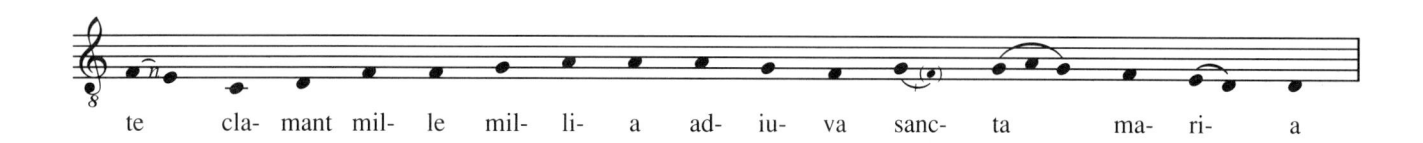

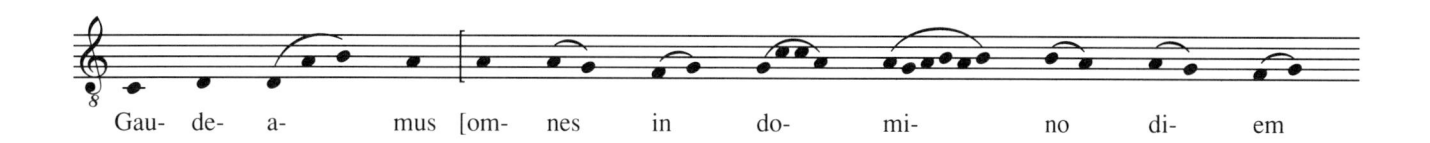

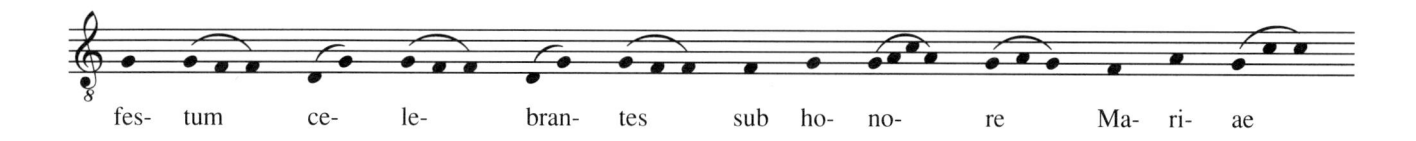

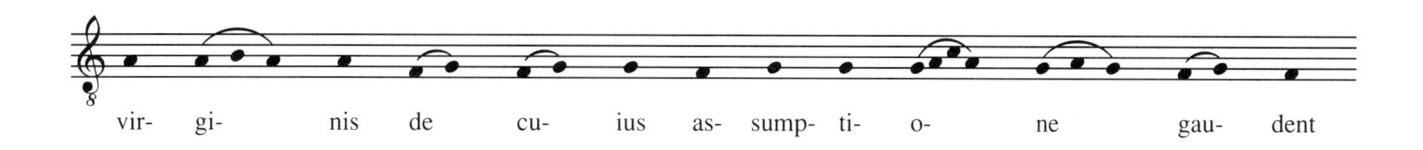

57. Introit: Gaudeamus . . . Mariae . . . assumptione
Ave beata Maria

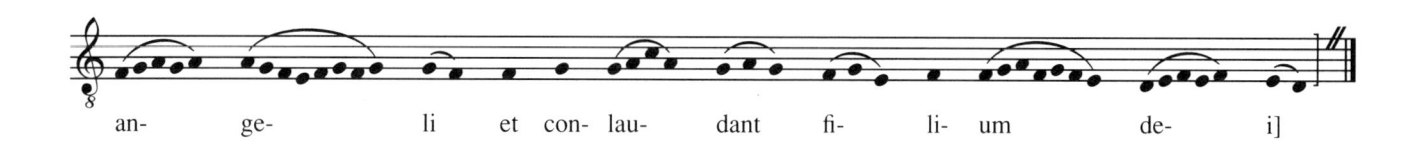

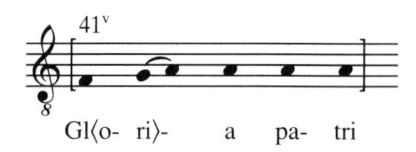

Rn 1343

A- ve be- a- ta ma- ri- a a- ve glo- ri- o- sis- si- ma

te cla- mant mil- le mil- li- a ad- iu- va sanc- ta ma- ri- a

Gau- de- a- mus [om- nes in do- mi- no di- em

fes- tum ce- le- bran- tes sub ho- no- re Ma- ri- ae

vir- gi- nis de cu- ius as- sump- ti- o- ne gau- dent

an- ge- li et con- lau- dant fi- li- um de- i]

Gl⟨o- ri⟩- a pa- tri

58. Introit: Gaudeamus . . . Mariae . . . assumptione
Nos sinus ecclesiae

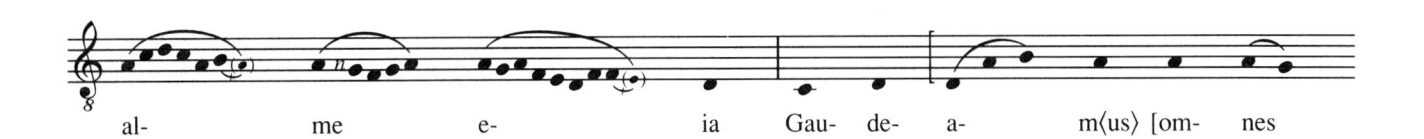

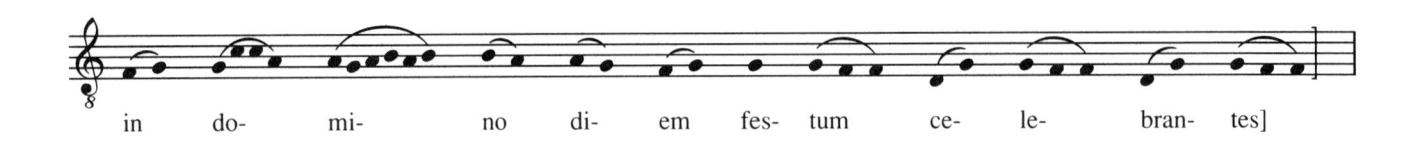

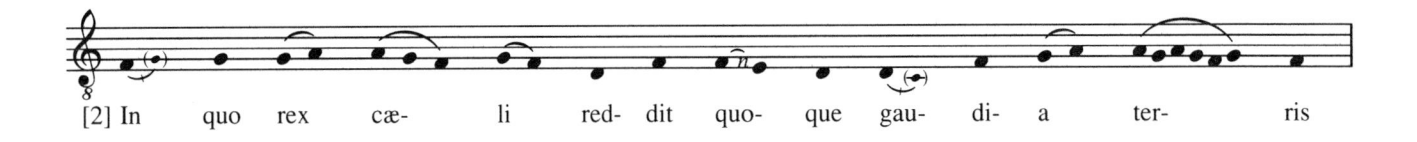

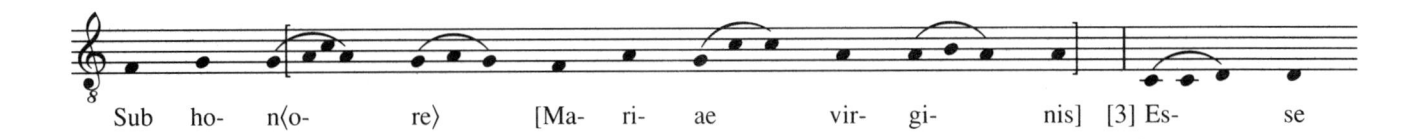

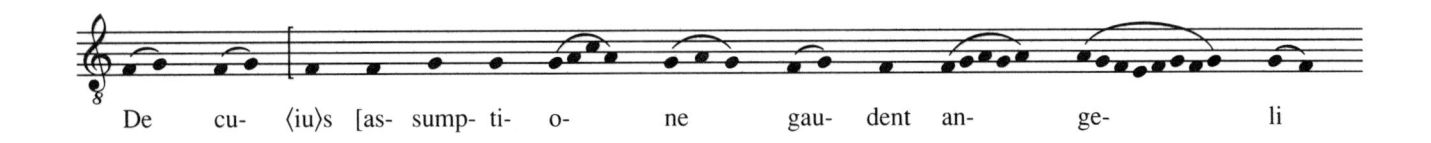

Rn 1343

[1] Nos si- nus æc- cle- si- æ ma- tris quos e- nu- trit al- me e- ia Gau- de- a- m⟨us⟩ [om- nes in do- mi- no di- em fes- tum ce- le- bran- tes]

[2] In quo rex cæ- li red- dit quo- que gau- di- a ter- ris Sub ho- n⟨o- re⟩ [Ma- ri- ae vir- gi- nis] [3] Es- se de- i ge- ni- trix que cre- di- tur om- ni- po- ten- ti[s] De cu- ⟨iu⟩s [as- sump- ti- o- ne gau- dent an- ge- li et con- lau- dant fi- li- um de- i]

59. Introit: Vultum tuum
O quam clara nitet

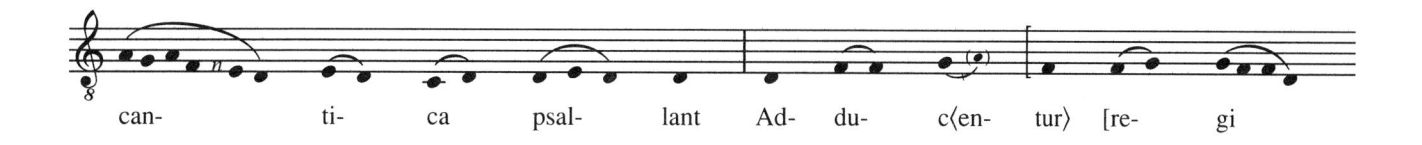

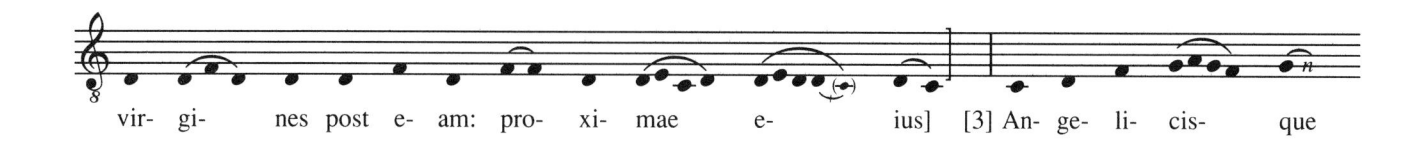

Rc 1741

[1] O quam cla- ra ni- tet ag- ni pul- cher- ri- ma spon- sa Vul- tum [tu- um de- pre- ca- bun- tur om- nes di- vi- tes ple- bis] [2] Ut cę- li in tha- la- mo sem- per no- va can- ti- ca psal- lant Ad- du- c⟨en- tur⟩ [re- gi vir- gi- nes post e- am: pro- xi- mae e- ius] [3] An- ge- li- cis- que cho- ris iunc- tę lę- ten- tur in e- vum Ad- du- cen- tur [ti- bi in lae- ti- ti- a et ex- ul- ta- ti- o- ne]

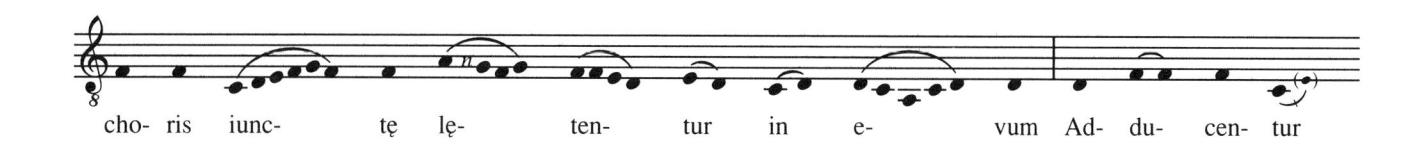

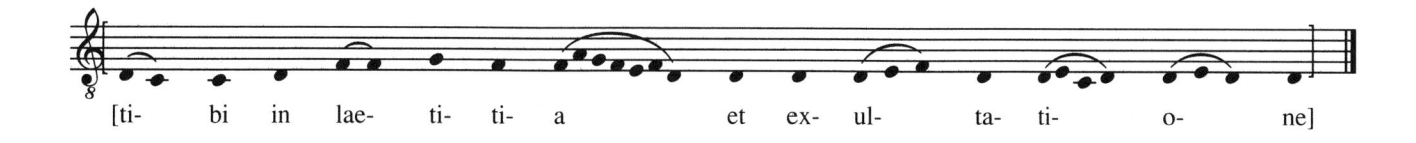

60. Introit: Benedicite dominum
Qui patris in caelo

[1] Qui patris in cae- lo nostris cognoscere vultum

Be- ne- di- ci- te [do- mi- num om- nes an- ge- li e- ius]

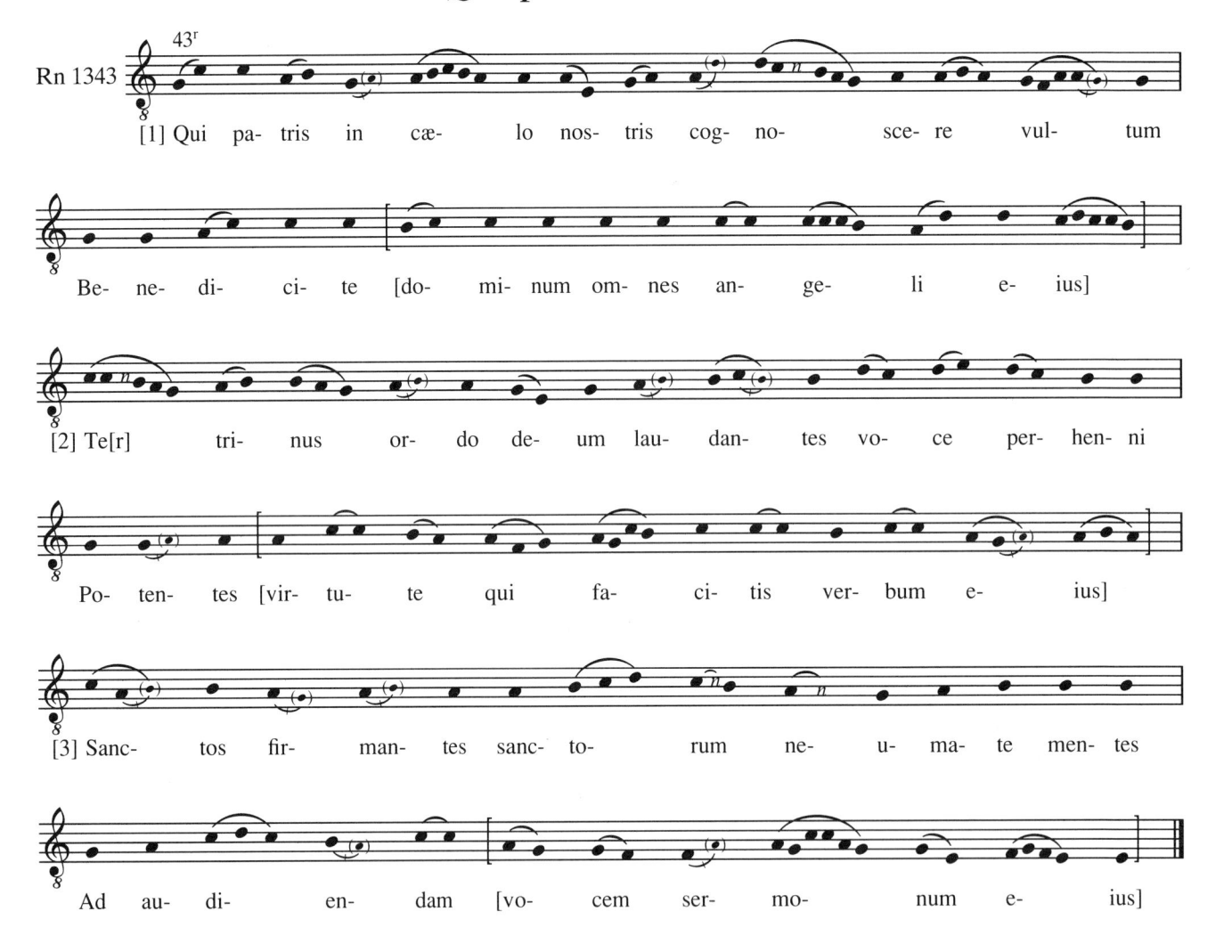

[2] Te[r] tri- nus or- do de- um lau- dan- tes vo- ce per- hen- ni

Po- ten- tes [vir- tu- te qui fa- ci- tis ver- bum e- ius]

[3] Sanc- tos fir- man- tes sanc- to- rum neu- ma- te men- tes

Ad au- di- en- dam [vo- cem ser- mo- num e- ius]

61. Introit: Mihi autem nimis
Nobile apostolici admirans

[1] No- bi- le a- pos- to- li- ci ad- mi- rans de- cus or- di- nis

al- mi da- vi- ti- cus psal- tes pro- cla- mat ta- li- a di- cens

Mi- chi au- t⟨em⟩ [ni- mis ho- no- ra- ti sunt a- mi- ci

tu- i de- us] [2] Quo[s] di- vi- nus a- mor ve- re ti- bi

iunc- xit a- mi- cos Ni- mis [con- for- ta- tus est

prin- ci- pa- tus e- o- rum] [3] Cæ- li- ca nam- que pi- is

red- dunt a- ca- ron- ta su- per- bis P[s.] D⟨o- mi⟩- ne p⟨ro⟩-ba- sti me

62. Introit: Mihi autem nimis
Admirans vates proclamat

Rn 1343

[1] Ad- mi- rans va- tes pro- cla- mat

vo- ce so- no- ra Mi- chi au- t⟨em⟩ [ni- mis

ho- no- ra- ti sunt a- mi- ci tu- i de- us] [2] Qui

ti- bi sunt iunc- ti di- vi- no neu- ma- te ple- ni

Ni- mis [con- for- ta- tus est prin- ci- pa- tus e- o- rum]

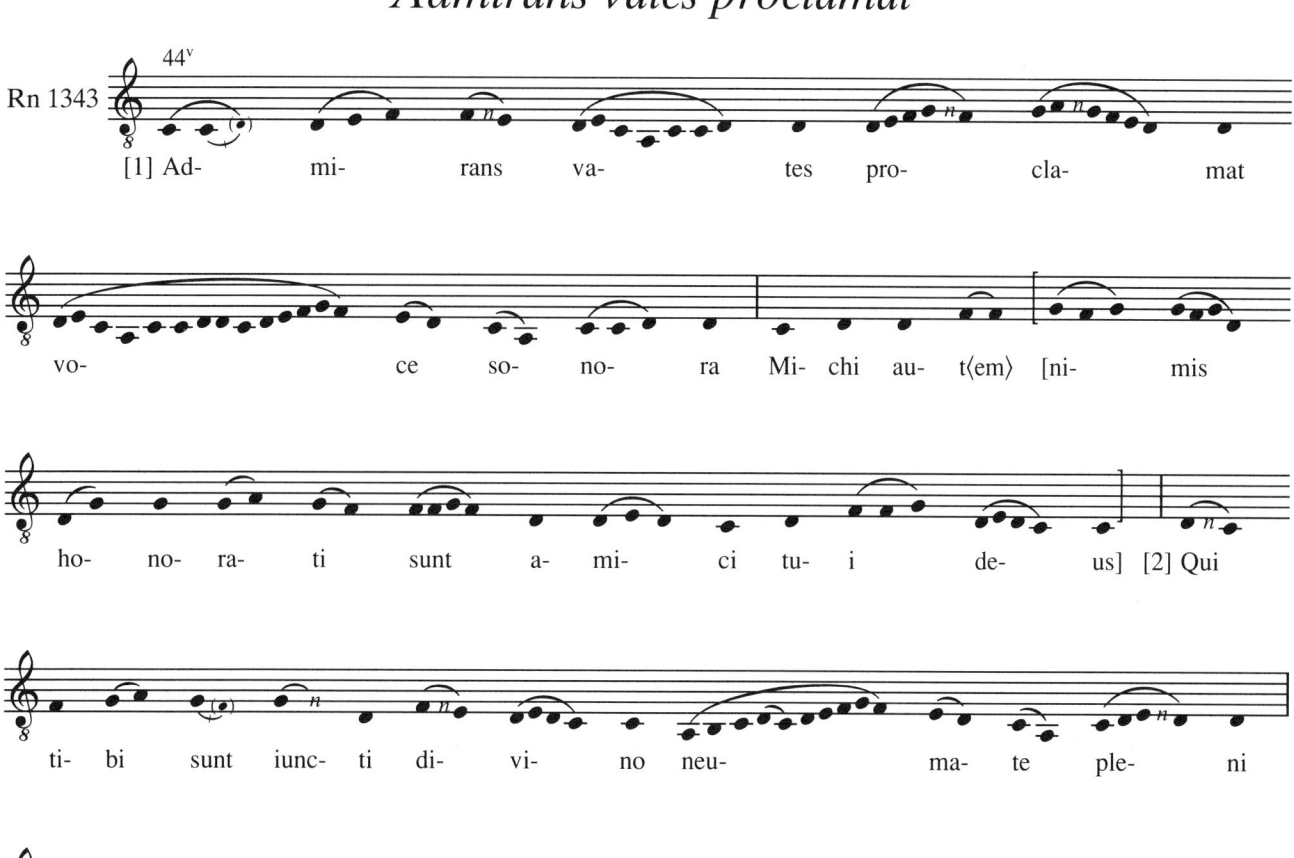

63. Introit: Mihi autem nimis
Consortes tuorum effecti

Rn 1343

Con- sor- tes tu- o- rum ef- fec- ti at- que so- ci- os

Mi- chi au- t⟨em⟩ [ni- mis ho- no- ra- ti sunt a- mi- ci tu- i

de- us ni- mis con- for- ta- tus est prin- ci- pa- tus e- o- rum]

64. Introit: Statuit ei dominus
Divini fuerat

Rn 1343

[1] Di- vi- ni fu- e- r[a]t quo- ni- am fer- vo- ris

a- ma- tor e- ia Sta- tu- it [e- i

do- mi- nus tes- ta- men- tum pa- cis]

[2] Et pac- tum vi- tæ fir- mum sta- bi- li- vit in e- vum

Et pri[n- ci- pem fe- cit e- um ut sit il- li sa- cer- do- ti- i

dig- ni- tas] [3] In- cen- sum- que su- æ con- dig- num

de- fe- rat a- re In æ- t⟨er- num⟩

65. Introit: In omnem terram
Festis nunc in apostolicis

Rn 1343

[1] Fe- stis nunc in a- pos- to- li- cis laus clan- gat e- ri- lis In om- nem [terram exivit sonus eorum] [2] An- ge- li- ci pa- tres cla- ri su- per e- the- ra ci- ves Et in fi[nes orbis terrae verba eorum] [3] Qui de- bri- ant e- van- ge- li- co so- phis- ma- te quos-mum [N]on sunt [loquelae neque sermones quorum non audiantur voces eorum]

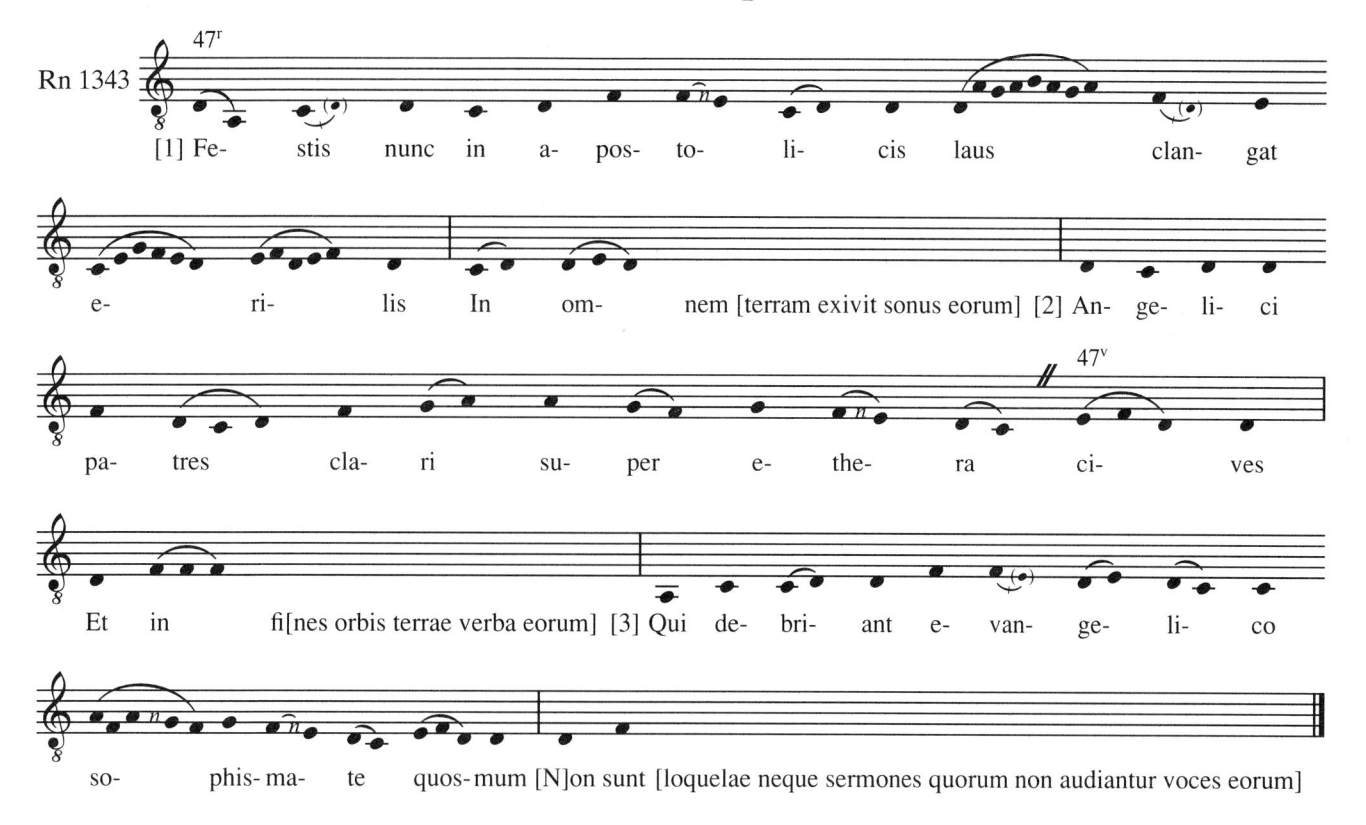

66. Introit: In omnem terram
Hodie beatissimus Andreas

Rn 1343

Ho- di- e be- a- tis- si- mus an- dre- as a- pos- to- lus plau- den- ti- bus an- ge- li- cis ag- mi- ni- bus cæ- lum pro- vec- tus est de- o gra- ci- as di- ci- te In om- nem [terram exivit sonus eorum Et in fines orbis terrae verba eorum Non sunt loquelae neque sermones quorum non audiantur voces eorum]

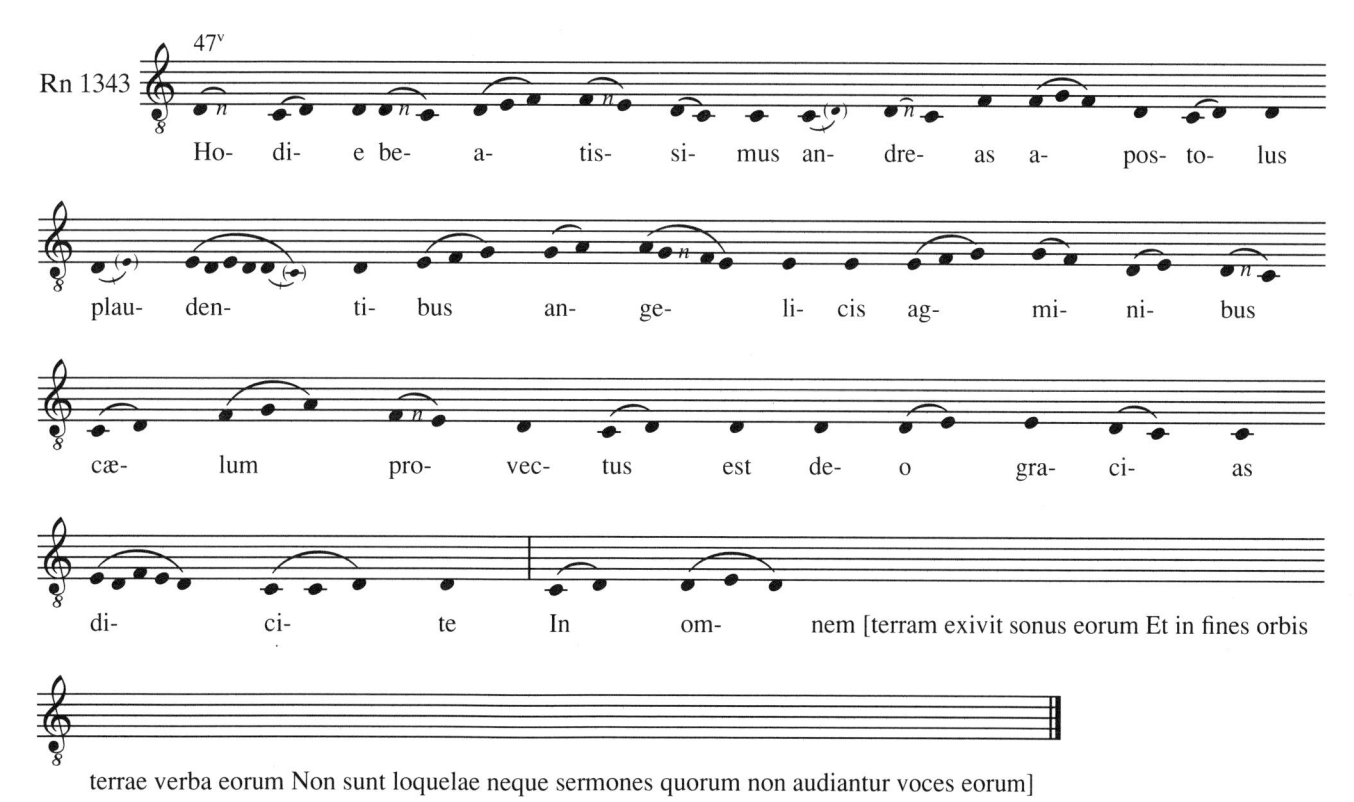

67. Introit: Benedicta sit
Splendor et imago patris

Rn 1343

[1] Splen- dor et i- ma- go pa- tris tri- nus et u- nus

Be- ne- dic- [ta sit sanc- ta tri- ni- tas]

[2] Pa- ter et fi- li- us et spi- ri- tus sanc- tus in u- num sunt

At- q⟨ue⟩ [in- di- vi- sa u- ni- tas]

[3] Tri- ni- tas et u- ni- tas de- i- tas

Con- fi- [te- bi- mur e- i] [4] Est

u- ni- ge- ni- tus sa- ba- oth no- men a- do- na- y

Qui- a [fe- cit no- bis- cum mi- se- ri- cor- di- am su- am]

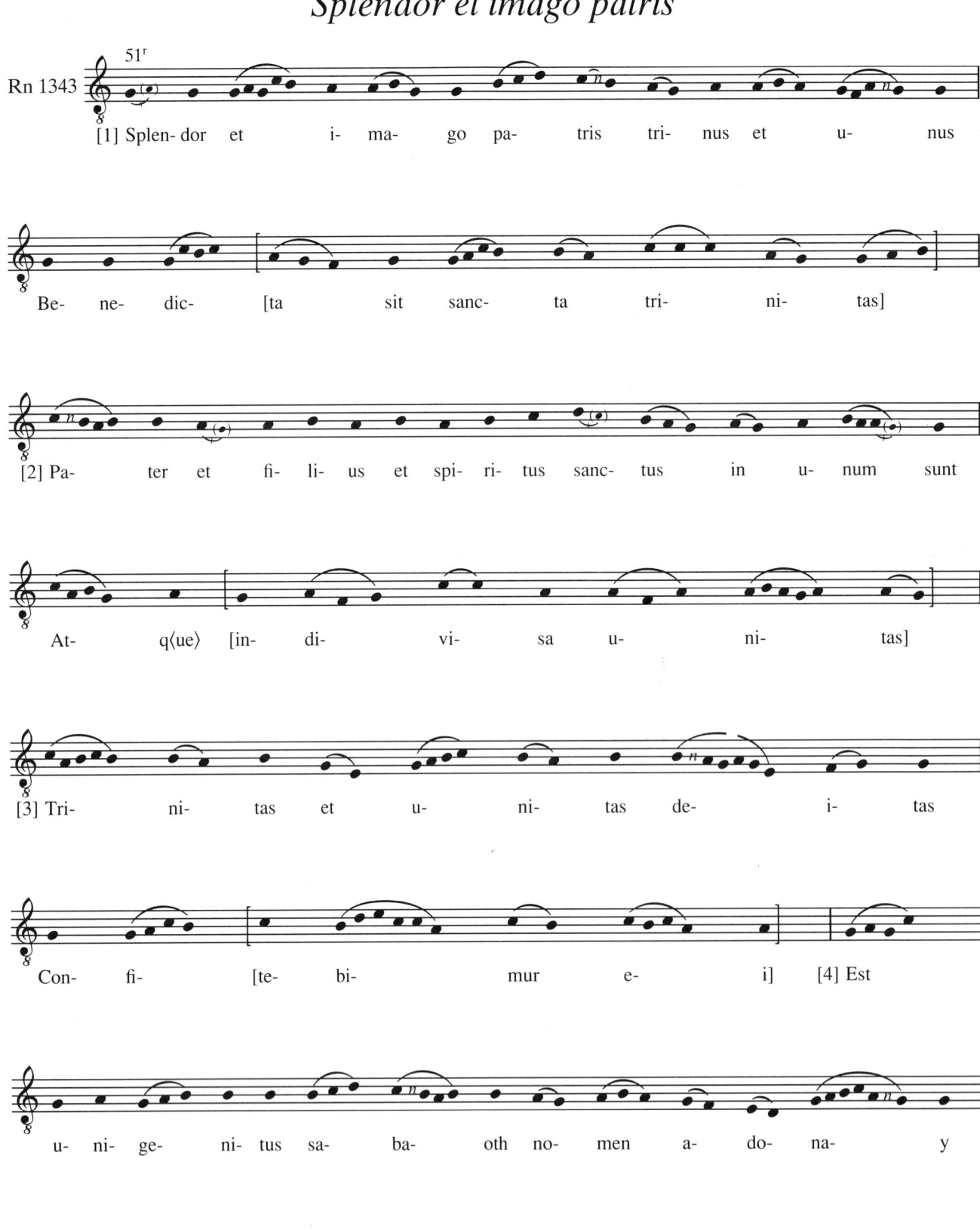

1. Gradual: Universi qui te exspectant
℣ Vias tuas domine

Prosula: *Venturum te cuncti dixerunt*

Rn 1343

Ven- tu- rum te cunc- ti di- xe- runt pro- phe- tæ nas- ci- tu- rum

es- se de vir- gi- ne mul- ti te ex- pec- tant ex om- ni ple- be

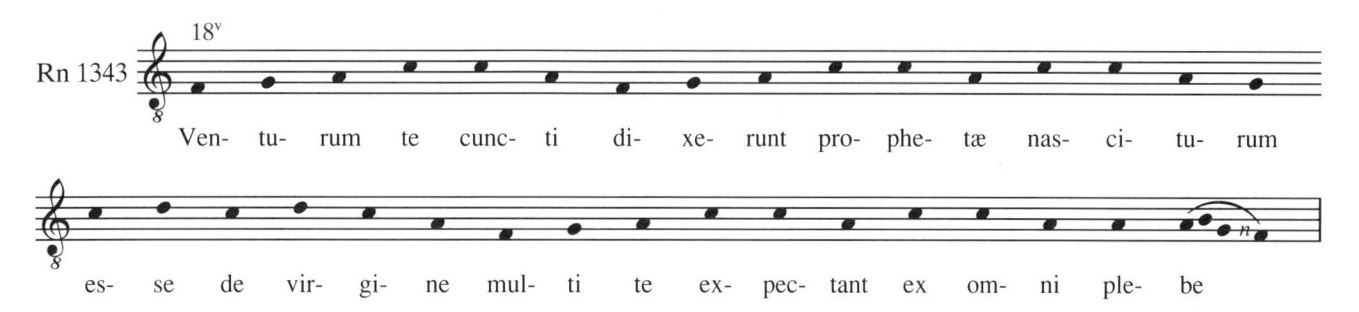

2. Offertory: Ad te domine levavi
℣2 Respice in me

Prosula: *Invocavite altissime*

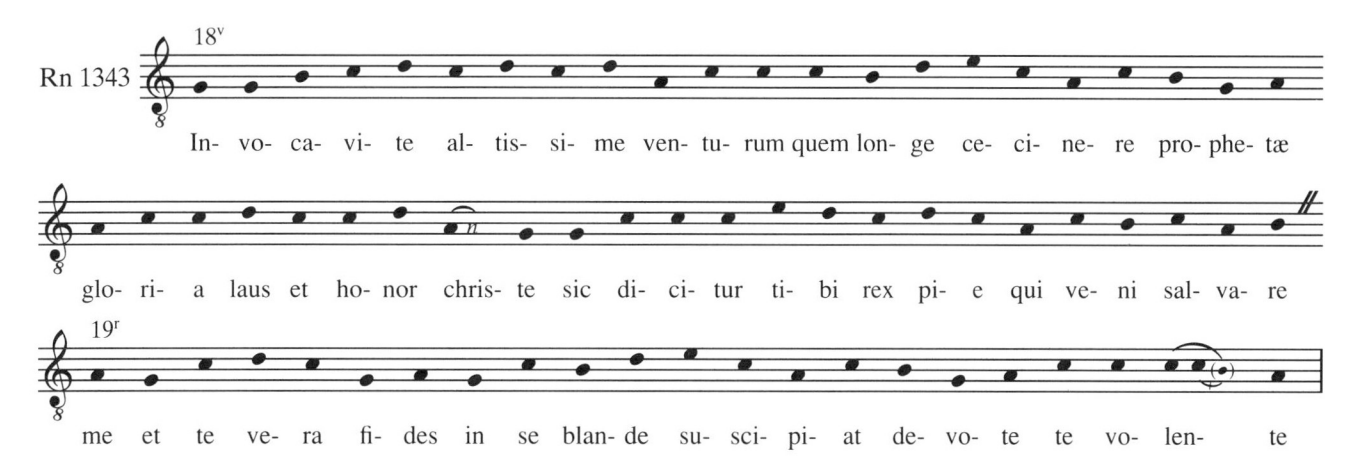

Rn 1343

In- vo- ca- vi- te al- tis- si- me ven- tu- rum quem lon- ge ce- ci- ne- re pro- phe- tæ

glo- ri- a laus et ho- nor chris- te sic di- ci- tur ti- bi rex pi- e qui ve- ni sal- va- re

me et te ve- ra fi- des in se blan- de sus- ci- pi- at de- vo- te te vo- len- te

3. Offertory: Deus tu convertens
℣2 Misericordia et veritas

Prosula: *Possessor polorum Deus*

Rc 1741

Pos- ses- sor po- lo- rum de- us qui nos de ter- ra o- ri- go fin- xit an- ge- li- co

cę- tu- i co- pu- la- vit et co- hę- re- vit cus- to- di- en- do e- ius prę- cep- ti-

-o- nem pro- me- re- a- mur nos cę- les- ti- co- las man- si- o- nes

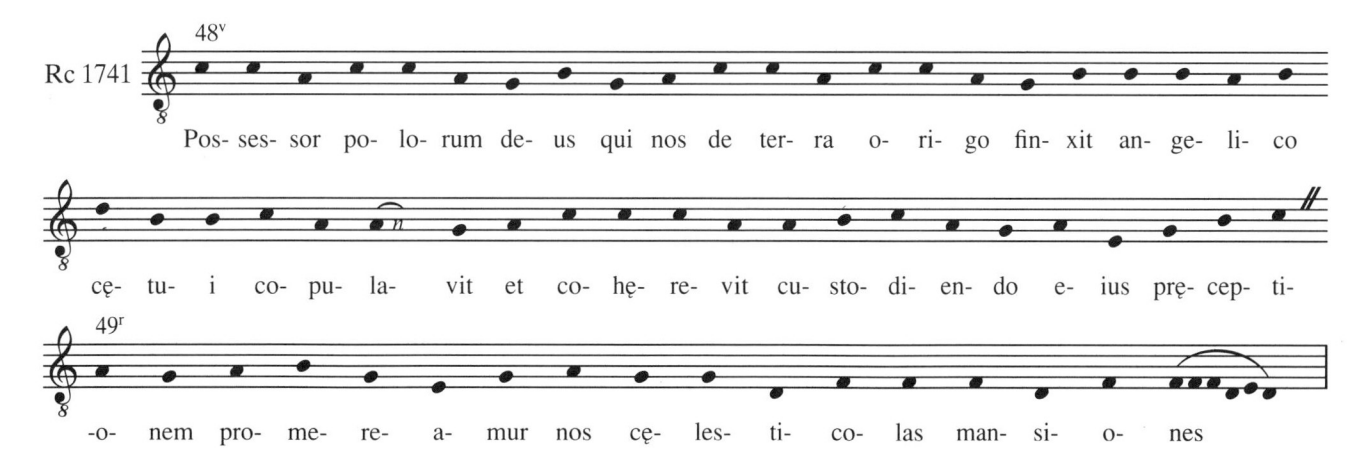

4. Gradual: Qui sedes domine
℣ Qui regis Israel

Prosula: *Qui sedes in alto throno*

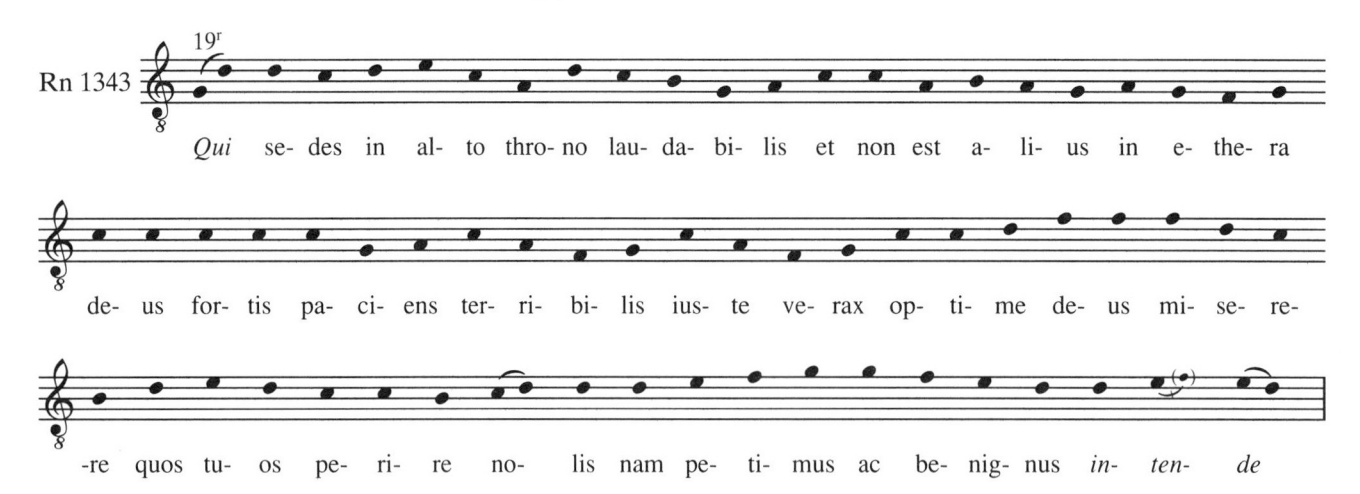

Rn 1343

Qui se- des in al- to thro- no lau- da- bi- lis et non est a- li- us in e- the- ra de- us for- tis pa- ci- ens ter- ri- bi- lis ius- te ve- rax op- ti- me de- us mi- se- re- -re quos tu- os pe- ri- re no- lis nam pe- ti- mus ac be- nig- nus in- ten- de

5. Offertory: Benedixisti domine
℣2 Ostende nobis domine

Prosula: *Misericors et clemens famulis*

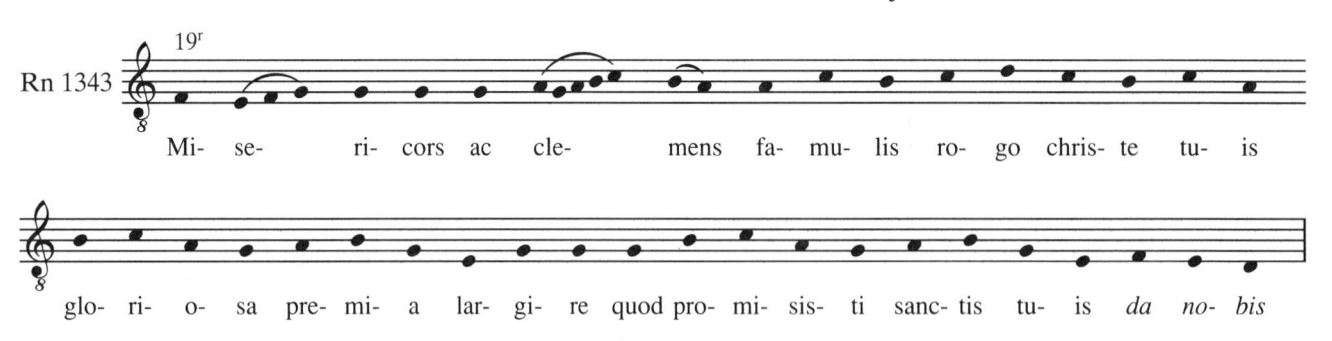

Rn 1343

Mi- se- ri- cors ac cle- mens fa- mu- lis ro- go chris- te tu- is glo- ri- o- sa pre- mi- a lar- gi- re quod pro- mi- sis- ti sanc- tis tu- is da no- bis

6. Offertory: Ave Maria
℣1 Quomodo in me

Prosula: *A supernis caelorum*

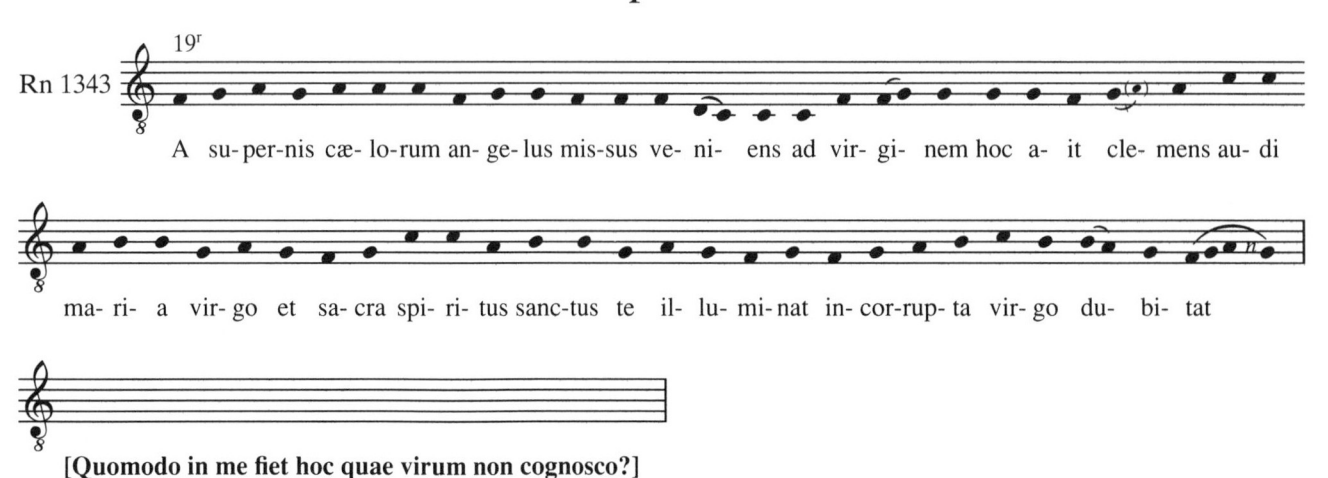

Rn 1343

A su- per- nis cæ- lo- rum an- ge- lus mis- sus ve- ni- ens ad vir- gi- nem hoc a- it cle- mens au- di ma- ri- a vir- go et sa- cra spi- ri- tus sanc- tus te il- lu- mi- nat in- cor- rup- ta vir- go du- bi- tat

[Quomodo in me fiet hoc quae virum non cognosco?]

7. Offertory: Deus enim fermavit
℣ 2   Mirabilis in excelsis
Prosula: *Dierum noctuque*

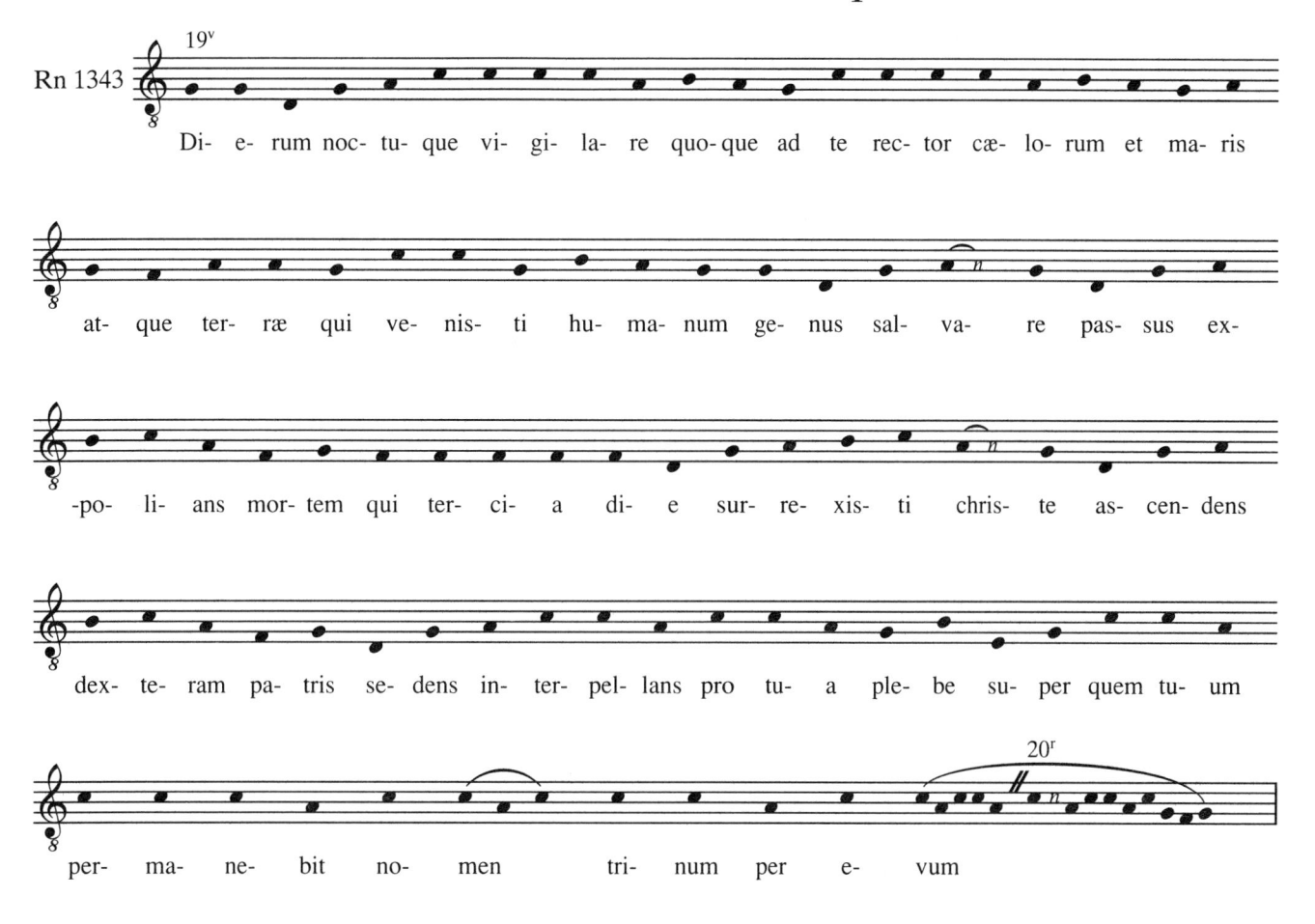

Rn 1343

Di- e- rum noc- tu- que vi- gi- la- re quo- que ad te rec- tor cæ- lo- rum et ma- ris

at- que ter- ræ qui ve- nis- ti hu- ma- num ge- nus sal- va- re pas- sus ex-

-po- li- ans mor- tem qui ter- ci- a di- e sur- re- xis- ti chris- te as- cen- dens

dex- te- ram pa- tris se- dens in- ter- pel- lans pro tu- a ple- be su- per quem tu- um

per- ma- ne- bit no- men tri- num per e- vum

8–9. Alleluia ℣   Dies sanctificatus
Prosulae: *Audi nos te deprecamur* and *Alme caeli rex immortalis*

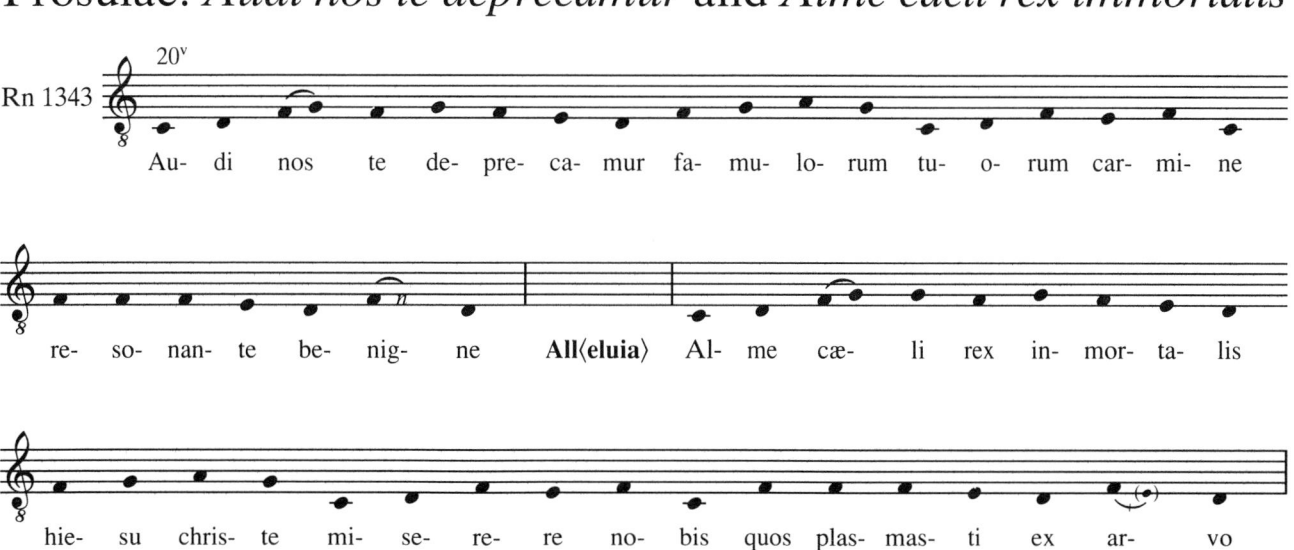

Rn 1343

Au- di nos te de- pre- ca- mur fa- mu- lo- rum tu- o- rum car- mi- ne

re- so- nan- te be- nig- ne **All⟨eluia⟩** Al- me cæ- li rex in- mor- ta- lis

hie- su chris- te mi- se- re- re no- bis quos plas- mas- ti ex ar- vo

10. Offertory: Tui sunt caeli
℣ 3   Tu humiliasti
Prosula: *Proles virginis matris*

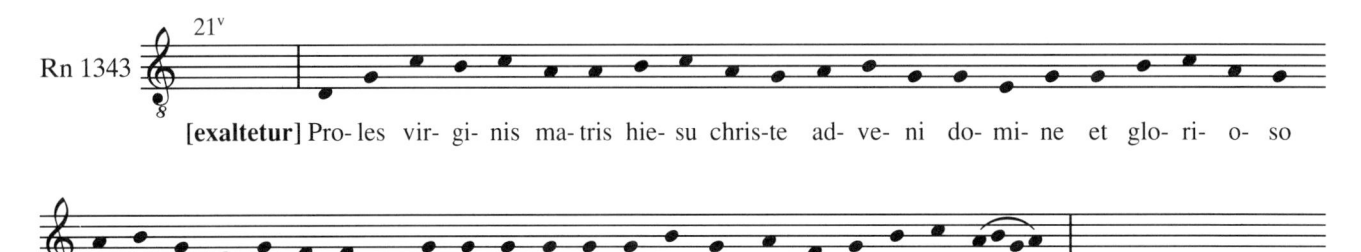

[exaltetur] Pro- les vir- gi- nis ma- tris hie- su chris- te ad- ve- ni do- mi- ne et glo- ri- o- so tu- o san-gui-ne nos re- di- me sau- ci- a- tum su-per-bum quip-pe hu- mi- li- ans [dextera tua domine]

11. Tract: Commovisti
℣   Sana contritiones eius
Prosula: *Sana Christe rex alme*

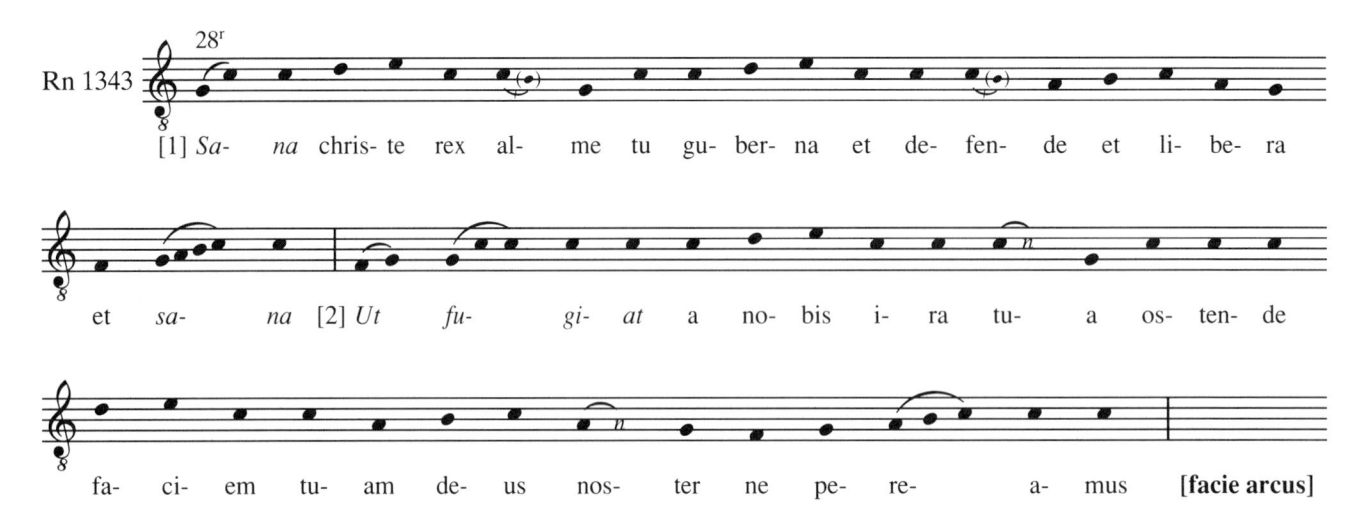

[1] Sa- na chris- te rex al- me tu gu- ber- na et de- fen- de et li- be- ra et sa- na [2] Ut fu- gi- at a no- bis i- ra tu- a os- ten- de fa- ci- em tu- am de- us nos- ter ne pe- re- a- mus [facie arcus]

12. Tract: Qui confidunt
℣   Montes in circuitu eius
Prosula: *Mons magnus est*

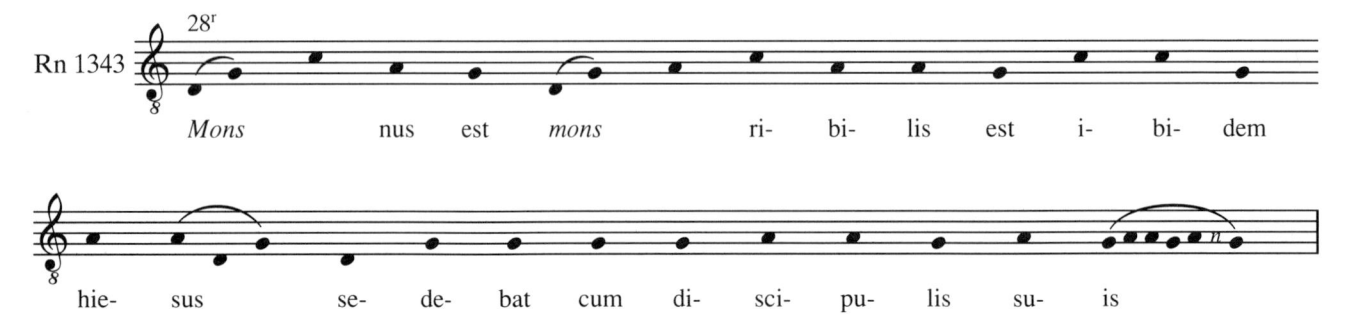

Mons nus est mons ri- bi- lis est i- bi- dem hie- sus se- de- bat cum di- sci- pu- lis su- is

13. Tract: Deus Deus meus
℣ Libera me de ore
Prosula: *Pater unigenitum tuum*

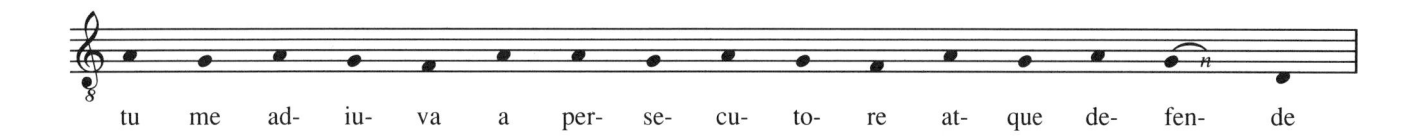

Rc 1741

[libera me] Pa- ter u- ni- ge- ni- tum tu- um fi- li- um- que

tu me ad- iu- va a per- se- cu- to- re at- que de- fen- de

14–15. Alleluia ℣ Pascha nostrum
Prosulae: *Iam redeunt gaudia* and *Christe tu vita vera*

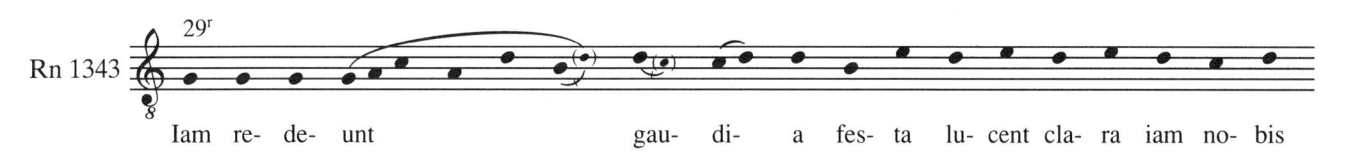

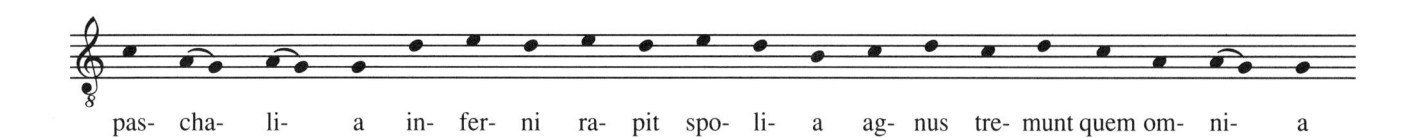

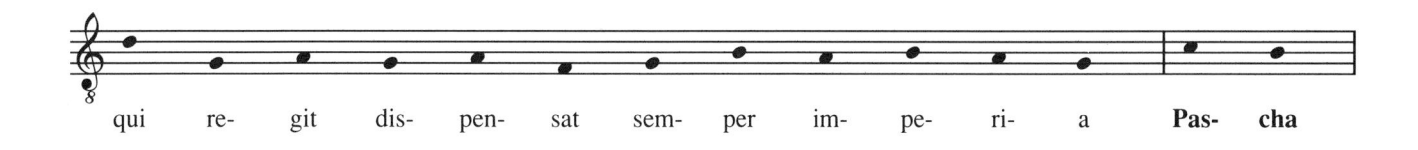

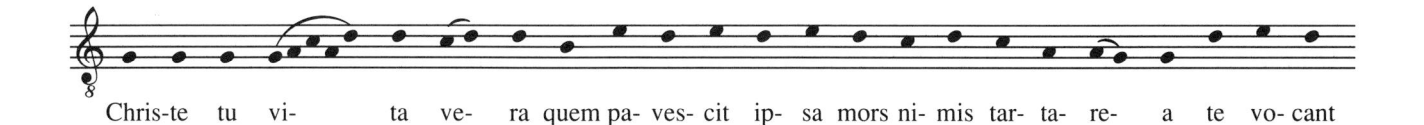

Rn 1343

Iam re- de- unt gau- di- a fes- ta lu- cent cla- ra iam no- bis

pas- cha- li- a in- fer- ni ra- pit spo- li- a ag- nus tre- munt quem om- ni- a

qui re- git dis- pen- sat sem- per im- pe- ri- a **Pas- cha**

Chris-te tu vi- ta ve- ra quem pa- ves- cit ip- sa mors ni- mis tar- ta- re- a te vo- cant

nos- tra nunc o- ra ut e- mun- des pre- cor- di- a qui re- gis e- the- ra laus ti- bi per se- cu- la

16. Offertory: Angelus domini
℣2   Iesus stetit
Prosula: *Christus intravit ianuis*

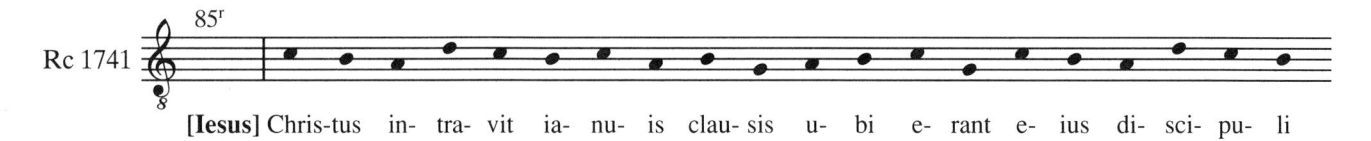

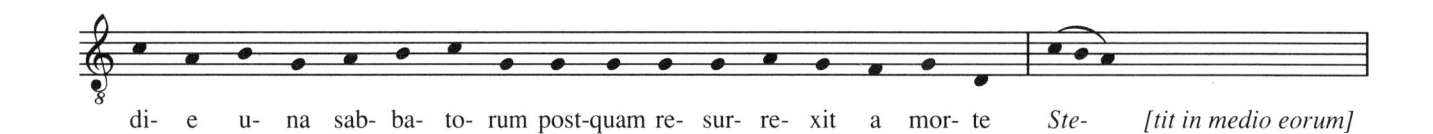

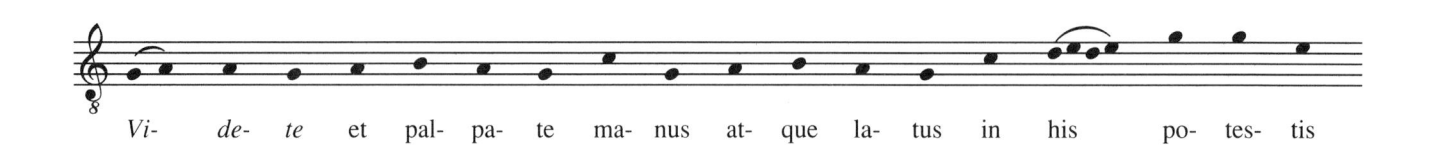

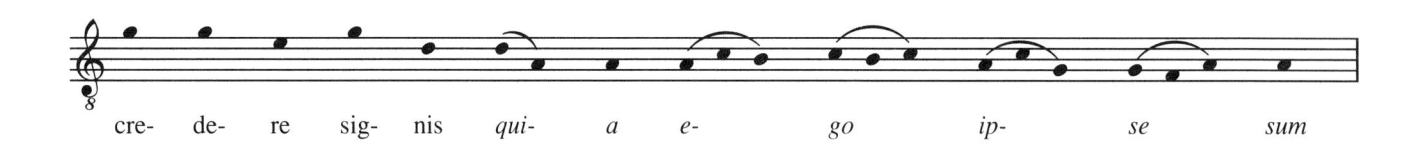

Rc 1741

[Iesus] Chris- tus in- tra- vit ia- nu- is clau- sis u- bi e- rant e- ius di- sci- pu- li di- e u- na sab- ba- to- rum post- quam re- sur- re- xit a mor- te Ste- *[tit in medio eorum]*

Vi- de- te et pal- pa- te ma- nus at- que la- tus in his po- tes- tis cre- de- re sig- nis *qui- a e- go ip- se sum*

17–18. Alleluia ℣ Vos estis
Prosulae: *Rex Deus omnipotens* and *Sicut tu Christe*

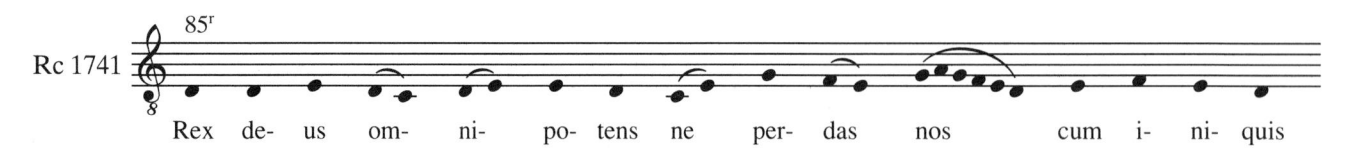

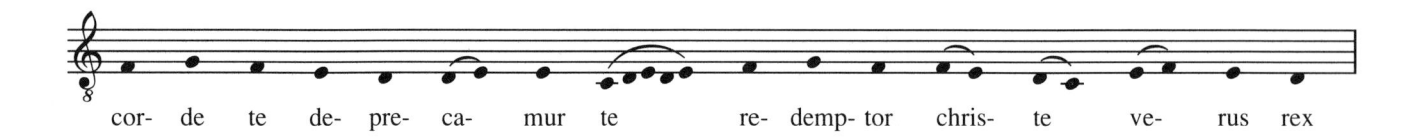

Rc 1741

Rex de- us om- ni- po- tens ne per- das nos cum i- ni- quis qui- a sci- mus nos pi- e- ta- tem tu- am mag- nam fo- re no- bis si pu- ro cor- de te de- pre- ca- mur te re- demp- tor chris- te ve- rus rex

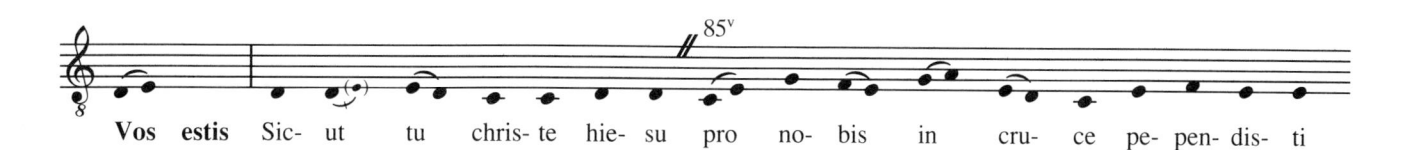

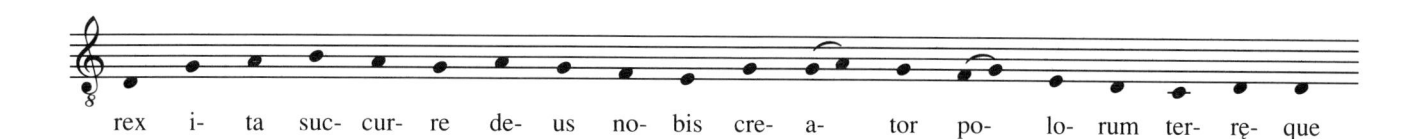

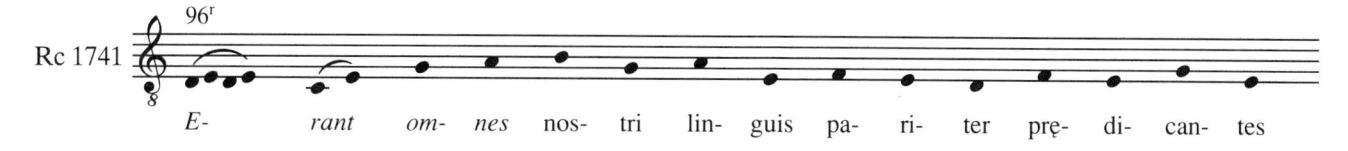

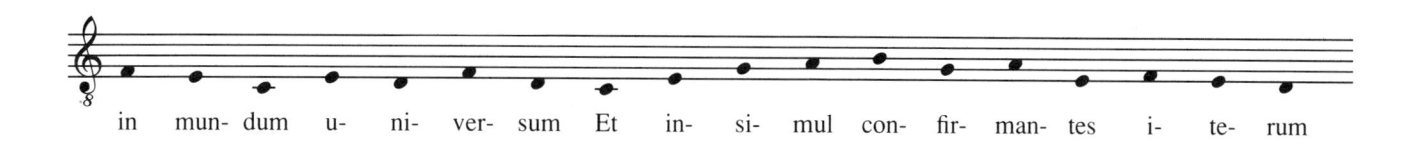

Vos estis Sic- ut tu chris- te hie- su pro no- bis in cru- ce pe- pen- dis- ti rex i- ta suc- cur- re de- us no- bis cre- a- tor po- lo- rum ter- rę- que in- ter- ces- si- o- que a- pos- to- lo- rum tu- o- rum no- bis pro- fi- ci- at do- mi- ne

19. Alleluia ℣ Dum complerentur
Prosula: *Erant omnes nostri linguis*

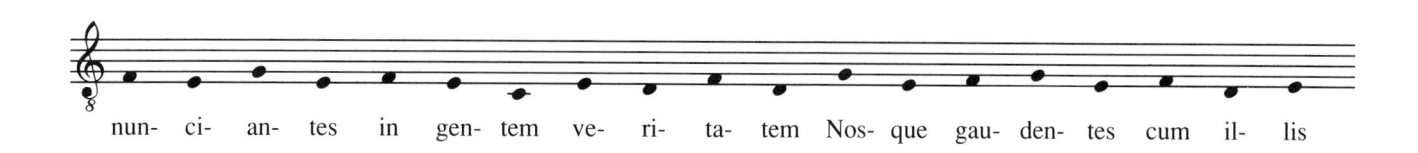

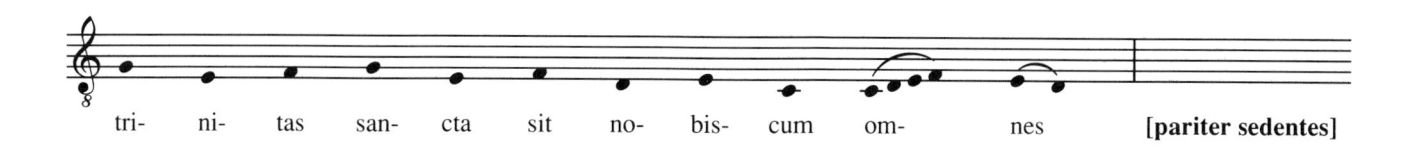

Rc 1741

E- rant om- nes nos- tri lin- guis pa- ri- ter prę- di- can- tes in mun- dum u- ni- ver- sum Et in- si- mul con- fir- man- tes i- te- rum nun- ci- an- tes in gen- tem ve- ri- ta- tem Nos- que gau- den- tes cum il- lis tri- ni- tas san- cta sit no- bis- cum om- nes [pariter sedentes]

20. Alleluia ℣ Dum complerentur
Prosula: *Pentecosten advenisse*

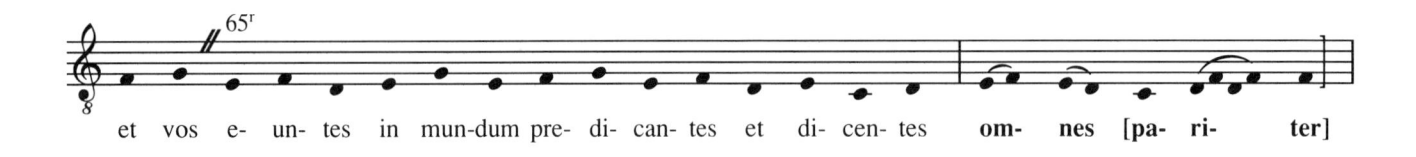

Bu 2824: Pen- te- cos- ten ad- ve- nis- se nos- ter cris- tus et di- cens ad a- pos- to- los om- nes non re- li- quam or- fa- nos vos sed va- dam et re- ver- tar et gau- de- bit cor ves- trum et vos e- un- tes in mun- dum pre- di- can- tes et di- cen- tes **om- nes** [pa- ri- ter]

21–22. Alleluia ℣ Serve bone et fidelis
Prosulae: *Alme cuncti sator orbis* and *Serve et amice bone*

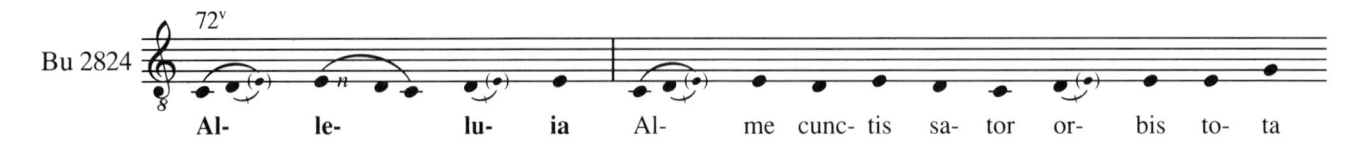

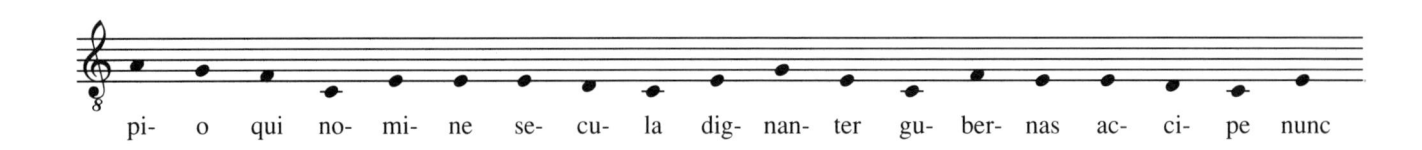

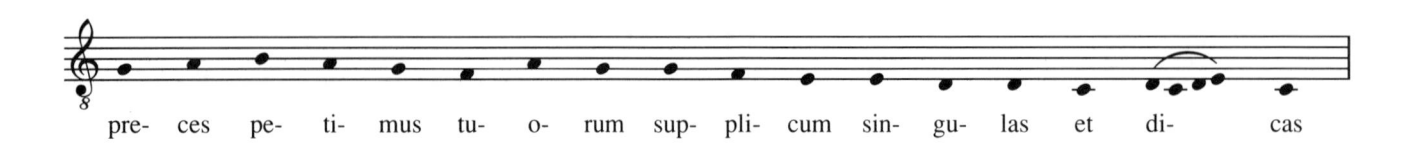

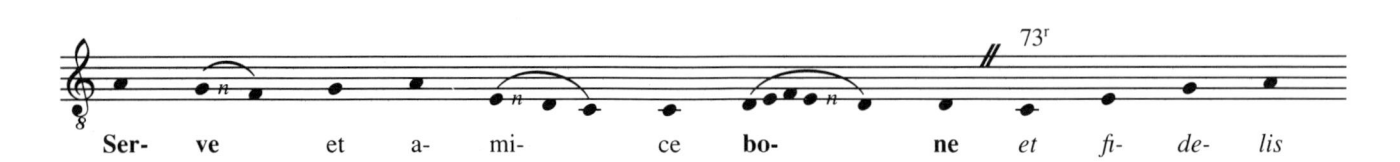

Bu 2824: **Al- le- lu-** ia Al- me cunc- tis sa- tor or- bis to- ta pi- o qui no- mi- ne se- cu- la dig- nan- ter gu- ber- nas ac- ci- pe nunc pre- ces pe- ti- mus tu- o- rum sup- pli- cum sin- gu- las et di- cas **Ser- ve** et a- mi- ce **bo- ne** *et fi- de- lis*

qui su- pra pau- ca com- po- si- ta mi- li- tas- ti pru- den- ter

In- tra in gau- di- um qui- a ta- len- ta tra- di- ta com-mu- la- ta- re fa- tu- is- ti fru- e- re

su- per- nis qua-prop-ter da- pi- bus per- vi- gil me- ri- to pre- pa- ra- tus **do- mi- ni**

Do- mi- ni tu- i re- co- len- tis qui- dem tem- po- re pros- tra- tus la- bo- rum

ac- ci- pe co- ro- nam sta- di- i bra- vi- um- que si- mul eu- ge per e- vum

23–25. Alleluia ℣ Concussum est mare

Prosulae: *Ante Deum semper gloriae, Concussum et percussum,* and *Angele Michael atque Gabriel*

Rn 1343

An- te de- um sem- per glo- ri- æ lux e- ter- næ om- nes an- ge- li- ci et

sanc- to- rum cho- ri im- plo- rent pro no- bis ve- ni- am con- ce- den- tem in se- cu- la

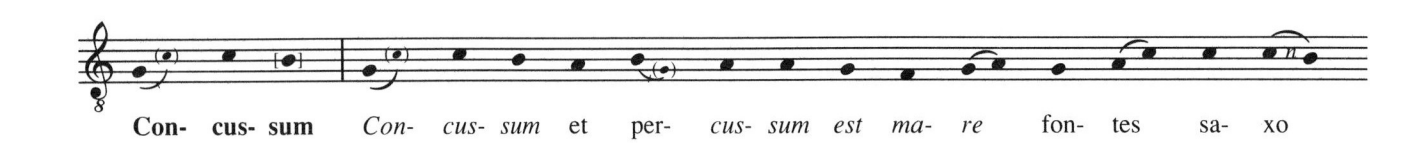

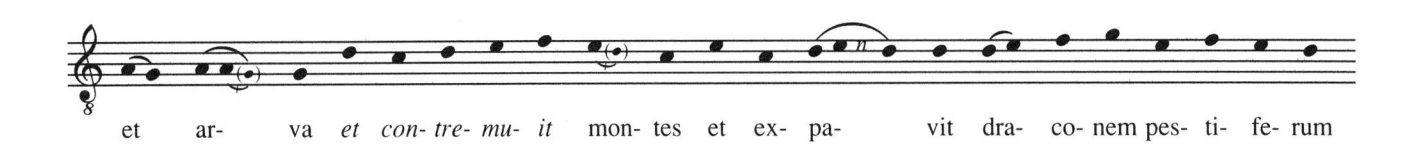

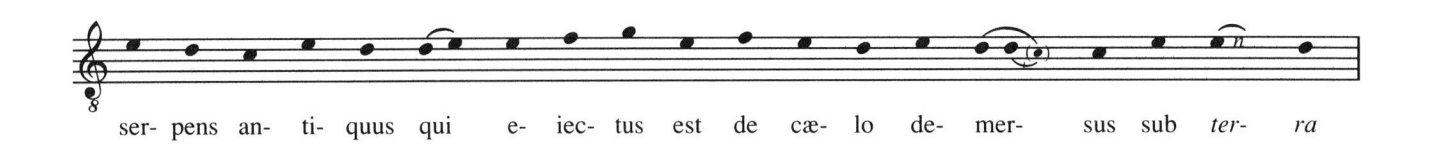

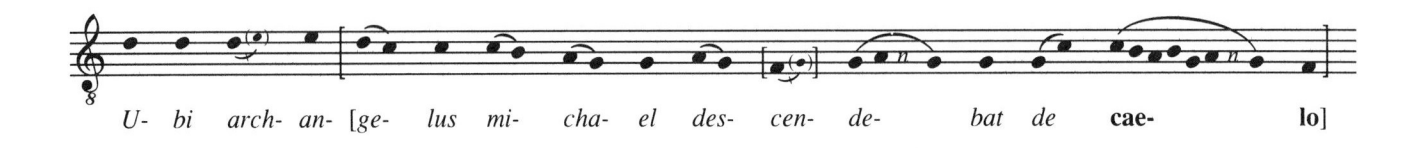

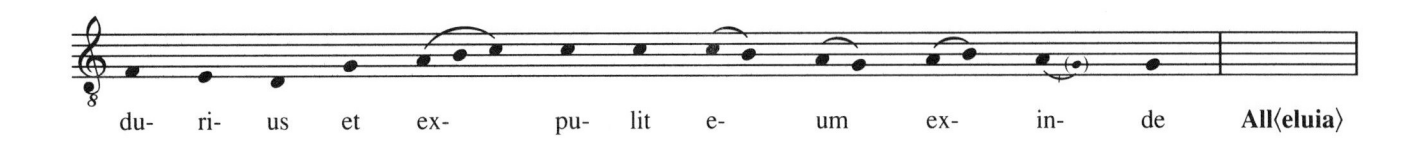

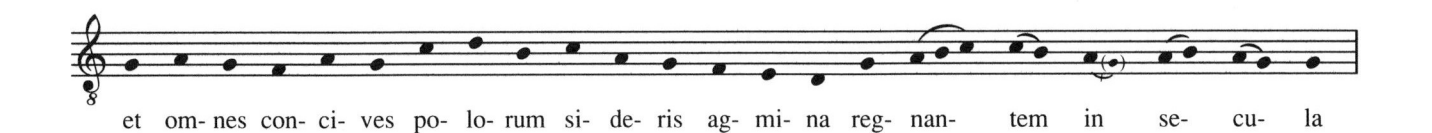

Con- **cus- sum** *Con- cus- sum* et per- cus- sum est ma- re fon- tes sa- xo et ar- va *et con- tre- mu- it* mon- tes et ex- pa- vit dra- co- nem pes- ti- fe- rum ser- pens an- ti- quus qui e- iec- tus est de cæ- lo de- mer- sus sub *ter- ra* U- bi arch- an- [ge- lus mi- cha- el des- cen- de- bat de **cae- lo**] In mon- te gar- ga- ni- co vic- to- ri- a chris- ti ex- pug- nan- tes cum sa- tan du- ri- us et ex- pu- lit e- um ex- in- de **All⟨eluia⟩** An- ge- le mi- cha- hel at- que ga- bri- hel si- mul- que ra- pha- el et om- nes con- ci- ves po- lo- rum si- de- ris ag- mi- na reg- nan- tem in se- cu- la

26. Alleluia ℣ O quam pulchra est
Prosula: *Psallat turba devota*

Rn 1343

[1] Psal- lat tur- ba de- vo- ta chris-to me- los at- que ca- nat dul- ce vir- gi- nis sa- cra- tæ cæ- le- brans of- fi- ci- um na- ta- lis sum- mi quo pro- ces- sit si- mul di- cat cor- de fi- de- li **O qua⟨m⟩** [pulchra est]

[2] Quæ su- is se- qua- ci- bus sa- lu- tem com- pe- ten- ter in ex- cel- sis con- do- nat æ- ter- nam an- ge- lo- rum- que dig- nos fa- cit con- sor- ci- o u- bi plau- dat at- que re- sul- tat **Cas- ta gen⟨eratio⟩**

[3] Vir- gi- num cor- rus- cat cho- rus an- te de- um sem- per vo- ci- bus de- co- ris nos- que ro- ge- mus in- ces- san- ter ut pro nos- tris in- ter- ce- dat se- du- le de- lic- tis **Cum cla- ri[tate]**

27. Alleluia ℣ Dilexit Andream
Prosula: *In dulcedine amoris*

In dul- ce- di- ne a- mo- ris re- demp- to- ris vo- can- tis du- os fra- tres de na- vi quo- rum u- nus fu- it pe- trus qui fu- it pis- ca- tor bo- nus at- que fra- ter an- dre- as hos do- mi- nus vo- ca- ve- rat qui fu- e- rant se- cu- ti o- do- rem **In** odo[rem]

28. Alleluia ℣ Verba mea
Prosula: *Alme domine noli claudere*

[1] Al- me do- mi- ne no- li clau- de- re au- rem tu- am sed ex- au- di **Ver- ba [mea]** [2] Ar- va cunc- ta et sa- ta tu gu- ber- nas o do- mi- ne re- demp- tor po- pu- lo- rum al- me [3] Cor- da nos- tra di- vi- ni ro- ris il- lu- stra tu de- us con- fir- ma

29. Alleluia ℣ Deus iudex iustus
Prosula: *Arbiter singulorum facta*

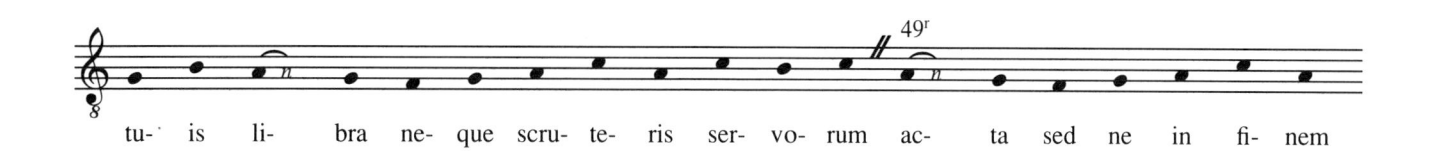

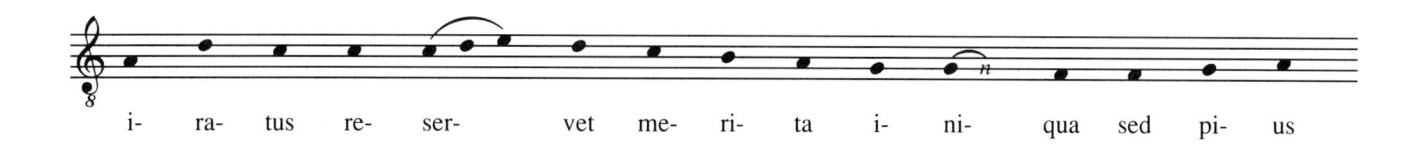

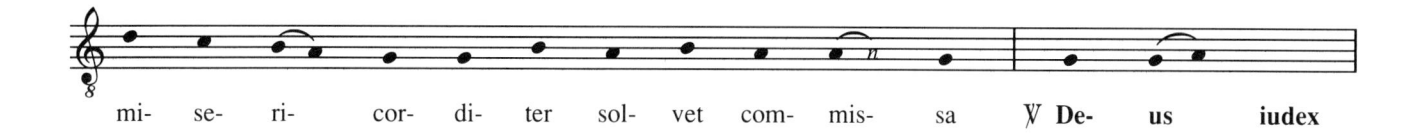

Rn 1343

Alleluia Ar- bi- ter sin- gu- lo- rum fac- ta qui pro- pe pen- sat in ex- a- mi- nis tu- is li- bra ne- que scru- te- ris ser- vo- rum ac- ta sed ne in fi- nem i- ra- tus re- ser- vet me- ri- ta i- ni- qua sed pi- us mi- se- ri- cor- di- ter sol- vet com- mis- sa ℣ **De- us iudex**

30. Alleluia ℣ Ad te domine levavi
Prosula: *Alma voce canamus*

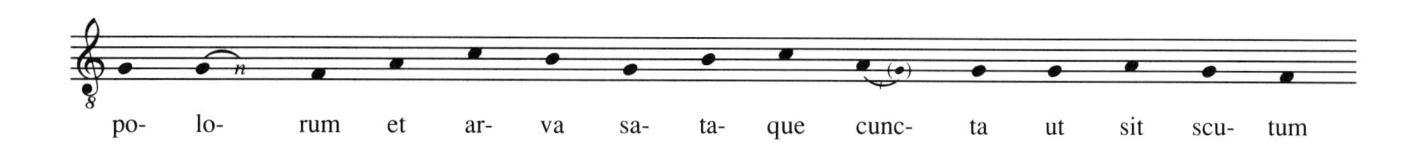

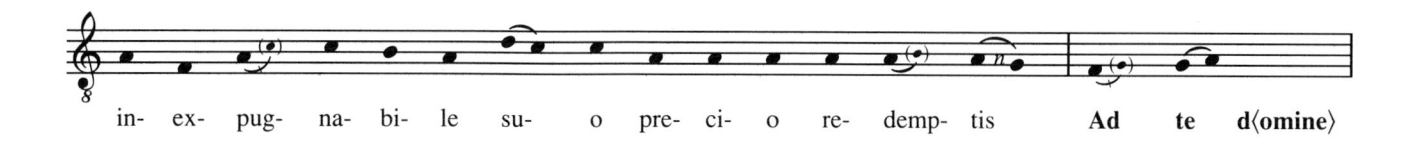

Rn 1343

Al- le- lu- ia Al- ma vo- ce ca- na- mus sup- pli- ces re- gi po- lo- rum et ar- va sa- ta- que cunc- ta ut sit scu- tum in- ex- pug- na- bi- le su- o pre- ci- o re- demp- tis **Ad te d⟨omine⟩**

31–33. Alleluia ℣ Eripe me

Prosulae: *Laudes debitas vocibus, Et ab insurgentibus Deus,* and *Lingua cor simul clamitet*

Rn 1343

Lau- des de- bi- tas vo- ci- bus dul- ci- so- nis om- nes

pa- ri- ter nunc mo- du- le- mur om- ni- po- ten- ti at- que pre- ce- mur

da- vi- ti- co spi- ri- tu di- cen- tes **E- ri- pe me**

Et ab in- sur- gen- ti- bus de- us for- tis rex es- to no- bis tur- ris

for- ti- tu- di- nis et cli- pe- us in- ex- pug- na- bi- lis

chris- te tu- os e- ri- pe ser- vos **Et ab in- sur[gentibus]**

Re- di- me nos pi- e chris- te qui re- de- mis- ti da- vid

pro- phe- tam de gla- di- o pes- si- mo sa- u- lis **All⟨eluia⟩**

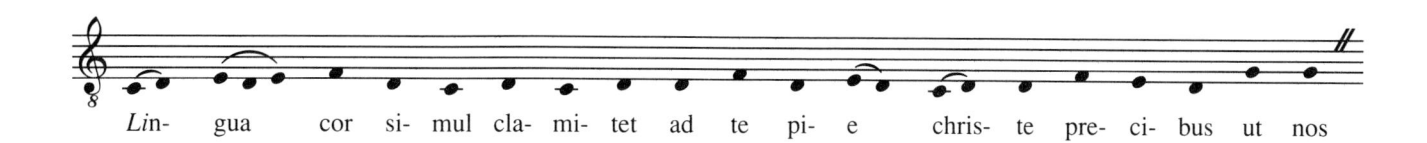

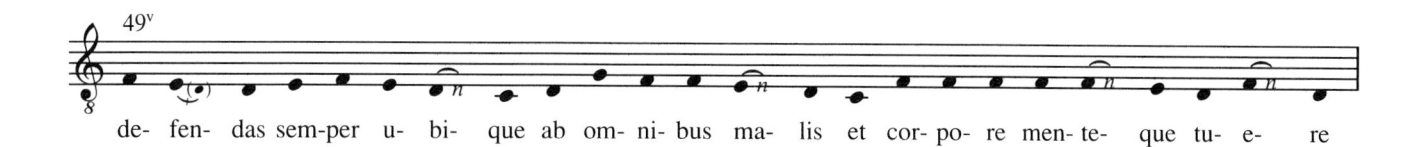

Lin- gua cor si- mul cla- mi- tet ad te pi- e chris- te pre- ci- bus ut nos de- fen- das sem-per u- bi- que ab om- ni- bus ma- lis et cor- po- re men- te- que tu- e- re

34. Alleluia ℣ Benedictus es domine
Prosula: *Semper sonet nostra lingua*

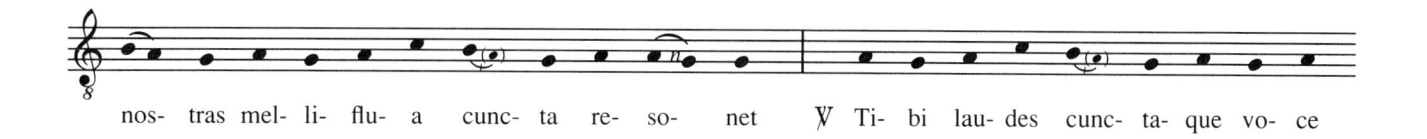

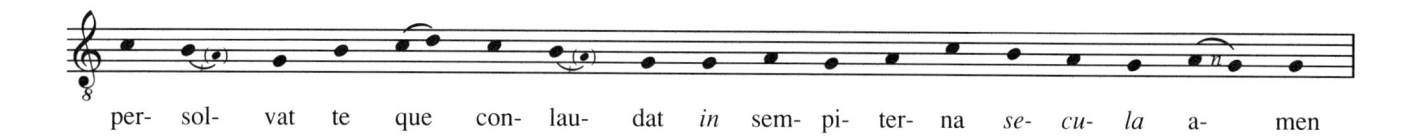

Bu 2824

Sem-per so- net nos- tra lin- gua que pu- ro cor- de ti- bi lau- dat quod vo- ces nos- tras mel- li- flu- a cunc- ta re- so- net ℣ Ti- bi lau- des cunc- ta- que vo- ce per- sol- vat te que con- lau- dat *in* sem- pi- ter- na *se- cu- la* a- men

Index of First Lines: Proper Tropes and Prosulae

The following abbreviations are used: C = Communion trope; I = Introit trope; O = Offertory trope; no. = number of the trope or prosula in this volume; Pr = Prosula. Verse numbers are given in brackets.

A domino impletum (I, no. 51, [1])
A supernis caelorum angelus (Pr, no. 6)
Ab increpatione et ira furoris (O, no. 34, [1])
Adest alma virgo parens (I, no. 27, [1])
Admirans vates proclamat (I, no. 62, [1])
Aeterno genitus genitore (I, no. 15, [1])
Agentes gracias illi qui (I, no. 36, [2])
Alma voce canamus supplices (Pr, no. 28)
Alme caeli rex inmortalis (Pr, no. 9)
Alme domine noli claudere (Pr, no. 26)
Almipotens verus Deus (I, no. 2)
Amor angelorum et gaudium (I, no. 17, [1])
Angele Michael atque Gabriel (Pr, no. 23)
Angelici patres clari (I, no. 65, [2])
Angelicisque choris iunctae (I, no. 59, [3])
Ante deum semper gloriae (Pr, no. 21)
Arbiter singulorum facta (Pr, no. 27)
Arctos et esperos auster (I, no. 28, [3])
Astra caeli dum conscendit (I, no. 53, [2])
Audi nos te deprecamur (Pr, no. 8)
Audite insulae et adtendite (I, no. 47)
Ave beata maria (I, no. 57)
Ave beata Maria praedixit (I, no. 56, [2])
Beatissimus petrus catenis in carcere (I, no. 48, [1])
Caelica namque piis reddunt (I, no. 61, [3])
Celsa nunc rutilant festa beati silvestri (I, no. 21, [2])
Christe tu vita vera quem (Pr, no. 15)
Christe tuus fueram tantum (I, no. 13, [3])
Christus de sepulchro resurrexit (I, no. 32, [1])
Christus intravit ianuis clausis (Pr, no. 16)
Christus iudicaturus est vivos (O, no. 34, [3])
Christus surrexit a mortuis (O, no. 34, [4])
Cibavit illum panem vitae (I, no. 16, [2])
Clara iam nobis adest hodierna (I, no. 46, [3])
Concussum et percussum est (Pr, no. 22)
Consortes suorum effectos (I, no. 36, [5])
Consortes tuorum effecti (I, no. 63)
Creator caeli et terrae (I, no. 1, [2])
Cui omnes occurrentes clamemus (I, no. 3, [3])
Cum apostolis cito properemus (I, no. 32, [2])
Cum essent apostoli in unum (I, no. 44, [1])
Cuncti fideles christi venite (I, no. 36, [1])

Dante suis palma post aspera (I, no. 37, [2])
Debitis laudibus venerantes (I, no. 36, [3])
Dedit me testem veritatis (I, no. 45, [4])
Deus exercituum et miliciarum rex (I, no. 48, [2])
Deus immensus et excelsus (I, no. 44, [2])
Deus pater clamat iohannem (I, no. 46, [2])
Deus pater filium suum misit (I, no. 9, [2])
Dierum noctuque vigilare quoque (Pr, no. 7)
Dilectus iste dominus iohannes (I, no. 18, [2])
Divina beatus Petrus erectus (I, no. 50, [1])
Divini fuerat quoniam fervoris (I, no. 64, [1])
Ecce iam Christus quem sancti (I, no. 3, [1])
Ecce iam venit hora illa (I, no. 6)
Erant omnes nostri linguis (Pr, no. 19)
Esse dei genitrix qu[a]e creditur (I, no. 58, [3])
Est unigenitus sabaoth (I, no. 67, [4])
Et ab insurgentibus deus fortis (Pr, no. 30)
Et hunc ad [a]eternum (I, no. 17, [3])
Et pactum vitae firmum stabilivit (I, no. 64, [2])
Exaudi virgo virginum hymnum (I, no. 56, [1])
Festis nunc in apostolicis laus (I, no. 65, [1])
Florebit iustus ut palma (O, no. 19)
Forma speciosissimus manuque (I, no. 25)
Generante filium vaticinando prophetando (I, no. 4, [3])
Gloria pangatur mundi hiesu (I, no. 42, [2])
Glorietur pater in filio suo (I, no. 9, [3])
Gracias agamus semper trinitatis (I, no. 42, [3])
Grandine lapidum mox moriturus (I, no. 12)
Haec est praeclara dies tribus (I, no. 26, [1])
Hic deus et homo caelorum (I, no. 40, [2])
Hic enim est de quo prophetae cecinerunt (I, no. 10, [1])
Hic est silvester papa (I, no. 22, [1])
Hodie beatissimus andreas apostolus (I, no. 66)
Hodie beatus laurentius levita (I, no. 53, [1])
Hodie descendit christus in iordanem (I, no. 24, [1])
Hodie exultent iusti . . . iohannes (I, no. 45, [1])
Hodie exultent iusti natus est filius (I, no. 9, [1])
Hodie inclytus martyr stephanus paradisum (I, no. 11, [1])
Hodie natus est salvator mundi cantemus (I, no. 10, [2])
Hodie redemptor mundi ascendit (I, no. 39, [1])
Hodie resurrexit leo fortis (I, no. 33, [1])
Hodie rex glori[a]e christus (I, no. 41, [1])
Hodie salvator mundi per virginem (I, no. 8, [1])

Hodie sanctissimi patroni nostri petri (I, no. 49)
Hodie spiritus sanctus procedens (I, no. 42, [1])
Hodie spiritus sanctus processit (I, no. 43)
Hodie te domine suggentes (I, no. 20, [1])
Hora est iam nos de somno surgere (I, no. 5)
Hora est surgite iubet domnus (I, no. 31)
Iam redeunt gaudia festa (Pr, no. 14)
Iam surgens aurora iam venit (I, no. 7)
Ille qui dixit aperi os tuum (I, no. 16, [1])
In brachiis sancti symeonis (I, no. 27, [4])
In cuius laude celsa voce (C, no. 35, [4])
In dulcedine amoris redemptoris (Pr, no. 25)
In iordane a iohanne baptizatus (I, no. 26, [3])
In iubilo vocis benedicto (I, no. 52, [1])
In principio erat et est (I, no. 9, [4])
In quo rex caeli reddit (I, no. 58, [2])
Incensumque suae condignum (I, no. 64, [3])
Ingresso hiesu in praetorium (I, no. 29, [1])
Insurrexerunt contra me iudeorum populi (I, no. 11, [2])
Invidiosae lapidibus oppresserunt me (I, no. 11, [3])
Invocavite altissime venturum (Pr, no. 2)
Laudes debitas vocibus dulcisonis (Pr, no. 29)
Laurenti post menbra soluta (I, no. 54, [2])
Laus et iubilacio per cunta (I, no. 55, [3])
Laus honor virtus deo nostro (C, no. 35, [1])
Laxare vincula strictum (I, no. 24, [3])
Leo fortis de tribu iuda (C, no. 35, [3])
Liberavit me salvator meus (I, no. 50, [3])
Lingua cor simul clamitet ad te (Pr, no. 31)
Lumen aeternum christum dominum (I, no. 27, [3])
Lux iusticiae in tenebris (I, no. 50, [2])
Magni consilii angelus eia iste (I, no. 8, [4])
Magnus et felix fuerat nimium ordine (C, no. 14)
Manet indeficiens (I, no. 21, [4])
Mentibus ergo piis cantemus (I, no. 15, [3])
Misericors ac clemens famulis (Pr, no. 5)
Mons magnus est mons terribilis (Pr, no. 12)
Monumenta aperta sunt (O, no. 34, [2])
Namque sophia struit sedem (I, no. 52, [2])
Naturas limpheas hodie mutavit (I, no. 26, [4])
Ne tuus in dubio frangar (I, no. 13, [4])
Neumate doctilogo cordis (I, no. 52, [3])
Nobile apostolici admirans decus (I, no. 61, [1])
Nomen eius hemmanuhel vocabitur (I, no. 8, [3])
Non derelinquam eum sed (O, no. 23, [2])
Non nullum nocui nec legum (I, no. 13, [2])
Nos sinus aecclesiae matris (I, no. 58, [1])
Nunc vivamus cum filio (I, no. 56, [3])
O admirabiles clementiae plene (I, no. 48, [3])
O quam clara nitet (I, no. 59, [1])
Oblatum purum non munere (I, no. 28, [2])
Olim promissus ac cupidis (I, no. 24, [2])
Omnes voce deo cantate et psallite (I, no. 15, [4])
Os tuum inquiens aperi meque (I, no. 18, [2])
Pater et filius et spiritus (I, no. 67, [2])

Pater unigenitum tuum filiumque (Pr, no. 13)
Peccata nostra ipse portavit (C, no. 35, [2])
Pectoris atque sacri pandit (I, no. 15, [2])
Pentecosten advenisse noster (Pr, no. 20)
Per ipsum illuminata est (I, no. 22, [3])
Personas omnes aequo discrimine (I, no. 51, [2])
Possessor polorum deus qui nos (Pr, no. 3)
Prestans linguarum peritiam (I, no. 44, [3])
Proclamemus omnes laudes (I, no. 27, [2])
Proles virginis matris hiesu (Pr, no. 10)
Prophetare in nomine ipsius (I, no. 45, [3])
Prunas extensa super craticulam (I, no. 54, [1])
Psallat turba devota christo (Pr, no. 24)
Psallentes legimus david (I, no. 28, [1])
Psallite fratres hora est (I, no. 33, [2])
Quem augustus constantinus statuit (I, no. 22, [2])
Quem creditis super astra (I, no. 38)
Quem euntem angelici (I, nos. 39 & 41, [2])
Quem magi hodie muneribus (I, no. 26, [2])
Quem quaeris mulier in monumento (I, no. 32, [3])
Quem quaeritis in sepulchro (I, no. 31)
Quem virgo maria genuit (I, no. 8, [2])
Qui cupit insontem morsu (I, nos. 29 & 30, [3])
Qui debriant evangelico (I, no. 65, [3])
Qui in stadio celebri meruerunt (I, no. 37, [3])
Qui me circumdedit consilio (I, no. 50, [4])
Qui patris in caelo nostris (I, no. 60, [1])
Qui primus meruit post christum occurrere (I, no. 13, [1])
Qui sedes in alto throno laudabilis (Pr, no. 4)
Qui tibi dedit laurenti tormenta (I, no. 55, [1])
Qui tibi sunt iuncti divino (I, no. 62, [2])
Quia veni vitam largiri regiamque (I, no. 4, [2])
Quo etherea pecierunt regna (I, no. 36, [4])
Quo panderetur omnibus lux (I, no. 17, [2])
Quo uniti sumus fide (I, no. 21, [3])
Quos divinus amor vere (I, no. 61, [2])
Regnum quod nullo defectu corrumpi (I, no. 24, [4])
Rex christe deus abraham deus yssac (I, no. 3, [4])
Rex deus omnipotens ne perdas (Pr, no. 17)
Sana christe rex alme (Pr, no. 11)
Sanctissimus namque Gregorius (I, no. 1, [1])
Sancto firmantes sanctorum neumate (I, no. 60, [3])
Sanguine sacrati christi (I, no. 37, [1])
Sed caeleri succurre michi (I, nos. 29 & 30, [2])
Semper sonet nostra lingua (Pr, no. 32)
Servum sibi iohanne me vocans (I, no. 45, [2])
Sicut tu christe hiesu pro nobis (Pr, no. 18)
Simulque consonis addatur hymnis (I, no. 55, [2])
Spiritus alme nostra semper (I, no. 42, [4])
Splendor et imago patris (I, no. 67, [1])
Statuam testamentum cum eo (O, no. 23, [3])
Statuit illi testamentum sempiternum (I, no. 16, [3])
Suam nos salvet per nativitatem (I, no. 3, [2])
Suscipe meum in pace spiritum (I, no. 11, [4])
Suspensus ligno patri (I, no. 30, [1])

Teneri exercitus pr[a]econia sparsisti (I, no. 20, [2])
Ter trinus ordo deum (I, no. 60, [2])
Terrestria atque superna (I, no. 44, [4])
Terrigenas summos affatur (I, no. 40, [1])
Trinitas et unitas deitas (I, no. 67, [3])
Unde et psalmist[a]e versus (I, no. 51, [4])
Usque in saeculum saeculi conservabo (O, no. 23, [1])
Ut caeli in thalamo semper (I, no. 59, [2])
Ut iugiter tra[c]tet quae (I, no. 51, [3])

Ut possimus contrariae virtuti (I, no. 1, [3])
Ut reddat cunctis gestorum (I, no. 40, [3])
Ut tua gloria in minimis (I, no. 20, [3])
Venite populi ad conlaudandum regem (I, no. 21, [1])
Venturum te cuncti dixerunt (Pr, no. 1)
Verbo altissimi patris genitoque (I, no. 4, [1])
Vide pater (I, nos. 29 & 30, [4])
Vitricem meruit palmam sertamque (I, no. 53, [3])

Index of Chants by Feast Day

The following abbreviations are used: C = Communion trope; I = Introit trope; O = Offertory trope; no. = number of the trope or prosula in this volume; Pr = Prosula.

Text Incipit of Trope or Prosula	Base chant: Text Incipit	Genre, Number
	First Sunday of Advent	
Sanctissimus namque Gregorius	Introit: Ad te levavi	I, no. 1
Almipotens verus Deus	Introit: Ad te levavi	I, no. 2
Ecce iam Christus	Introit: Ad te levavi	I, no. 3
Venturum te cunti dixerunt	Gradual: Universi qui te exspectant ℣ Vias tuas domine	Pr, no. 1
Invocavite altissime	Offertory: Ad te domine levavi ℣ 2 Respice in me	Pr, no. 2
	Second Sunday of Advent	
Possessor polorum Deus	Offertory: Deus tu convertens ℣ 2 Misericordia et veritas	Pr, no. 3
	Third Sunday of Advent	
Qui sedes in alto throno	Gradual: Qui sedes domine ℣ Qui regis Israel	Pr, no. 4
Misericors et clemens famulis	Offertory: Benedixisti domine ℣ 2 Ostende nobis domine	Pr, no. 5
	Fourth Sunday of Advent	
A supernis caelorum	Offertory: Ave Maria ℣ 1 Quomodo in me	Pr, no. 6
	Christmas I	
Verbo altissimi patris	Introit: Dominus dixit	I, no. 4
	Christmas II	
Hora est iam nos	Introit: Lux fulgebit	I, no. 5
Ecce iam venit hora	Introit: Lux fulgebit	I, no. 6
Iam surgens aurora	Introit: Lux fulgebit	I, no. 7
Dierum noctuque	Offertory: Deus enim fermavit ℣ 2 Mirabilis in excelsis	Pr, no. 7
	Christmas III	
Hodie salvator mundi per virginem	Introit: Puer natus est nobis	I, no. 8
Hodie exultent iusti natus est	Introit: Puer natus est nobis	I, no. 9
Hic enim est de quo prophetae	Introit: Puer natus est nobis	I, no. 10
Audi nos te deprecamur	Alleluia ℣ Dies sanctificatus	Pr, no. 8
Alme caeli rex immortalis	Alleluia ℣ Dies sanctificatus	Pr, no. 9
Proles virginis matris	Offertory: Tui sunt caeli ℣ 3 Tu humiliasti	Pr, no. 10
	St. Stephen	
Hodie inclitus martyr Stephanus	Introit: Etenim sederunt principes	I, no. 11
Grandine lapidum	Introit: Etenim sederunt principes	I, no. 12
Qui primus meruit	Introit: Etenim sederunt principes	I, no. 13
Magnus et felix	Communion: Video caelos apertos	C, no. 14
	St. John Evangelist	
Aeterno genitus genitore	Introit: In medio ecclesiae	I, no. 15
Ille qui dixit	Introit: In medio ecclesiae	I, no. 16
Amor angelorum et gaudium	Introit: In medio ecclesiae	I, no. 17
Dilectus iste domini	Introit: In medio ecclesiae	I, no. 18
Florebit iustus ut palma	Offertory: Iustus ut palma	O, no. 19
	Holy Innocents	
Hodie te domine suggentes	Introit: Ex ore infantium	I, no. 20
	St. Sylvester	
Venite populi ad conlaudandum	Introit: Statuit ei dominus	I, no. 21
Hic est Silvester	Introit: Statuit ei dominus	I, no. 22
Usque in saeculum saeculi	Offertory: Veritas mea	O, no. 23
	Epiphany	
Hodie descendit Christus	Introit: Ecce advenit	I, no. 24
Forma speciosissimus	Introit: Ecce advenit	I, no. 25
Haec est praeclara dies	Introit: Ecce advenit	I, no. 26

Text Incipit of Trope or Prosula	Base chant: Text Incipit	Genre, Number
Purification		
Adest alma virgo	Introit: Suscepimus	I, no. 27
Psallentes legimus	Introit: Suscepimus	I, no. 28
Sexagesima Sunday		
Sana Christe rex alme	Tract: Commovisti	Pr, no. 11
	℣ Sana contritiones eius	
Fourth Sunday in Lent		
Mons magnus est	Tract: Qui confidunt	Pr, no. 12
	℣ Montes in circuitu eius	
Palm Sunday		
Ingresso Iesu	Introit: Domine ne longe facias	I, no. 29
Suspensus ligno patri	Introit: Domine ne longe facias	I, no. 30
Pater unigenitum tuum	Tract: Deus Deus meus	Pr, no. 13
	℣ Libera me de ore	
Easter		
Hora est surgite/Quem quaeritis	Introit: Resurrexi	I, no. 31
Christus de sepulchro resurrexit	Introit: Resurrexi	I, no. 32
Hodie resurrexit leo fortis	Introit: Resurrexi	I, no. 33
Iam redeunt gaudia	Alleluia ℣ Pascha nostrum	Pr, no. 14
Christe tu vita vera	Alleluia ℣ Pascha nostrum	Pr, no. 14
Ab increpatione et ira	Offertory: Terra tremuit	O, no. 34
Laus honor virtus	Communion: Pascha nostrum	C, no. 35
Octave of Easter		
Christus intravit ianuis	Offertory: Angelus domini	Pr, no. 16
	℣ 2 Iesus stetit	
First Sunday after Easter		
Rex Deus omnipotens	Alleluia ℣ Vos estis	Pr, no. 17
Sicut tu Christe	Alleluia ℣ Vos estis	Pr, no. 18
Ss. Senesius and Theopontius		
Cuncti fideles Christi	Introit: Gaudeamus . . . Senesii	I, no. 36
Sanguine sacrati Christi	Introit: Gaudeamus . . . Senesii	I, no. 37a
Ascension		
Quem creditis super astra	Introit: Viri Galilaei	I, no. 38
Hodie redemptor mundi ascendit	Introit: Viri Galilaei	I. no. 39
Terrigenas summos affatur	Introit: Viri Galilaei	I, no. 40
Hodie rex gloriae Christus	Introit: Viri Galilaei	I, no. 41
Pentecost		
Hodie spiritus sanctus procedens	Introit: Spiritus domini	I, no. 42
Hodie spiritus sanctus processit	Introit: Spiritus domini	I, no. 43
Cum essent apostoli	Introit: Spiritus domini	I, no. 44
Erant omnes nostri linguis	Alleluia ℣ Dum complerentur	Pr, no. 19
Pentecosten advenisse	Alleluia ℣ Dum complerentur	Pr, no. 20
St. John the Baptist		
Hodie exultent iusti . . . Iohannes	Introit: De ventre matris meae	I, no. 45
Deus pater clamat Iohannem	Introit: De ventre matris meae	I, no. 46
Audite insulae	Introit: De ventre matris meae	I, no. 47
St. Peter		
Beatissimus Petrus catenis	Introit: Nunc scio vere	I, no. 48
Hodie sanctissimi patroni nostri Petri	Introit: Nunc scio vere	I, no. 49
Divina beatus Petrus	Introit: Nunc scio vere	I, no. 50
Alme cuncti sator orbis	Alleluia ℣ Serve bone et fidelis	Pr, no. 21
Serve et amice bone	Alleluia ℣ Serve bone et fidelis	Pr, no. 22
Translation of St. Benedict		
A domino impletum	Introit: Os iusti	I, no. 51
In iubilo vocis	Introit: Os iusti	I, no. 52
St. Lawrence		
Hodie beatus Laurentius levita	Introit: Confessio	I, no. 53
Prunas extensa	Introit: Confessio	I, no. 54
Qui tibi dedit Laurenti	Introit: Confessio	I, no. 55

Text Incipit of Trope or Prosula	Base chant: Text Incipit	Genre, Number
	Assumption	
Exaudi virgo virginum	Introit: Gaudeamus . . . Mariae . . . assumptione	I, no. 56
Ave beata Maria	Introit: Gaudeamus . . . Mariae . . . assumptione	I, no. 57
Nos sinus ecclesiae	Introit: Gaudeamus . . . Mariae . . . assumptione	I, no. 58
	Birth of the Blessed Virgin	
O quam clara nitet	Introit: Vultum tuum	I, no. 59
	Michael Archangel	
Qui patris in caelo	Introit: Benedicite dominum	I, no. 60
Ante Deum semper gloriae	Alleluia ℣ Concussum est mare	Pr, no. 23
Concussum et percussum	Alleluia ℣ Concussum est mare	Pr, no. 24
Angele Michael atque Gabriel	Alleluia ℣ Concussum est mare	Pr, no. 25
	Ss. Simon and Jude	
Nobile apostolici admirans	Introit: Mihi autem nimis	I, no. 61
Admirans vates proclamat	Introit: Mihi autem nimis	I, no. 62
Consortes tuorum effecti	Introit: Mihi autem nimis	I, no. 63
	All Saints	
Sanguinis sacrati Christi	Introit: Gaudeamus . . . sanctorum omnium	I, no. 37b
	St. Martin	
Divini fuerat	Introit: Statuit ei dominus	I, no. 64
	Common of the B.V.M.	
Psallat turba devota	Alleluia ℣ O quam pulchra est	Pr, no. 26
	St. Andrew	
Festis nunc in apostolicis	Introit: In omnem terram	I, no. 65
Hodie beatissimus Andreas	Introit: In omnem terram	I, no. 66
In dulcedine amoris	Alleluia ℣ Dilexit Andream	Pr, no. 27
	Trinity Sunday	
Splendor et imago patris	Introit: Benedicta sit	I, no. 67
Alme domine noli claudere	Alleluia ℣ Verba mea	Pr, no. 28
	Sundays after Pentecost	
Arbiter singulorum facta	Alleluia ℣ Deus iudex iustus	Pr, no. 29
Alma voce canamus	Alleluia ℣ Ad te domine levavi	Pr, no. 30
Laudes debitas vocibus	Alleluia ℣ Eripe me	Pr, no. 31
Et ab insurgentibus Deus	Alleluia ℣ Eripe me	Pr, no. 32
Lingua cor simul clamitet	Alleluia ℣ Eripe me	Pr, no. 33
Semper sonet nostra lingua	Alleluia ℣ Benedictus es domine	Pr, no. 34